# 9 Lives

*An oral history*

## By AARON ELSON

**first edition**

# About the World War II Oral History Web Site

Since it was started in 1997, the WWII Oral History site has become one of the most popular and entertaining military history destinations on the Internet.

The web site was launched by Aaron Elson, whose father, Lieutenant Maurice Elson, joined the 712th Tank Battalion as a replacement in Normandy and was wounded twice.

After his father's death from a heart attack in 1980, Elson

Members of D Company, 712th Tank Battalion, in England, July 1944, before going into combat.

Art Horn, 11th Cavalry, and friend, Camp Seeley, Calif., 1941. "This horse is the only loving I get out here," Horn wrote to his future wife, Margaret.

attended a battalion reunion, hoping to find some veterans who remembered his dad. He found three, and was so moved by their stories and the other stories he heard that weekend that he returned the following year with a tape recorder. He has been preserving veterans' firsthand accounts ever since.

**WWII Oral History**
**www.tankbooks.com**

## Also by Aaron Elson

**Tanks for the Memories:** An oral history of the 712th Tank Battalion in World War II.

**They were all young kids:** The story of Lt. Jim Flowers and the 1st platoon, C Company, 712th Tank Battalion, in the battle for Hill 122.

**A Mile in Their Shoes:** Conversations with veterans of World War II.

For information on ordering any of these books, call 1 (800) 807-8265

The author's father, Lt. Maurice Elson

Aaron Elson's work has been compared to that of Studs Terkel, Stephen Ambrose and Tom Brokaw. For more than a decade, he has been preserving veterans' stories in a way that few other historians have, and in the last few years he has made many of those stories available on the Internet.

Web sites by Aaron Elson:

www.tankbooks.com
www.kasselmission.com
www.audiomurphy.com

to Lisa

Chi Chi

# Nine Lives
**ISBN 0-9640611-5-5**

Printed at
Ted Weiss Printing
409 Bridgeton Pike
Langhorne, PA 19053
(800) 635-0215

Published by
Chi Chi Press
PO Box 914
Maywood, N.J. 07607
(800) 807-8265

Chuck Hurlbut, far right, with fellow D-Day veterans of the 299th Combat Engineer Battalion, from left: Sam Trinca, Jim DePalma, Bill Secaur, and James Burke, and the author. The monument, in Auburn, N.Y., honors six members of the battalion who were killed on D-Day.

# Table of Contents

# Preface

When I first saw Arnold Brown, at a reunion of the 90th Infantry Division, he was carrying an album that said "Oberwampach" on the cover.

Places like Oberwampach, a village in Luxembourg, don't get mentioned much in the histories of World War II, or even in histories of the Battle of the Bulge. But Oberwampach – where Arnold Brown's rifle company and two platoons of the 712th Tank Battalion, my father's outfit, held off nine counterattacks over a three-day period – means a great deal to me, and it means even more to the men who fought there.

I knew that Brown – who bears a striking resemblance to the late Colonel Sanders – was going to be one of my favorite interviews almost from the moment I asked him his name.

"Arnold L. Brown," he said.

"What does the 'L' stand for?"

"Lee."

"Was that after Robert E?" I asked.

"I don't know of any ancestors named Lee, so it could have been."

After pausing, he added, "I hope the Arnold wasn't after Benedict Arnold."

I also met Vern Schmidt at a reunion of the 90th Division. The 358th Infantry Regiment, which was part of the 90th, has a ritual which, perhaps, only people who have been in combat can fully appreciate: At the end of their annual lunch, which at that reunion in 1994 had nine or ten tables, the emcee would announce a table number, and table by table the veterans of the 358th rose and paraded past the podium, pausing to announce, "My name is So and So and I was wounded at Such and Such a place." Every now and then someone said, "I don't know how they missed me, but I didn't get a scratch," usually eliciting roars of laughter. But most of the seventy or eighty veterans who made their brief statements were wounded once, twice, and some of them several times. The 90th Division suffered the third highest rate of casualties of any division in the European Theater of Operations.

At the end of the procession, the emcee asked if anybody else would like to speak. That's when Vern Schmidt came to the podium.

He said he'd like to tell a story, and apologized for the time it would take. The emcee assured him it was okay.

"On my trip to Germany in 1993, my wife and I visited a little home in the Siegfried Line where my squad had stayed for three days while holding a bridge over the Prum River," he said.

"We knocked on the door, and this couple came to the door. I said, 'I was in this house in 1945,' and the woman said, 'You were an American soldier?'

"I said, 'Yes.' We came on in. They were overwhelmed that someone would come back and visit. And she said, 'Can I tell you a brief story that took place, that you may not have put together?'

"She said, 'When you came in' – our squad had a big tall Texan as a sergeant; I can't remember his name, but it might have been Webster.

"When we'd go into a building we'd generally throw a grenade in to clear the place out until we knew it was safe. Somehow, this big tall Texan walked in, and he saw a cellar. He walked down to the cellar with his M-1, and it was dark. It was a square cellar. He shined his light, and there were 24 civilians sitting on the dirt floor and their eyes were wide, wondering, 'What's this guy going to do?' And then he saw that on the wall opposite him was a crucifix. He said, 'Are you Catholic?'

"And the lady who we met when we returned, her father said, 'Ja, Ich bin Catolisch.' And it was like it was a magic word. The GI dropped his rifle, he reached into his pocket, and he pulled out a rosary, and he said, 'I'm Catholic, too.' And for three days, the people in this cellar were taken care of. We gave them food, we took care of their wounds, and reminiscing back almost fifty years, this lady put her arms around us and hugged both my wife and myself, and said, 'You know, doesn't this do wonderful things in our life? It brings us together. Once we were enemies, and now we are friends.' "

Jim Koerner and I have a ritual, too. He calls me very early in the morning once every few weeks and says, "Don't you hate it when the phone wakes you up?"

I tell him he can call me anytime and I ask him how he is.

"Not bad for an old fart," he says.

If I don't hear from him for a couple of months, I know he's used up another of his nine lives. He only had two left at the end of the war, and has expended six or seven since.

When I went to take pictures for the cover of an audiobook I produced from our taped conversation a few years back, Koerner spread out some of his memorabilia on a coffee table. Among the items was a manuscript written on yellow legal paper. He said it was an account of his experiences that he wrote shortly after the war, while everything was fresh in his memory. It is much more detailed than the interview, and his comments are precious. In the manuscript, he changed the names of some of his officers. For this book, I have used mostly the memoir, with portions of the interview edited in.

I found Chuck Hurlbut through the Internet. He doesn't own a computer, but his name was listed on a web site containing contacts for various veterans' alumni groups, and I was looking for some information about an incident in the Battle of the Bulge involving the 299th Combat Engineer Battalion. I phoned him, and he gave me the name of a fellow engineer who could tell me more about the incident. We talked some more, and suddenly I realized that here I was on the phone with a veteran who had been on Omaha Beach on D-Day. He said Dan Rather interviewed him for a documentary; I had seen the documentary, but it was four years earlier and I didn't remember him specifically.

Halfway through my interview with Hurlbut, as he was describing the landing on Omaha Beach, I suddenly remembered the story he told Dan Rather, and I said, "Was that you?!" It was a story about a buddy of his, Tom Legacy of Niagara Falls, who wore a gaudy tie underneath his field jacket for the assault. Someone had sent him the tie from home, and although it was hardly regulation, he remarked, "What can they do, court-martial me?" and Chuck and Tom shared a good laugh.

Later that morning, after a raft full of explosives blew up behind him and he dragged a severely wounded buddy to safety, Hurlbut was in a state of near exhaustion and shock when he looked out from the dune line and surveyed the vision of Hell that was spread out before him. He saw someone staggering towards him 60 or 70 yards away, his jacket in shreds, half his face torn off, and yet there was something about him that made Hurlbut think, "I know that guy."

And then he saw the tie.

When I launched the World War II Oral History web site, my goal was to publicize a pair of books I had written, but soon the site took on a life of its own. A high school student in Arkansas sent me an e-mail asking if there was a veteran he could interview on line. I sent him the e-mail address of a B-17 crew member who had contributed a couple of stories to the site. In 1998, Patsy Giacchi of Clifton, N.J., asked his daughter to do a web search on "that ship" he was on. She found my interview with Angelo Crapanzano, a survivor of LST 507, which was sunk during the ill-fated Exercise Tiger. It turns out the two veterans live in neighboring counties, and the web site brought them together.

"When are you going to interview some women about the war?" Helen Grottola asked me several years back.

"How about now?" I replied.

I still haven't transcribed my interview with Helen, whose late husband, Joe, was one of the 712th Tank Battalion's postwar chaplains, but she heightened my awareness that World War II was waged not just by men. At a Florida mini-reunion of the 712th a few years back, I interviewed Jeannie Roland, whose late husband, Jack, had been a sergeant in the battalion's Headquarters Company. Her story is included in this book, as is a narrative drawn from my interview with Kay Brainard Hutchins, who joined the Red Cross while two of her brothers were missing in action.

One of those brothers, 2nd Lt. Newell Brainard, survived one of the most spectacular aerial battles of World War II only to be murdered on the ground by slave labor camp guards, who later were executed for war crimes.

The Kassel mission bombing raid in which Kay Hutchins' brother took part is one of the great little-known stories of World War II. There are brief references to it in a number of books, often with slight inaccuracies. What is most often noted about the battle is that on Sept. 27, 1944, the 445th Bomb Group of the 2nd Air Division sustained the heaviest one-day losses of any bomb group in 8th Air Force history.

I learned of the Kassel mission while researching the life of Lt. Edward L. Forrest, an officer my father knew briefly during the war. Ed Forrest had nothing to do with the Kassel raid, other than the fact that he was killed in the village of Heimboldshausen, Germany, on April 3, 1945, and Heimboldshausen is only about 20 kilometers from Friedlos, where Walter Hassenpflug lives. I met Hassenpflug on my trip to Heimboldshausen in 1996, and after helping me with my own research, he took me to the Kassel Mission Memorial, in a clearing in the Hesse State Forest.

It was a cold February afternoon, and there was a dusting of snow on the ground. A fading bouquet of dried flowers rested in front of one of the three stone slabs, on which were inscribed the names of 118 Americans and 23 Germans who died in or as a result of the battle.

Frank Bertram and George Collar survived the Kassel mission, in which 35 B-24 Liberators strayed off course and were ambushed by as many as 150 German fighter planes. Both bailed out of their planes and became prisoners of war.

All Kay Hutchins knew until 1986 – and all her mother ever knew – was that

Newell Brainard was missing in action, and that he was later reclassified as killed in action. When Kay's mother died, Kay discovered a newspaper clipping from Sept. 28, 1944, in her desk drawer. The article was about the bombing raids of the day before, in which more than 2,000 planes hit various targets in Europe. It was the only clipping from the war in the desk, and Kay believes her mother must have had some sort of extra-sensory perception.

When Patsy Giacchi bobbed up in the English Channel following the torpedoing of LST 507, he looked up at a gun turret where only moments before he had seen the body of a dead sailor. Suddenly he saw his mother saying to him in Sicilian, "Patsy, save yourself!"

Arnold Brown, after describing several harrowing incidents in which he escaped death by what often seemed a miracle, says: "And then I had my vision."

Jim Koerner, George Collar and Frank Bertram are all former prisoners of war. Collar, Bertram and Hutchins are all connected to the Kassel mission. Giacchi is a survivor of Exercise Tiger, which, like the Kassel mission, has been denied its place in history because it was an incident that never should have happened. Arnold Brown and Vern Schmidt were both in the 90th Division. Brown and Hutchins both had educations that were cut short by the Depression. Although the stories in this book will seem disparate at times, there are many threads that tie them together.


When I began interviewing World War II veterans, I described my avocation as being "like oral history." Then one day a friend said, "It isn't like oral history. It *is* oral history."

Although the stories I have preserved represent a tiny but important piece of the lore of World War II, it was not out of any sense of history that I recorded them, but rather because I found them simply to be great stories, stories that touch upon every aspect of the human condition.

*"A shell exploded nearby and a piece of shrapnel struck a boy in the head. He was somewhere between 18 and 21 years of age. I can hear him today, his cry out and the way his voice trailed off as he dropped dead. He said, "Mommmm." It gave me the chills. That was my first casualty. He was one of the 405,399 to be killed in World War II. He became a statistic. He was a statistic to everyone except his mother and his other loved ones."*

**Arnold Brown**
**Retired colonel,**
**company commander**
**358th Battalion,**
**90th Infantry Division**
**Interviewed in**
**Owensboro, Ky.**
**Sept. 8, 1997**

They say the infantry is cannon fodder. This is true. And I was in a specific situation that would bring this out.

There was a certain village that the division thought it was important to capture. They knew that it was occupied and filled with Germans, and it would be too much for an infantry force alone, so they were going to use an armor and infantry team. But there was some critical terrain on the left of this village that they wanted to secure.

My mission was to take my company across this open field in front of this village, go over a little ridge, and take the woods on the other side.

I don't know what is there, but I know that I've got to make this attack with my right flank exposed, and close enough that the Germans can fire at us. Of course, we're going to have them under artillery fire. And we were so close that some big hunks of shrapnel from that artillery fire fluttered across and landed among us, but that's the chance we had to take.

I organized two platoons forward, and I said, "When we leave this covered position, we're not going to stop until we take our objective." Because I knew if we ever stopped in that open field, we'd be under a crossfire.

This is strictly an old infantry assault – standing up, marching fire to the front; my third platoon was in line where they could march-and-fire sideways into a building on the right.

We launch this attack and sure enough, here comes some fire from the village, but we had enough artillery fire on it to make them inaccurate; they couldn't enjoy their shooting. Then on this little ridge where the road came down a couple of Germans jumped up and ran back to those woods which were our objective. As we came over the ridge, I could see some white smoke rings coming from the edge of the woods, a couple of hundred yards away. So I started yelling to the men, "Fire everyplace you see those smoke rings!"

One of them said, "That's our own artillery!"

I said, "That's enemy artillery!"

And it was. Because then they depressed those guns and started firing at us point blank. They fired at my right platoon, and they missed the men and the projectile went into the ground and exploded. The ground was soft. These were guns placed there to knock out tanks, so their shells didn't let out as much shrapnel as the regular 88.

I was still moving forward, and I was close enough that I could look down the muzzle of the gun that had fired at my right platoon. If I'd have been a private I would have hit the ground. I would have disobeyed the company commander's orders. But what could I do? As the company commander, I could never show any fear to my men. So I stood up and moved forward. But ours was a small group, apparently, so the gun swung over and fired at my left platoon. It got a direct hit on a man; blew him all to pieces. The biggest part was a leg from midcalf down with the combat boot on; it blew it up in the air a few feet and it fell, and when it landed it looked to me like it kind of quivered. I can close my eyes and see that today.

When the Germans saw they were not going to stop us, the gun crew put their hands up. And I said, "Shoot the sonofabitches!" At the time I was so damn mad that I wanted to. But my men didn't do it. They took them prisoners. The other German gun crews left their guns and ran down through the woods, and my men were chasing them trying to shoot them down, and I finally had to stop them because they were getting scattered out and disorganized, and the Germans might be going to attack us.

I was born and raised in Ohio County, Kentucky. On a farm. I was a teenager back during the Depression years. I got tired of eating cornbread and molasses three times a day so I decided to go into the Army. I left home with 50 cents in my pocket and an eighth-grade education. I went out in the bushes and waited till the first freight train came through, and when it slowed down I jumped inside one of these boxcars. It was dark inside, and there was a professional hobo in there. He said, "Where you goin', sonny?" Like to scared me to death. But he turned out to be a very nice hobo, because he told me when and where to get off the train when I arrived in Louisville so that the security forces wouldn't pick me up. Otherwise I probably would never have made it into the Army.

In those days, we were an all-volunteer force. Some of the men were individuals like me, and there were other young men who would get into some type of minor trouble with the authorities. A judge would give them a choice of paying their fine and spending 15 to 30 days in jail or going into the military. So a lot of them would take the military. And in those days, the basic training in the military was to weed them out; in other words either make a man and a soldier out of them or out they would go. Later on, I ended up being a recruiting instructor in the same outfit I enlisted in. And this was quite a problem, because as a corporal in those days I had more authority than the majors had later on as far as disciplinary actions were concerned. If we had a problem recruit, we could take him down and put him in the guardhouse and leave him there overnight, with no charge. He didn't know how long he was going to be there and this would scare the heck out of him. When he came back, he'd turn out to be a good soldier. Can you imagine trying to do that today in this type of Army? No.

While I was drilling recruits, I had trouble with one soldier. I did everything I could to discipline him. One of the things they would allow us to do was to have the recruit hold a rifle over his head and run down to the parade ground, around the flagpole and back, and if you do this for a little while you're really tired out. I had him do that a few times and it didn't help, so I reported him to the lieutenant. And the lieutenant said, "Take him behind the garbage rack."

If you had a problem with an individual, they had an area behind the garbage rack where you could fight it out, as long as you used your fists, and when it's over you're supposed to get up and shake hands.

I said, "Did you look at this one? He's over 6 feet tall and he's from the mountains" up in Virginia. These are some of the comical things.

I enlisted on March 18, 1936. And it took me a year and 11 months to make private first class. But it wasn't too long after that until I made corporal. The reason I got promoted was that a World War I sergeant committed suicide, and this left a vacancy for sergeant, so when they promoted one of the senior corporals, it left a vacancy for a corporal.

I proceeded and got to buck sergeant, served as platoon sergeant, and I was getting ready to leave the service. I'd already met my future wife. I was stationed at Rockford, Illinois, and I was going to be separated from the service in March of the following year. In the military at that time a sergeant made $72 a month. On my pay I certainly couldn't afford a wife, so I was planning on getting out. I was in a position where I could take a trade school, and I qualified and even had a job lined up. I didn't want to wait, so we decided to get married.

We got married on Thanksgiving Day. It was November 20, 1941. On December 7, Pearl Harbor was attacked, so I couldn't get out.

Everyone was real mad at the Japanese, and volunteers were pouring in. The volunteers were just about as plentiful as the draftees were. It unified the country. In other words, this was a war that we had to win.

It's been said that compared with later wars, World War II was a good war. There's no such thing as a good war. World War II was a "must" war. We had to win. I think even among those who were in combat there was never any doubt in our minds but that we were going to pursue it until we won.

After Pearl Harbor, they started calling in reserve officers. Now, I don't want to put any reflection on any  individuals. They were educated, they were smart, but they knew very little about the military. And there was this one lieutenant, he was reading in the manual, trying to learn something. He said, "I understand why we have officers and non-commissioned officers, but who are these 'Bar' men?" Browning automatic rifles.

I thought, "Good gosh, these people are going to be leading me in combat?" And here I already had five years of training. So I applied for officers candidate school.

You had to make 110 on the Army General Classification Test to qualify, and they also required a high school education. They had a board of officers there to make the selections to OCS, so they observed me in my handling of my platoon, etcetera, and they gave a waiver for me to go OCS at Fort Benning, Georgia, in spite of my not having finished high school. And I might add that I graduated in the upper 10 percent.

When I graduated, they assigned me to a new infantry division that was being formed. They sent five of us shavetails into this company, and the company commander gave us a form to fill out, giving our experiences and our preference of assignment. I put down "rifle platoon leader." I'd been a platoon sergeant and I knew the platoon A to Z, so I knew I could handle this job in spite of my limited education. All the other officers put down company executive officer. Well, who do you think they chose for company exec? I should have known, because that's the Army system: If you want something, tell them that's what you don't want.

After being in that position for three months, they promoted me to first lieutenant. It wasn't long after that until they were forming another new division, so now we had to send a cadre to this new division. The company commander called me in. He said one of us would have to go as a company commander in the new division. Then he said, "Since this is my first company, I'd like to stay here." In other words, I had no choice. I was cadred out to help form another division.

After holding that position for six months they promoted me to captain. So when I first went in, it took me a year and 11 months to make private first class; now I go from second lieutenant to captain in 11 months. I said, "I must have been a dumb private and a smart officer."

At the time I got my orders to go overseas, I was working for the assistant division commander. We were running rifle platoons through a live firing field problem and I had to rate them as to whether they were qualified for combat. If they weren't, they had to go back and take some more training.

I was able to rate all the platoons except one. This platoon did everything wrong as far as issuing their orders and taking advantage of the camouflage. Everything they did was wrong except one thing: They hit every target. So I went to the assistant division commander, a general, and asked him to help me make this decision. And he wasn't much help; he's still going to leave it up to me. This is what I said: "The cover of your own rifle fire is the best cover you can have, and when you're killing the enemy they're not killing you. So how can I rate them unsatisfactory?"

He said, "Good."

So we rated them qualified.

This is what I was doing when I got orders on the 16th of June, 1944, to ship out as a replacement officer because of the high rate of casualties they were having in Normandy.

They put us on a troop ship to ship to England, and we were in a convoy. There were so many ships in this convoy that you could look in any direction almost going over the horizon, and the freighters and tankers had the perimeter. In other words, if submarines made an attack on us they were supposed to take it rather than let them get to the troop ships.

The ship that we were on was an old German ship that had been scuttled by the Germans in Africa, and we had salvaged it. We were out two days; our convoy was taking a zigzag course, and they were making a turn to the left when the steering mechanism on our ship went out. We couldn't turn. And there was one of those tankers crossing in front of us. They put our ship in reverse and it was like it was jumping up and down to stop from hitting this tanker that's filled with high-octane gas.

I hoped they would turn around and take us back to repair the ship, because the convoy just went off and left us, but we were already at the point of no return. So they left us there and they left one destroyer with us. He was circling us all the time while we were getting our repairs done, and occasionally he'd take off and drop a few depth charges. I don't know whether there was an enemy sub there; the radar picked up something, it might have been a school of fish.

They got the ship repaired before daylight the next morning, and we caught up to the convoy without any further incident.

We landed in England, but I was only there a few days because they needed replacements badly. They shipped me through and right on up to the front lines. It was so confused I don't even remember the date, but it was around the end of June. They assigned me to the 90th Infantry Division. They assigned me as company commander of Company G in the 358th Infantry Regiment. This company had lost all of its officers and 50 percent of its enlisted men during a prior engagement.

My mission was to organize replacements into this demoralized company and make an attack three days later. That was the most trying time I've had in my entire life. I thought, if I live through this, I'd have to have some help from the Supreme Being, and I believe He came to my rescue.

After the reorganization, when we were moving up to the front, we were under long-range artillery fire. A shell exploded nearby and a piece of shrapnel struck a boy in the head. He was somewhere between 18 and 21 years of age. I can hear him today, his cry out and the way his voice trailed off as he dropped dead. He said, "Mommmm." It gave me the chills. That was my first casualty. He was one of the 405,399 to be killed in World War II. He became a statistic. He was a statistic to everyone except his mother and his other loved ones. I've often wondered, how is the selection made? He hadn't seen an enemy. He hadn't fired a weapon.

My first major battle was the battle of the Island of Seves.

The regiment made two attacks on that island and they were repulsed with heavy casualties. The regimental chaplain put up a white flag and started walking across toward the enemy lines. A German officer put up a white flag and they met out in no man's land. They organized a truce, so both sides could pick up their casualties and get medical treatment for them. They came back and took the white flags down and we started making more casualties.

It was there that I learned my first big lesson.

After making the first attack and getting ready for the second attack, there was one sergeant, I couldn't get him out of his foxhole to join us for this attack. He was squatted down below ground level, and he was frozen with fear. After this attack, which was also a failure, I went back to check on him. There he was, crouched down in that foxhole in the same position I'd last seen him. The only difference was, he had a hole in his steel helmet. For him to get killed like that it took a treeburst artillery shell, and a piece of shrapnel had to go straight down into that foxhole. The lesson I learned was, if it's your time you cannot hide. I decided that I may get it, but I'm going to be doing my job when I do. If he had joined us in the attack, he might be alive today. Of course, with the condition he was in he wouldn't have been any help. Some people just could not take it. The public doesn't realize all the types of killing there is in a war, and the ruthlessness of it. There are some men who couldn't take it mentally, while other men who could take it, who knows why they could take it?

After the two failures, the regiment wanted to make another attack – with just one rifle company – and they chose my company to make it. I wondered if the tactics were correct, because here's a strong point three miles long. I was always taught that you attack the weak points, not the strong points. If you surround them, they'll fall without any casualties. But here they're going to order one rifle company to take an objective that the whole regiment had failed to take and one battalion surrendered half of its men on that island.

They promised me a smokescreen and an artillery preparation so that they could blind the enemy and make him keep his head down while we crossed this open field and the river we had to wade to get to this strong point.

I keep waiting for the smoke and the artillery and I never see it. The battalion commander orders me to go anyhow. I questioned him on that. And these are his words. He said: "If we don't get some men on that island, I'll be relieved, the regimental commander will be relieved, you'll be relieved."

I said, "Colonel, I think my responsibility goes a little deeper than that. I'm responsible for 150 men."

I don't remember saying this but in my mind I knew that was what I felt.

He ordered us to go, so what am I going to do? Take a chance of being court-martialed for disobeying an order to go on a hazardous duty? I couldn't do that. I remembered the old infantry credo – I said, "Follow me!" I thought it would be sure death, but I had no choice.

I got out about 50 yards, and the Germans opened up on us with machine guns, even some tank firing. I look back, and there are three men following me. So I hit the ground. Now what the heck are me and three men going to do? I lay in a prone position, and one machine gun was cutting grass over my legs and I believe if he had searched up any higher he'd have cut the cheeks of my butt off. But he searched back and killed one of the men that were following me.

Also, someone was firing at me with a burp gun; what we called a burp gun, it's like our Thompson machine guns. It wasn't high-powered and it was firing at its maximum range. So they're on line with me but they're falling about three feet short. The bullets were bouncing. I could see them. I was holding my carbine, and I felt something roll across my hand, and I caught three of those bullets. Now who's going to believe that you caught three bullets in combat?

After a while they stopped shooting. Either they thought we were dead or they could see that we were no threat to take the island. I told these two men to run back for cover, so they dashed back. I should have gotten up and gone with them, but I lay there until they reached cover. Then I got up, and these Germans were ready for me. I had three machine guns firing at me, like you see in a movie. They ripped up the dirt on the right side, the left side, I could hear the bullets like hornets all around me. And I didn't zigzag, I just took off as fast as I could dash. It was fifty yards, and I didn't get a scratch. So I figure the guardian angel was working for me there.

They had an investigation after that. They had me make out a report on the battalion commander's action. Now, pardon my General Patton language, but I said in the report that they were so damn screwed up that none of them knew what the hell they were doing. That's the way I expressed it. The battalion commander got relieved of his command and so did the regimental commander.

When I issued that attack order and most of my men refused to go, actually my sympathy was with them. They were correct. Suppose I order you to walk out in front of automobiles. Are you going to do it? To cross the highway with high speed automobiles? The principle is the same. You don't have to obey an illegal order, and I wondered what my chances would have been if I had disobeyed that order.

Shortly after that was the Normandy breakout, and the armored forces were pursuing the Germans twenty to thirty miles a day. We in the infantry were trying to keep up. We were marching down the road, single file, on each side of the road, and here comes a jeep. My first sergeant said, "Do you know who that is?"

I said, "No."

He said, "That's General Patton!"

I'd heard a lot about General Patton but I'd never met him. He got right even with G Company and said, "Driver, stop here."

I thought, "I don't see how anything could be wrong." My biggest responsibility at that time was keeping the stragglers moving. Mine was the rearmost company, so some of the stragglers were from other companies.

General Patton got out of the jeep and said, "Who's the blankety blank commanding officer of this blankety blank outfit?" You can fill in the blanks.

At that time I was hoping the Germans would start shelling us so I could jump in a hole. And then I was thinking, if he relieves me of my command, with the experiences I've had, he'd be doing me a favor.

I stepped out and reported to him and said, "I am, Sir."

He looked me over and made a few comments. Then he got back in the jeep and drove on. It was just his way of letting everybody know that he's in charge of things and he's up there. So I'm one of those who could brag about being chewed out by General Patton.

In August, we had moved into a bivouac area, and they decided they would have a little break and pay the troops. They told me to go back to the division rear and pick up the payroll.

By the time I got back to my company, it was late afternoon. I started paying off the troops. Most of them would take a few dollars, and they had a system where you could put some of the money back and send it to your family.

I got through one platoon, and we got an emergency order. We've got to move right away. I had to stop paying off the troops and move into this other area. By the time we got there and got situated it was dark, and I could hear the Germans out in front of me. I could hear their vehicles and tanks running around. This was during the closing of the Falaise Gap. The Germans had broken through in one spot, and they wanted to plug the hole with us.

During the night, I get orders that we're going to make a daylight attack. What am I going to do with this payroll? I can picture me galloping across this field with a .45 pistol in one hand and the payroll in the other. I thought about it and thought about it. Finally, I turned this payroll over to my driver, who was a Pfc. He was a pretty reliable guy, and I told him, "Guard this with your life."

We launched this attack, and we came under mortar fire. A mortar round exploded nearby, and I felt something jerk my trousers below my knee. I jumped in a hole until the mortar barrage lifted, and when I started to move out, uh-oh, something's wrong with that leg.

I look down, and pull the britches leg up. There's a piece of steel sticking in my left leg, just below the knee. So I took my first aid packet, and thought through my first aid training. The first thing I did was to sprinkle this sulfa powder around the wounded area. I put a bandage around it. Then I took my sulfa tablets and drank half a canteen of water.

This thing's got to come out of my leg before I can go any farther, so I call the executive officer over and put him in charge of the company going into this attack, and I go back to the aid station. On the way back, I run into a Mexican who was in my company. His right hand was shredded, and it looked like there was no meat on his fingers. He said he was throwing a hand grenade and it hit an apple tree and bounced back, and he picked it up to throw it again and it exploded.

We had to cross an open field to get back to the aid station, and whenever we got into the field a German machine gun opened up on us. So we ducked down in this ditch. We lay there a little while, then we got up to move again, and the Germans opened up with that machine gun a second time.

There was no way we could get across this field with that machine gun shooting at us. So we lay down again, and got up a third time, and the same thing. Now this Mexican takes his carbine in his left arm, and he's up there looking for that machine gun.

I told him, "Stay down here! There's no reason to commit suicide." So we lay there awhile longer. Of course, my company and the other elements of the battalion were moving forward with the attack, so the Germans must have gotten out of there. Eventually we got up, they didn't shoot at us, and we got back to the battalion aid station.

They had quite a few casualties there. The battalion surgeon looked at me. I wasn't hurting and I wasn't losing any blood, so he just put another bandage on top of the one that I had put on. Then he gave me six sulfa tablets and told me to drink half a canteen of water. I said, "I've already done that, Captain."

He said, "We've got to get it on the record." So I took the six tablets.

Then they sent me back to the regimental clearing station. Here again they had heavy casualties, and I'm waiting for them to treat everybody. Finally they looked at me, and all they did was give me six more sulfa tablets.

The doctor at the battalion aid station had forgotten to put it on my tag – you can understand in combat how they forget these things. I had to take the tablets, and by this time I was more concerned about overdosing on sulfa drugs than I was about my wound.

I went back to the division collecting station. There they had hospital tents set up. Here again, they take care of the most seriously wounded first, including the Germans. I was the last one that they took into surgery.

I was wounded at 9:30 in the morning and here it is midnight. When they removed the bandages from my leg and pulled that piece of steel out, blood squirted up. That hot steel had cut my artery and sealed it at the same time. You see what would have happened if they'd pulled that out any other place? This is the sort of luck I had all through this war.

At the division collecting station, you saw all types of injuries. You saw tankers who had been burned, and they were bandaged up to the top of their head; all you could see was their eyes, just like a mummy. At midnight a Red Cross girl came around and lit a cigarette for them.

From the division collecting station I was evacuated to England, and within two weeks I was back at the front line. All this time I was wondering what happened to that payroll.

When I came back through the division rear, I went in to see the intelligence officer, and I kind of whispered to him, "What happened to that payroll?"

"Ohhh," he said, "We had a heck of a mess with that! We counted it up and $82 was missing. We started wondering whether to charge you or not."

I was getting ready to say, "You aren't charging me for nothing! I couldn't help that."

Then he said, "We had a little slush fund back here so we put in the $82." But all I could figure out, the Pfc that I turned the bag over to – a Pfc got about $82 a month – he must have taken out his $82 and forgot to sign the payroll.

After I came back, they assigned me to Company C of the 358th Regiment. And this company had the best non-commissioned officers. They had good morale. In other words, they're combat-trained now; they know what they're doing. And that helped boost my morale, too.

I had a few skirmishes, but the next thing of importance was the period of time when they ran out of gas. [In September 1944, gasoline was diverted from Patton's Third Army to Operation Market Garden in Holland.] We were in a bivouac area, and the rumor was that we were going to bed down for the winter and make a spring attack. I realized later that this was just a ploy to fool the enemy, but we were even cutting down logs and building log cabins and hauling straw in so it would be comfortable for the men. All the activity that was going on was just some patrolling by each side.

While we're going through all this, we get a message from the regiment: "All officers report to the division rear." They had a sports arena back there and they got all of the officers in the entire division together. I thought, "They're taking quite a chance. What if somebody dropped a bomb?" You can imagine how many officers were in that building. It has a stage up in front, and we're all waiting to see what's going to happen.

The first thing, here comes old General Patton walking across the stage. He walks from one end of the stage to the other, then he walks back and stops. And he says, "Men, this is it!"

I'm not going to quote all his curse words. He said, "We're going to cross that damn Moselle River at 2 o'clock in the morning."

He said, "I want to tell you a little bit about the enemy over there. Now, in these fortress battalions, the Germans don't have their best troops. Their armored forces, their crack troops, are back in reserve. Some of the fillers in these fortress battalions are old men."

He said, "Kill the sonofabitches."

He said, "Some of them have been slightly wounded in combat, or maybe they've got a crippled leg or one arm missing, but they can man those machine guns in these forts. Kill the sonofabitches."

Then he said, "There's this business about taking prisoners. When you accept an enemy as a prisoner, and you've searched him and disarmed him and he's in your possession, you treat him according to the Geneva Convention.

"But there's nothing that says you can't shoot the sonofabitch before you've accepted him as a prisoner. Some of those snipers will take camouflage in a tree, and some of them are going to let you pass and are camouflaged behind you, and they'll kill a few of your men. Then, when you locate his position, he wants to come out and surrender. Don't accept that sonofabitch. Kill him."

The Moselle River was flooded at that time, and the ground was wet. We had to carry the assault boats from our covered position, to keep it secret from the Germans. I helped carry one of the boats; the terrain was rough, and my shoulder was black and blue for two or three weeks.

When we got down to the river we had to plug in a large cable that was insulated and waterproof. We plugged that into our telephone line, and when we began to row across, as we'd roll this cable off from the rear of the boat, the current kept swinging us downstream. And these men weren't skilled oarsmen to begin with. I said, "Throw that damn wire overboard!" When we got across we were 100 yards down from where the company was. It's a good thing there was no enemy there. And it was a complete surprise because we had to wake the Germans up to tell them we were over there. So the strategy worked, but nobody had thought about how strong the current was.

My mission in the Moselle crossing was to capture the little town of Bessehahn. The battalion was attacking Fort Koenigsmacher, and Bessehahn was where the battalion wanted to move everything into.

A and B Companies made the attack on Fort Koenigsmacher, and they had so many casualties that they couldn't go forward. So now they're going to commit me, and also G Company on the other side.

Prior to us making this crossing, they were doing away with the old cannon company. The regimental cannon company was artillery. Some of its officers were sent to the infantry. And they sent me an officer whose name was Lieutenant Gordon.

The old infantry style is to attack with two platoons forward and one in support. So I put Lieutenant Gordon in charge of my support platoon until he could get his feet on the ground and get acquainted with his men.

When they were getting ready to make this attack on Fort Koenigsmacher, I took all of the officers on a reconnaissance into the area that A and B Companies had already captured and occupied, to see what the situation was. When I got back and issued an attack order, Lieutenant Gordon was missing. I reported it to the battalion commander.

We captured Fort Koenigsmacher and started setting up our defenses, because the Germans have a habit of trying to attack you before you get organized on your objective. Just as we got reorganized, I got a message to call the battalion commander.

He said, "We located Lieutenant Gordon." He claimed he was shellshocked. The battalion commander said, "Do you want me to send him back up there?"

I said, "If you send the sonofabitch up here I'll shoot him myself!"

"Then I'd better not send him up there."

Now, while we were on that reconnaissance there were a few harassment artillery shells, but none of them hit close, so how could he have gotten shellshocked? I've seen men shellshocked. They're just as likely to go forward as backward; they don't know what they're doing, and he knew what he was doing.

Then they sent me a two-page questionnaire to fill out. The last question on it was: "Even though this officer is unqualified for combat, do you think he's qualified for a rear area job in administration, supplies, or communication?"

I said, "No."

They said, "If your answer is no, state why? "

I wrote, "In my opinion, the purpose of Army officers is to lead troops in combat. There's only one test of that ability. If they fail that test, they do not deserve a commission in any capacity, period."

It turns out Lieutenant Gordon was some big shot's son back in the States, so they assigned him to a rear area job. And I and all of the officers, whenever we'd go back to the rear and had to see him, he'd want to be friends, but we just gave him the cold shoulder.

Some time later I was reading an article in Stars & Stripes. It was an article on how to fight the Germans in the city. I said, "This is very good. This is the way I've been coaching my troops."

Who do you think signed it? Lieutenant Gordon! You talk about wanting to go back there and shoot him myself, and all he knew about it was what I briefed the company when we were going across the river to take Bessehahn. Now today, he's a veteran, with all privileges. Where's the justice?

Now I'm going to tell you about another incident that stands out very strongly in my memory.

The battalion commander called me back and said the division is organizing a special operation, and that they need one rifle company. He said they requested that the 358th Infantry Regiment supply the rifle company, and that the regiment called on our battalion to supply the  company, and he said they specifically suggested that I take it.

The mission was a guerrilla warfare type operation. They would assign me an objective behind the enemy lines, and my mission was to take this rifle company to that location, take that objective at night, and the division would attack – when I say division, I mean they would designate somebody from our battalion to attack – at daylight the next morning.

I suppose that I was successful in these operations. If I had not been successful, I wouldn't be able to tell the story.

On one of those operations, so many unusual things occurred that I would like to present it in detail.

My mission was to sneak through the German lines at night and occupy a piece of critical terrain that was overlooking a German village that sat behind the dragons' teeth in the Siegfried Line. The battalion would attack at dawn to capture this town. I would be in a position where when they started their attack, I could fire into this town and also deny the Germans use of this critical terrain.

Before I started out, they sent me a new artillery forward observer. I received a call from battalion, regiment and division telling me that this was this lieutenant's first experience in combat and for me to look out for him, that he was a general's son.

To accomplish the mission I had to make a map reconnaissance during daylight, to be able to guide the company to its location. There was no road or trail to guide on, so I had to do it from the outlines of the vegetation, the trees, and the contour of the land.

It so happened that this particular night was one of those nights that was so dark you literally could not see your hand before your face. And since I'm the only one who can get this company to that location, we proceed in one line, by holding hands.

Now, can you picture 150 men lined up behind me holding each other's hand?

As we moved up through the first wooded area we had to go through, there were evergreens. If you've ever been around evergreens on a moonless night with no stars, can you realize how dark this is?

As we were moving through this group of evergreen trees, we heard some Germans approaching our position. And by the sound of it, they were going to cross somewhere in this line of troops behind me.

I cannot give orders. That would give our position away. All I could do was whisper to the man behind me to pass the word along to take care of these Germans wherever they crossed.

A short while later I heard a few muffled rifle shots. These men had laid there in a prone position and let these Germans – I don't know if it was two or three of them – walk right on top of them, and gut-shot them.

These Germans were carrying some hot chow down to one of their security posts that we had bypassed. And the story the men told me was that the guys who shot those Germans sat there on their bodies and ate those hot sandwiches.

Then we get up and move out again, and we come to the end of these evergreens. Now we have an open field to cross before we get into this high ground and wooded area that was our objective. From the edge of the wooded area it was clear down to the village, and we were to take a position along the front of the woods. But I looked and listened before I moved out from the cover of the evergreens. I realized that even though it's dark, we could be silhouetted against the skyline. And I could hear a group of Germans talking in clump of bushes to my right front.

I had to do something. So I called up two men with automatic rifles. I said, "Do you hear those Germans jabbering over there in that clump of bushes?"

They said, "Yeah."

I said, "When we start across this open field, I want you to spray the bushes with automatic rifle fire."

Being in the service I knew, what do these Germans do? They're going to do just like anyone would do. If somebody suddenly opened up on me, I'm going to hit the ground and head for cover. So these automatic rifles started spraying that clump of bushes and we moved across that open space to those other trees and they didn't fire one round at us. And I said, "Look, we're behind their lines. They don't know whether this is one of their own units making a mistake or what." So I begin to realize – I've been on two of these operations previously – that actually, this is a lot better behind their lines than it is attacking a fortified position when they're waiting for you with their guns zeroed in, so if you don't get too scared, in a way it can be fun.

We got in position on the edge of those woods, on this high ground that sloped down into this village. All we've got to do now is sit there and wait.

While we were waiting, a group of Germans left the village. It was only a small patrol but they were approaching our position. Now this is going to give us away before we want our presence to be known. So I have to do something.

I called up three men that had rifle grenades and had them put phosphorous grenades on their rocket launchers. I put them in position and gave them the angle; my idea was that I would fire these phosphorous grenades where they would land behind this group that's approaching us. This field had some grass growing, it would set that on fire, and that way we can see them and they can't see us. And sure enough they walked right under this; the rifle grenades went up and exploded behind them. They didn't shoot one round at us. Those that weren't killed dashed back to the village.

Now they know we're here.

Later on, there was a German straggler, or someone from the village who was worried about his friend. He's coming up from the village, and as he's approaching where we were in those woods, he was hollering for somebody by the name of "Heinie, Heinie, Heinie," walking right into our laps. Here again, I can't holler, I just know these men are trained; the first guy he comes to is either going to capture him or kill him. And lo and behold we had one recruit, this was his first day out, and if this wasn't the one he approached. The recruit froze, and the German reached over and started pulling his pant leg, as if he thought it was another German and he was trying to shake him. Then the squad leader jumped up and hit that German over the head with his rifle butt and captured him.

At daylight they started sniping at us, and the only one they hit was that German. He was laying there on the ground, and let me tell you where they shot him: right between the legs. I'd never heard anybody groan and moan like he did. There was nothing we could do except give him a shot of morphine, and one of the men said, "Don't worry about it, your own men shot you." That was very cruel. And he died.

Now I get a call from battalion. They tell me they're not going to launch this attack.

I'm behind the enemy lines, my neck's stuck out and they're going to leave me there. And the reason was – after we got in position I could hear tanks and vehicles rolling around, and there was a big crowd of Germans in that village – they said intelligence had reported that position had been reinforced with a German armored division and we cannot take it. They said to stay up there and withdraw under cover of darkness.

Well, this sounded good if the Germans would cooperate. But like I said, now they know we're there. So they start firing 120-millimeter mortars. And we're so close to them that we could hear the mortars popping out of their tubes. I sent a man to the right flank and another man to the left flank to shoot an azimuth, where they could hear the mortar rounds coming out of the tubes. They brought those azimuths back and I plotted them on a map, and it showed a bunch of gullies in that area. I figured that would be a good place to set those mortars up. Then I gave the location to this lieutenant – the artillery forward observer I was supposed to look out for – and he went up and established an observation post, and he observed the artillery fires and got them on those gullies. And the Germans stopped firing.

There was a bunker – the Germans had those scattered all over – so we had the command post set up there, and the lieutenant came back down to the bunker, and we were just sweating it out now, hoping that they don't bother us anymore so we can bug out when night gets here.

Later on that afternoon, those mortars open up again, and I hear them popping out of the tube. They were coming from about the same place. So I told this lieutenant to refire that concentration. And all he needed to do – they had already zeroed in on that location, and we'd given it a number – all he had to do was call and say, "Fire concentration, 235," and then go up to the observation post. Instead, he decides to go up to the O.P. and then call in the fire order. And on his way up, one of those mortar rounds landed between his legs. Can you imagine the shape he was in? I went up there, and one leg was thrown this way and the other one that way, and I talked to him. At that time, shock hadn't set in yet.

I said, "I'll have a medic come up to take care of you." But when the medic got up there, he was already dead.

The Germans didn't bother us after that. We fired that concentration, and the mortars stopped shooting.

We waited until night, and they told us to bring all of our equipment and bring our casualties back. This lieutenant was 6 feet tall if he was an inch. He graduated with honors from college and got an appointment to West Point, his father's a general, he's general material, he needs to get this – we call it punching their ticket, combat experience – and then to get killed on his first day out, it's embarrassing for me, but how can I stop this? It's his time, that's all there is to it. I'm around that area where the mortars were firing; why didn't one of them fall between my legs? How do you understand these things?

We had only two men killed, one Pfc and this lieutenant, and we had to carry them out.

To this day I don't remember the lieutenant's name. General Patch lost a son in the war about that time and it could possibly have been General Patch's son.

When we got back to our lines, I was challenged, and I didn't know the password. They took me all the way down to the battalion command post so they could identify that I wasn't a German in an American uniform.

In another one of those operations I went on, we were going in to take a village. Let me add that during these operations, Patton had the Germans on the run, and we were hitting so hard that they were never able to set up any good security or defensive positions.

As we're moving down on the village, the Germans are moving out. They were sending a towed antitank weapon into position to cover this withdrawal, and it was horse-drawn. They hadn't put it in position by the time we arrived, so we knocked out this crew of that horse-drawn weapon and moved on in.

Can you picture now men going into buildings to see if there's Germans in them? It's night, walking in a room and turning on a flashlight to see if anybody's in there? They did this at one house – the squad leader went in there and informed me. He said when they went in this bedroom, there was a man and woman in bed, so he was getting ready to say, "Excuse me," and he said the man was jumping up and he started putting his clothes on, and he's putting on a German uniform. So they took him prisoner.

Another of these missions was a daylight operation. In moving to our objective, we ran into a German security outpost, and we captured it. They didn't have any communications, to even send word to the rear. So the Germans didn't know that we were approaching.

We were screening out through some woods. I'm approaching with two platoons following the scouts out, and when we reached the edge of the woods, I said, "Stop!" I wanted to observe before we proceeded across the open ground. I went forward, and with my field glasses I searched the first hundred yards back and forth. It must have been thousands of yards across this open space. And then I searched back another hundred yards, and so on until I looked way down to the end of of this rolling terrain where this other strip of woods were, and I saw a movement. We saw some Germans were leaving that patch of woods and approaching us. And if they stayed on this little trail that they were on, they'd come right up in front of these woods and turn right in front of us.

I said, "This is an ideal ambush." So I got busy. I put my two light machine guns in position first. I said, "I'm going to blow a whistle to start this. You start at the front of the column and search back, and you start at the rear of the column and search forward." Then I placed some automatic rifles in position, because I knew as soon as we opened up, they're going to hit the ground. And then I positioned my support platoon, and I had my mortars in position. And I said, "When I blow the whistle a second time, everybody cease fire." The support platoon now will dash out with fixed bayonets and grab anybody that's alive as a prisoner."

Now can you imagine these Germans walking along there, laughing, talking, and then all of this hits them at once? And this was in the winter, it's snowing. When the platoon dashed out there, they said there wasn't any fight left in the Germans, and they're laying in the snow, praying.

There was one man in that group who got away. He started running back across the field, and the machine guns were firing at him, you could see the tracers, and not one of them hit him. I felt bad about that; we let one of them get away. And then I thought, man, let him get back there and tell them what happened to the rest of them!

But you don't plan these things. You're out there, and something's occurring, you just do what you have enough training to do. They taught me when I received my tactical training that the worst thing you can do in combat is nothing, to do something, even if it's wrong.


We crossed the Saar River early in December of 1944. Our objective was Dillingen, Germany. We crossed it on assault boats. It was at nighttime. And in taking the first building that we approached, there's a stairway outside the building, and this squad went up the stairs through that building. I heard somebody running down those steps just as hard as they could go, and I'm wondering what happened. I started stepping down the foot of the stairway. About that time I'm hit on the shoulder and there was a German running down there, and before I could get my gun up to get him he ran out through the dark.

In this little suburb of Dillingen, I forget the name of it, there was a pillbox. I assigned one platoon to knock out this pillbox. They assaulted the pillbox and came under fire from a second pillbox. So I took my support platoon, and we maneuvered up through these buildings, and we got up into the second story of a building from which we could look across and down onto this pillbox.

There was a German in a trench outside the pillbox with a rocket launcher. I had a man with an automatic rifle in the platoon, and I told him to get in the window and shoot the German. He shot at the German and missed.

Now the German is swinging that rocket launcher around to fire into the room where we are. I didn't have time to take any other action except to take him out myself. And I shot him with a .45 pistol. There was another German who shot back at me, because I felt the wind from that bullet as it went between my neck and right shoulder. And I had shot through a plate glass window, that's about 70 yards. The effective range of a .45 pistol is 50 yards, so I had my guardian angel helping me there, although I was an expert pistol shot.

When I felt that bullet go over my right shoulder, I turned around, and there's a soldier dead behind me.

In Dillingen, we cleared out these buildings on one side of a large railroad track. This railroad yard was two or three hundred yards wide. There was a German pillbox sitting right out in the middle of the railroad tracks, and the Germans occupied the buildings on the other side of the tracks. So we had a little wait here, since they hadn't gotten the bridge across the Saar River, and the Army Times gave us a writeup as the longest bridgehead without getting any rations. We all laughed about that, and the reason was this: There was a meat packing company in this part of the town, and we were cutting off choice steaks and having steak and eggs three times a day.

But eventually we were going to cross the railroad tracks to take the rest of the buildings. So I'm walking up and down the front line of my company trying to boost morale, like any commanding officer would be doing, and I come across a building which I thought would give me good observation into the German occupied part of the city.

I went up two flights of stairs, and I said to myself it was a good observation post because there was an artillery team up there. There was a forward observer and a radio operator, and they were observing for targets in enemy territory.

Just as I arrived at that position, I saw a vision.

It was just like observing a wide angle TV screen. I can see these Germans, in their uniforms, with their distinctive steel helmets. They had a radio and it was letting out beams, and they were beaming in on my position, according to my vision. It was all in my mind. Nobody else could see this but me, but it was just as clear as watching a TV set. I saw them transmit this information to their fire direction center. I could see the German fire direction center communicating. I saw them send this fire mission out to one of their guns. I could see these Germans getting ready to fire that gun.

I hesitated. I thought, "What should I do? Should I tell these men to move? If I tell them to move and nothing would happen, they'd think I was cracking up and I wouldn't be effective as a commander."

When I hesitated, I felt something pushing me toward the stairway, just like wings, pushing me. When that occurred, I didn't hesitate.

When I got down off the last step, an artillery shell exploded in that room and killed both of those men.

This was my evidence that I was going to survive this war, and that I did have a guardian angel.

My first operation in the Battle of the Bulge was in the town of Niederwampach, in Luxembourg. A and B Companies had attacked Niederwampach and they were held up, so the battalion asked me to go around the left flank and attack from the rear.

In an attack position such as this, I always attacked with two platoons forward and one in support, and my position is always in between and slightly to the rear of the two attacking platoons, so I can keep abreast of what's going on and if I need to commit my support platoon, I'll know where to do it.

In approaching Niederwampach, the two platoons split up a little, so the village in my immediate front had not been cleared. I entered a building with my command group; when I say command group, that was just myself, my communications sergeant, the radio operator and my messenger.

We entered the barn part of this building, and when I first entered, I turned around and started to say, "I don't believe there's anything in here." There was a platform of hay on the right side; the platform was about waist high, and the hay was a little higher than that, and this hay started to move. So we squared off toward that hay with our weapons, and a German said, "Nicht schiessen! Nicht schiessen!" Which meant, "Don't shoot."

I said, "Hande ho!" Put your hands up. So they put their hands up and came out and surrendered; there must have been ten or twelve Germans.

There was another group of four or five men who came out from the stall behind us, and they surrendered. I heard a commotion over my head and I looked up and there's a German descending from a rafter, and he had hand grenades around his waist belt; he came down and surrendered.

I bring this out just to show you how lucky I was all through combat.

Then I had my other platoons clear out the other buildings, and we captured Niederwampach.

From Niederwampach, we were to go and take Oberwampach.

Before we left, the battalion commander informed me that the situation was serious, but it wouldn't become critical as long as we could prevent the Germans from widening the gaps in our lines. They were sending me into Oberwampach, which was on the shoulder of this breakthrough, with orders to hold it at all costs.

In moving across the open fields to get to Oberwampach, we came under machine gun fire from a position on our right front. So I told the radio operator who's carrying the SCR300 radio on piggyback right beside me to call for artillery fire to neutralize this machine gun fire. This radio operator now is shot through the head and falls dead at my feet while I'm on the transmitter making that message.

Instead of getting artillery that time, one of the tanks that we had in support took care of the machine gun nest.

Another man picked up the radio and we moved on into Oberwampach, which we took with very little resistance. It was about dusk, and before I got my security all arranged, a German halftrack towing a 120-millimeter mortar and a crew of 12 moved into our midst. We didn't know it at the time, but they moved into one of the buildings. They didn't know we were there and we didn't know they had moved in until I sent my messenger back to one of my other platoons, and he went back to the building where this platoon had originally been. He opened the door, and the building was full of Germans.

Two platoons were going into position, so I took my other platoon and gave them the mission of knocking out or capturing these Germans, and I told everybody in the company to keep their heads down because it looked like we were going to have a fight right in our midst.

This platoon got in a semicircle around that building, and they opened up on it. They fired a few rifle grenades, and when the rocket launchers fired, one of these Germans put up a white flag. But only six of them surrendered. That's what the Germans will do sometimes; some will surrender while the others get away. The other six escaped through the darkness when we stopped shooting.

Well, these Germans are all 6-foot blonds, and they have Adolph Hitler shoulder patches. They were part of Hitler's elite guard. In other words, up until this time they had been protecting Hitler's headquarters, and this is the first time I guess that they had actually been committed to hard fighting.

So we were literally fighting Hitler's supermen. They all had the same blood type, so that if they had to have a transfusion, they didn't have to check it out, they'd just take one man to another.

I questioned them, and found out that they were part of an armored division that was moving into this area. Then I sent them to the rear.

Based on that information, I asked the battalion commander to send me some more weapons to defend against an armor type attack. He sent me up a platoon of tanks and a platoon of tank destroyers, and I deployed them. And it's a good thing, because the Germans launched an attack at 3:30 in the morning. If we hadn't rushed up those tanks and tank destroyers, they would probably have overrun us the first night.

This little knoll, the high ground on our right, gave us good observation of one of the Germans' supply routes to the troops that surrounded Bastogne, and we were shooting up those vehicles. So they sent elements of a panzer division to knock us out. And we ended up in somewhere between a 36 and a 72 hour battle, night and day. When the Germans were not making a ground attack, they were bombarding us with artillery fire and direct tank fire.

All of their attacks were at night except one. And this was their last attack. I'll get into that in a moment. But when these battles were going on, two of my senior platoon sergeants came to me and said, "Captain, this is the roughest that we've ever experienced. We think we had better withdraw. If not, we'll probably have to surrender."

And I had to tell them that we're going to hold until the last man.

I was no hero. Those were my orders. Knowing that at some time, if the Germans got these tanks into our position, we're out of ammunition, and there's nothing we could do to resist, I would surrender or tell the men to bug out. But I couldn't tell these men that at that time.

Now, these sergeants were brave. They'd fought the Germans longer than I had. They'd fought the Germans from Normandy through the French Maginot Line, the German Siegfried Line. So they were just stating the facts, and I agreed with them. But I had to do what my job was.

We did hold. And rather than go into a lot of these operations up until the last attack, it was either on the 18th or the 19th of January, the Germans made their main effort to overcome us, and they made this attack in daylight hours.

They hit my right flank where I had a platoon on this knoll with four tanks and I estimate a platoon of infantry. Coming across a big long rolling ridge to our front we could count 11 German tanks. There was infantry riding on the tanks. There was infantry in halftracks following over this ridge just as far as we could see, and they were shooting everything they had while they were moving in.

I got on the telephone with the battalion commander, and I asked him to give me all the artillery fire he had available.

He turned me over to the artillery liaison officer of the battalion, and he asked me to zero one gun in on this target.

I had two observation posts set up, one in the right platoon and one in the left platoon, with wire communications to them, so through them we relayed information. We zeroed this one gun on this target, and the artillery officer said, "Fire for effect."

He had nine battalions – that's 108 artillery pieces – that hit that target at one time.

You never saw such a slaughter in all your life. These Germans turned around and withdrew. They didn't make a tactful withdrawal, it was every tank and every man fleeing for his life. Nothing could have overcome that. It's impossible. Some of my men were firing standing up, like shooting ducks in a pond, but they were so far away they'd be lucky if they hit anyone.

The Germans didn't fool with us anymore.

One other incident took place that I think is of interest.

I had my company command post in Oberwampach set up in the home of the Schilling family. When the Germans were shelling us, a five-year-old boy got excited and dashed out the front door, right into the impact area of the artillery. A 20-year-old soldier dashed out to rescue the little boy.

They were both mortally wounded.

The soldier asked someone to rub his left arm; he claimed it hurt him. I rubbed his arm, and he turned blue and died.

The little boy died slowly in his mother's arms, and to see this – you read about these things – but to see the grief this mother was going through of her son being killed by something she had no control over, it really brings some strong lessons to you.

This soldier's name was Sergeant Whitfield. I recommended him for a Distinguished Service Cross and he got it. Now he was a true hero. He gave his life trying not to defend his own life, but to rescue an innocent little boy, and truly he earned his decoration.

After the battle, we picked up a German soldier who had been wounded. He had been shot in the leg with a .50-caliber bullet, and he had lain out overnight in this freezing, subzero weather. Both of his arms and both of his legs were frozen stiff as a board. He begged us to shoot him.

I couldn't do it. I asked for a volunteer. Even if he survived, he'd have to have both arms and both legs amputated, and this could have been a mercy killing. But these battle hardened soldiers that had been fighting Germans a few minutes before would not volunteer. One soldier, out of sympathy for the suffering and bravery of this soldier, lit a cigarette and held it to his lips. Another soldier brought him a hot cup of coffee and held it so he could get coffee until we got the litter jeep up there and sent him to the rear.

I've always been curious to know what happened to him, but I believe he would have died before they got him back to the aid station.

After this battle, the division decoration section came down and they said that with what happened down there the men deserve some medals. They said, "We want to write you up for a DSC."

I said, "No. Every man in the outfit deserves it as much as and some of them more than I do," and I was being honest about it. I wasn't trying to collect medals.

I was trying to save as many of these men as I could from getting killed in this terrible war. I don't know whether I would have received it or not, but I wouldn't even let them write it up. I told them about the experiences of this platoon on the right flank – I had to withdraw them a couple times because the Germans wrestled that knoll from us and we retook it – that there were some heroes up there and for them to check that out and see if they could find out who deserved it from that group.

A couple of weeks later, the battalion commander informed me that there was to be an exchange of foreign decorations, and that a British Military Cross would be presented to one officer per infantry regiment, and that our regiment had asked that each battalion submit the names of two officers for their recommendations and their preferences. From among those names they chose me to receive the British Military Cross. I take this as the best compliment that I could have for my experiences during World War II.

*"Got caught in an air raid and spent 15 minutes huddled with four other PWs near an air raid shelter. One PW made a break for the woods.*

*"When the raid was over the corporal of the guard counted heads and threatened to blow our heads off if we didn't tell him where he went.*

*"I honestly told him I didn't care. I said if he lived to be a hundred in Germany he couldn't have enjoyed life equal to fifteen years in our USA."*

### Jim Koerner
**Sergeant,
10th Armored Division,
former prisoner of war
Interviewed in
Kenilworth, N.J.
Oct. 31, 1997**

*(This narrative is taken from a manuscript Koerner wrote in the early 1950s, with excerpts from the interview woven in.)*

It was a beautiful summer day, this May 9, 1941. I was due for the draft sometime in the near future prior to my volunteering.

I was given the honor of being assistant group leader to Fort Dix.

Thirteen men left from our draft board from Roselle, N.J. We were piled into a chartered bus amid tears and farewells.

I was 21 years old; wouldn't be 22 until May 26, 1941.

Before long, we were hearing the oft spoken, "You'll be sorry," "Watch your back," etc.

Into tent city and the strange new life that was to be home for the next four years, five months and 15 days.

That first night, and long into the morning, the low and muffled sound of sniffles could be heard throughout our five-man tent.

To me it was new, but I'd done a lot of camping and lived the so-called outdoor life and it seemed natural, but to some it was the shaking of the apron strings.

When the first reveille sounded and we were dressed and out for breakfast it seemed as though we all were hungry but untalkative.

After five days at Dix, we were shipped by train to sunny Florida. Camp Blanding, Fla., to be exact.

This was the sandy and red bug center of the world.

We got a cadre of regular army soldiers from a pack artillery outfit in Panama. They were really tough but this outfit left a vivid memory in later Army life.

We had 155 millimeter rifles, World War I vintage, with hard rubber tires, tractor-drawn.

We had good basic training, and in September of 1941 we made the North Carolina maneuvers. All our equipment, or most of the modern parts, was on paper. We had signs for .30-caliber machine guns and .50-caliber machine guns.

Back to Camp Blanding amid rumors of the 28-year-olds going home for good. Then they started being sent home. All got stripes to take home. Some were single and wanted to see Miami, so the married boys got an earlier start.

I went into Stark, Fla., in civvies to see the movie "All This and Heaven Too" on Dec. 7, 1941. I came out to hear the lobby buzzing with the sinking of the Arizona, and wondered what movie they had seen that in. I hit the street and heard the loud MP public address telling all soldiers to get out of civvies and back to camp as all leaves and passes were void.

The next few months were nightmares with our alerts. Clear camp, pack everything in trucks and ride 10 miles, then back to start all over again in a few days.

Five non-commissioned officers – I was a corporal, another corporal and three sergeants – decided we'd never make it overseas with our present outfit, so we volunteered for the paratroops.

Here the toughest training anyone ever had began.

Five weeks in Fort Benning paratroop school is equal to 25 weeks' training elsewhere. I've seen men spit in the sawdust judo pit and have to eat it on command of our training sergeant. I've seen men fall out of five-mile speed marches and vomit and get back in and run. I've seen in judo a man get his shoulder broken and finish his period in pain, but silent pain.

I broke my ankle on a training jump and each day I'd get it strapped so I could get a boot on to jump.

I went into the final stage pulling my bad ankle up and sitting hard on my rump. I wanted to graduate with my class, which was forming the 101$^{st}$ Airborne Division.

I had made it up with a buddy that if I or he couldn't make the grade we would get out together. He had a fear of heights. And at that time you got six months in the stockade for freezing (a natural fear of not getting out of the plane; it happens to longtime jumpers).

After three jumps we joined a casual company where we again volunteered for a so-called colonel's hand-picked mission, which ended up as cadre for the 55$^{th}$ Armored Engineer Battalion, 10$^{th}$ Armored Division, in the Sand Hill area of Fort Benning, Ga.

There we had a colonel who was so tough he used to beat the officers up. I only went through the second year of high school because when I was 14 my father killed himself and I had to work to help keep my family together. And when I'd go out on reconnaissance I had to figure out the capacity of the bridges. One day the colonel said to me, "You're supposed to be pretty good at this. I'm gonna ask you, how good are you?"

I said, "When I say the bridge will take it, it'll take it."

He said, "Well, I'll prove it. The first tank that goes over that bridge, you're gonna be underneath the bridge."

He used to have us run in the morning, at 5 o'clock, get up and doubletime down the street yelling "Bang! Bang! Bang! Bang! I'm Sergeant Koerner and I'm the toughest man here!" And the guys would open the barracks up and say, "Shut up ya son of a B, let us sleep!"

This same colonel, his name was Spangler, they shipped him over to Africa because he got so many complaints. He got over there, and they were taking up mines in this engineer outfit he commanded, and he said, "You're not making enough time. You've got to go like this. ..." Poom! Four more guys to heaven. He was a West Pointer, too. Everybody was saying it couldn't have happened to a nicer guy.

I had a boxing instructor at Fort Benning by the name of Leopold. He was a race car driver in real life, and he had scars all over his face from the accidents he was in.

I'm on tranquilizers. My wife, God bless her, she has to remind me, "You didn't take your tranquilizer today," because if I don't take it, I bite heads. People don't realize that haven't been in the service, when you spend four years learning how to kill people, and to try to save the ones that you've got under you, it's not easy to return to society. I've walked away from fights that I could kill somebody.

Before I left to go overseas, I had a pretty good reputation. I used to tell my men, "I want you to do something for me. Do me a favor." And a couple of big guys would say, "Are the stripes talking?"

I'd say, "They come right off."

We had a platoon in the engineers, in a different barracks. And we had a wooden goat; they used to take that goat and put it in front of the platoon that was the worst platoon in the battalion. These guys were so tough that were in this platoon, they burned that goat.

Before we went overseas, the colonel called me in and said, "Sergeant Koerner, you're taking over the third platoon."

Well, the third platoon was the platoon that burned that goat. They were so mad at the sergeant that was in charge of them, one time when he was out there was a guy sitting with a loaded tommy gun, he was going to kill him when he came in.

I said, "Sir, no. I'm not taking over the third platoon. I'll take private."

He said, "Well, you'll take it over as a private. How do you like that?"

I said, "I'd like it better as a staff sergeant," because my mother was a widow; I was sending money home.

Most of the men in that platoon were from the hills. In the Appalachians, those people are the proudest people, and they're the best soldiers. But when they've got a guy that doesn't appreciate them, and all he did was drink and chase women, they're going to be trouble.

Before I took over I had a couple of sergeants in the platoon that had more seniority than me. There was one regular Army sergeant and I knew he was looking to take over the platoon. I explained to him, "Look. I'll never give you anything to do that I won't do myself. And I'll prove it to you. If you'll help me, I'll help you."

He said, "Okay." That was Sergeant Wiley. I used to say, "The blue grass of Kentucky is in his eyes." He had beautiful blue eyes.

I had two big guys in two different outfits, but in this one outfit, I said to this guy, "I only want three guys lining up over there" to get a haircut. The fourth guy gets up, so I said to him, "Hey, get back on the job."

"Stripes are talking."

I said, "Okay." Off they went, and I turned around and I dropped him.

He went to the colonel. So the colonel called me over. He said, "Sergeant Koerner, did you lay hands on a man?"

"That's right," I said. "If I asked that man to get out of that line – if I tell him to kill somebody – do you think he's going to kill him when he goes overseas?"

"You've got a point, but you've got a week's special duty."

Another time I was on guard duty, and the carpenter said, "Hey, we don't have a ring here for you to train in. Let's get the lumber while we're out here."

I said, "Okay." He built me a ring in the center of the camp. Because we had Chuck Taylor, who fought for the championship when he got out; in the 10th Armored he was the champ, and they wanted me always to fight him. And I said I'll fight him for money. I'm not fighting him for nothing.

Somebody reported that lumber was missing, and I got called in by the colonel. He said, "Sergeant Koerner, when you were on duty, did you see anybody take anything?"

I said, "Yes, I did, Sir."

And he said, "You stood there and you watched them?"

I said, "No, Sir. I helped them unload it."

He said, "Well, I'll tell you what. You just got yourself some more extra duty."


After months of training we went on Tennessee Maneuvers and from there we returned to Camp Gordon, Ga., and then finally in August of '44 we headed north to New York for three days. Then off we went to beat the hurricane out of New York.

One night we went into Weymouth, England, where the misty banks of France seemed to haunt our dreams.

Early departure and the announcement we were to land direct in the harbor of Cherbourg, France. The harbor looked very dreary with its submarine pens and battered ship and gun emplacements.

So over the side to the LCIs [landing craft-infantry] and the grating of the sandy beach under our keel.

While standing on the beach I watched a slow flotilla of LSTs [landing ship-tanks] come into view. I thought, "Boy, wouldn't it be something to see my brother's boat? He's been away over 18 months."

All at once into view came the 345. What a thrill! We were going out only 12 miles to bivouac in the beach area where we were to get our indoctrination of actual mine removal, so my first sergeant said.

Bright and early the next morning found me standing in our hastily erected orderly room.

Captain Garwood listened and was very much the good Joe. Lt. Hanel, my platoon leader, and myself headed for Cherbourg.

We got there about 10 a.m. and with a little persuasion by Lt. Hanel we got a Coast Guard boat to take me out to the 345, at anchor in the harbor.

The port side as we neared was quite a mess with shell marks.

I saluted the deck officer and asked to see Chief Machinist's Mate Ted Koerner.

He looked perplexed and said, "When's the last time you heard from Ted?"

I half-muttered, "Why?"

"Well, Ted's on his way back to the States on rotation by now. He's been in England waiting for the past two weeks."

I was introduced to Ted's replacement, Jim Brown, and given a nice look-see all over the LST.

About that time we had an alert emergency engine start, as our boat was dragging anchor right at a sister ship.

I thought the boat seemed rough, but I heard they were always rough riding so I didn't know a good storm was on us.

The Coast Guard blinker contacted the 345 that my lieutenant, who was waiting for me, was going to leave and for me to stay till I could get ashore.

I spent the night sleeping in my brother's old bunk. Even the blankets had his name on them. I felt near to all my family here.

After a very good breakfast, deluxe to any soldier's idea of food, the captain had a boat put over and back to French soil I returned.

After a hitchhike and some walking I located our bivouac area.

Much to my surprise, all that remained was our garbage dump sign and latrine marker. So I stood bewildered in the middle of nowhere, with no idea of where they had gone.

By the convoy tracks I saw they had headed west. And west I started.

I'd gone about three miles when a jeep screeched to a halt and there was my driver, T/5 Prejean. I sure was glad to see him.

We had gone about 40 miles to a small seashore resort where we were to get our baptism of mine removal.

All along the block were grim reminders of what lay ahead inland.

There were jeeps blown to pieces. There were remains of clothing and bodies.

The Jerries had 16-inch naval shells for mines on the beach near the water. There were schu mines and further inland there were jumping Jennies, or bouncing Betties as they were better known. And also teller mines, pressure release and pressure type.

Every farmer in the peninsula seemed to have a pasture or farm yard to check and clear of mines.

We could have started a junkyard with the pieces of steel we picked up and treated as mines till they were seen.

We even picked up some remote control tanks for observation.

The third platoon needed an extra trailer for our own use. So all of us put our heads together and decided to do something.

We tried supply, but to no avail. One day while on a reconnoitering mission, I noticed set back in a heavily wooded area a group of jeeps and three-quarter ton trailers setting near this house. We stopped and took a run up through the alley and peered into the back of each trailer. They were all new and also empty.

That night Sgt. Marks, a Connecticut cop, and myself asked the motor sergeant, Grimes, an Ohio boy, for a jeep.

Meanwhile we borrowed a can of white stencil paint and a can of green O.D. [olive drab] paint and a "Co. C" stencil from the supply sergeant.

We were all set to move out when Sgt. Grimes, who knew our intent, decided he had a new jeep here and he was going to do the driving.

We headed out to the scene of the crime.

It was a fairly dark night with an occasional moon. We were near our location about 11:30 and the lights were seen dimly through the drawn shades. We waited nearby till 12:15 and then turned on the key and pulled slowly up to the area of the trailers. Sgt. Marks and myself hopped out and Sgt. Grimes backed up to the trailer hitch.

When a burst of moonlight shone through the clouds I looked at the sign hung before the big house. It read, "Normandy Beach MP Headquarters." That sure sped our mission.

We both almost broke our backs lifting the supposedly empty trailer.

We hooked it up and I shoved Sgt. Grimes over and yelled to let me drive. He protested but gave ground.

I put it in first and felt a heavy lurch as we took off with no lights.

All at once we heard a loud "Halt!" to our rear.

I gave it another burst and shoved it into second.

I don't know if we were shot at because of the noise of our motor and the dragging behind of the big one-ton trailer.

Sgt. Grimes kept yelling, "Take it easy! You'll burn my new jeep up!" I still poured it on.

We must have gone a half-mile before Sgt. Marks, who was looking out the side, yelled, "Here they come on the fly!" I put more coal on and flipped off our blackout lights.

By now we were wide open, going nearly 50 mph. And every turn or bump I'd have my head on the side to see better.

We must have gone ten miles before the offering of a side road into the woods gave us the break to lose them.

We took and painted the trailer olive drab and gave it a half-hour to dry, and then we stenciled our "C Company" name and number on.

Back to camp we went. When we looked into the trailer we noticed it was filled with a large walled tent, and also big tarpaulins. They sure came in handy.

The third platoon made a nice meeting room out of the trailer.

We had it all of two days when our battalion supply officer very nicely told us the battalion was taking it for their use, as they were short a trailer.

This same captain got the Bronze Star at a later date for the wonderful way he supplied the battalion. We had men lose eyes and legs and their action didn't warrant a reward. That's war I guess.

Finally we got the big news that we were to head into battle indoctrination at the fortress city of Metz.

We relieved the 95th Division on a front near Metz (I've come to find out a very good Pennsy Buddy, Dave Hughes, was killed near here and I didn't even know he was overseas).

We (our platoon, 44 men) covered a front of roughly a half-mile. We had booby traps put out by the 95th in our front with no outline of places or types.

We had two patrols hit by Jerry charges (nails wired to a charge). One lieutenant had 40 or better holes in him from the first patrol.

We lost, that is, the division lost quite a few men by mortar fire, also by small arms fire and booby traps.

It rained and rained here; for three days and nights I stood in water and didn't sleep as I had a medic in my foxhole who had a bad case of nerves. He was on first night watch when a boobytrap blew up near us. He panicked and blocked my exit to crawl out of the cave we had in the rear of the hole. He finally saw the light with the help of a size 9 boot.

Just as I put my head up someone threw a grenade that tore my helmet off and gave me a hissing in my left ear that still remains with me. Eight lives to go.

After three days I had a nice case of trench foot.

The doc said if I couldn't clear it up I'd have to be evacuated.

I finally had to shed my shoes (my toes were too swollen to put them on), so I had a heavy pair of socks and galoshes that fit very good.

The news came late one night that we were being relieved and sure enough we were the next day. Bright and early we started out. Well spaced and double time was passed down. Sure found out why as we headed up the open road. The Jerries had taken all the high ground and wanted to use us for target practice for their 88s.

It sure felt good to get back to our farmhouse headquarters. We had a big job of cleaning up a week's growth of dirt and mud.

It wasn't a week before we headed for the big front up northeast. We were to be used by Patton's Third Army as a spearhead in first the Moselle River crossing, then the Maginot Line and the Saar River fake crossing, too.

On the Moselle River crossing we lost our platoon's first man, T/5 Glass. A real good man. We had to furnish a man from each platoon as an assault boat driver. Glass was our man from the third squad, Sgt. Wicket's.

From later reports we found out they had to ferry infantry boys over the Moselle under some small arms, mortar and artillery fire. When last seen, Glass' boat had been hit and he was riding it down the river upside down. He never was heard from again.

Here also one of our boys, a sergeant, shot his first collaborator.

While crossing the river he noticed a shade go up on the riverfront. Soon all hell broke loose near his boat and other boats.

On his next trip back he stayed while one boat headed out. Again the shade on the third floor went up to reveal a small lamp. Again, heavy fire.

So into the building went the sergeant and two men. On the third floor they shot up a door and located a sad-eyed individual who claimed France for a home. He had no home on this earth five minutes later.

We got a Bailey bridge job to do the next day, as the engineer outfit that started it had twenty or thirty percent casualties. We were a lot luckier. We had two B Company men hit and quite a few near hits.

We also had a break when the Jerries moved out and did a poor demolition job on a building that spanned a canal.

Our Major Clapp grabbed the opportunity by having a tank dozer knock the building down and we used this as a crossing for our tanks. We hit the Jerries so hard we were 30 miles into and behind his lines before he could get a force together to stop us.

We took our first decent load of prisoners here. They really struck us as being cocky and in the pink of shape.

We really got to see our share of dead Jerries and quite a few of our boys. I think everyone had their fill here. We were in a small village over the Moselle and our dead salvage crew piled truckload after truckload a few houses down from our kitchen. We had a good time the first couple of days just looking at parts and ways death was achieved.

I managed to add quite a few German weapons and a few of ours to our supply trucks. In fact, the supply corporal told me if we added any more guns he'd have to get rid of some of his engineer tools.

I also got a good double sleeping bag from a lieutenant that had no future needs.

I saw the remains of a Catholic church that was looted clean of valuables by the retreating Jerries. Also picked up some more new Jerry weapons.

Our fame had spread as quite a few of the headquarters crew had orders in for souvenirs. The platoon filled them all in short time.

Even the battalion supply officer put in an order for a Garand rifle. Filled this, too.


One time, we went through a minefield, and the minefield was a mile and a half wide. It was built all by slave labor. We got up there at night. And the thing that stands out with me – one of the big flashbacks that wakes me up many a night – we had to go out to get information. We wanted to know what outfit it was. And they had a horse-drawn gun there.

They'd throw the artillery a hundred yards ahead of us, so we wouldn't have to run into something we didn't expect.

We went through this minefield. The horses were dead – they were hit with artillery – the gun was all shot up – and I saw a body on the ground. A flare went up and lit up the area. And I reached down to find out if he was alive or not, and I put my hand where the head used to be, and I got a handful of blood.

The Germans would put white marking tape all the way across where the clear spot was so that they could turn around and go back through without running into mines. We started laying artillery down, and two of the guys that were in there turned around and started to go back and they hit their own mines, and one of them fell back and lost a leg. He had a tourniquet on it. And he took out pictures of his wife and his kids, and he died with that. The second one was the same way, but he had hit two of the mines. He just about got his pictures out on the ground, and that was it.

Another time we went through a minefield with tanks, at night. And Sergeant Wiley – the one who I said the blue grass of Kentucky was in his eyes – was out in front with his squad, and he cleared a path. He came back to tell the first tank to go through. He was looking at the tank, telling it to come forward. It was dark, and the tank was resting on a mine. When it started moving, the mine went off and it blew one of Sergeant Wiley's eyes out.

I didn't know it at the time. I was in another section. And there was a wounded German out there who was yelling that he wanted to turn himself in. We had a bugler who spoke German, so I said, "You tell him if he's got anything plotted out there, I'm going to kill him." The bugler told him in German. So I went out, and I put him on my back and I brought him back.

It turned out the German had a P-38 in his pocket. Seven lives to go.

That night, I heard Sergeant Wiley got hit. I went running to the rear aid station, and Sergeant Wiley was on the floor. He was all bandaged up and he was bleeding. Meanwhile, I'd brought that German back and the doctor was fixing him up; he was shot in a couple of places. I pointed to Sergeant Wiley and said, "Doctor. Take care of that man."

He said, "I'll do what I want. I'm almost finished."

I said, "Take care of that man, or I'll take that German outside and I'll kill him."

He said, "You won't do it."

I said, "Watch me."

He said, "I want your name and rank. You're going to hear about this."

I said, "You'll get my name and rank. If you don't take care of that man, I'll kill him." And I meant it, too.


We pulled out for a new mission, which was to blow up a bridge on the Saar River.

We were really pinned down hard getting to do this job.

We got into town by shooting up everything that moved and headed for the bridge with a halftrack load of TNT. Got pinned down by heavy fire from a machine gun. We returned fire and knocked out same.

A five-man patrol was sent out to reconnoiter the bridge: Lt. Hanel, Lt. Sherry, Sgt. Marks, Cpl. LeWeek and myself. We met Jerries walking down the middle of the road smoking and laughing. They got in the first burst with a burp gun. We hit the ditch just in time as our lead tank opened up with its .30-caliber machine gun. We were pinned for five minutes till I crawled to yell disapproval. The gunner apologized. Good boy. (Six lives to go.)

Just as we got our wits together the Jerries knocked us down with an explosion that shook the town. We headed to the bridge and saw the Jerries had blown it up. Good boys there, sure saved us a lot of work and probable casualties.

Slept in a good soft bed for a change. Next day the town was alive with MPs, a sure sign all was under control.

Army boys spent the next week giving Jerries jitters by making smoke pot false river crossings while we went across to the north and south.

Rumors of us getting rest soon. Proved true in the next three days.

Pulled back into small factory town for rest and to await replacements.

One of our boys on the third floor got a pass to go home by way of a discharged gun on the first floor, which blew off two toes.

One other boy cut his foot in half with an axe cutting wood.

Some of the luckier boys got to shoot German deer with carbines. You had to be a good shot or you couldn't stop them with normal bullets; best shot in head. Had venison feast (real good).

Some of the boys were getting to plot the Siegfried Line on patrol. Real heavy forts there. Getting real cold mornings and evenings now. Feels like winter at home.

No packages of late but hear tell by letter that my foul weather gear is coming before Christmas.

Dec. 16, '44. Hot mission coming up. All big brass running around (rumored big push coming off). Grabbed all NCOs, told to be on two-hour alert to move out.

News came down to load. Must be big; convoys started off like first race at Belmont. Traveled all day and into night; even had convoy headlights on. Pulled into small town in middle of night and told we were to be here for night. Picked out red schoolhouse for most of platoon, private house for Lt. Hanel, myself and two corporals.

Boy invited us home, told us to expect air raid, but no bombs, only pictures. Sure enough, he was right. He told us we were here in Luxembourg to stop Von Runstedt's drive.

All taverns open, even ice cream, most all spoke English. Seemed like transferred U.S. town.

Bright and early next a.m., off for unknown. Saw MPs chasing jeep loads of soldiers, said they were Jerries dressed as our boys. What a shock this was.

Went all day and into night at full pace. Around 11 p.m. ran through town, saw sign to Bastogne, went right through and out onto highway to Ste. Margarethe – now could see and hear heavy shelling. Convoy came to halt and orders went out to get security out in all directions.

I was in second halftrack from rear vehicles, radio truck. Slept on hood as motor was always running, nice and warm. Sure felt more and more like snow.

Truck came roaring out of rear. Could hear rear guards halt and check same. Was gas truck from Bastogne, driven by colored GI.

Was all out of breath and shook up, claimed Jerries rode into Bastogne in civilian clothes and he was last to get out.

Loaded last truck with gas. Also our halftrack and one in front of us was busy loading Sherman tanks when the sky lit up like day. Got report Jerries lay on side of road and threw grenades into gas.

As soon as truck lit up road we were clobbered by everything that fired.

Sgt. Marks, myself and one corporal and one private set up a heavy water cooled .30-caliber machine gun. I had a light air-cooled .30 MG set on a little rise. Caught a patrol going back to their lines across open field. We cross-fired till my .30

light was showing a very nice hook as each tracer hit the dawn sky.

We were now getting a constant stream of 106th Infantry and 9th Armored Division wounded and combat shocked troops. Must have been 500 laying from one side to the other of the road as fire increased or decreased from both sides.

We had a constant battle going between ourselves and German infantry. We had gotten an M-90 .50-caliber equipped six-wheeled armored car and we put the turret over a knoll and with a 105 self-propelled gun that had a track gone. We managed to yell fire commands as the need arose. Which was getting closer and closer.

Now we looked to dig into the hill for night security, but our shovels just bounced back.

The town behind me had five houses that were in our hands and the Jerries had the rest. We started to pick up equipment. We now had an extra jeep that we got from a field. And we had a mean run to get to our ammunition trailer on the road, getting potted at as we ran.

Next step was to head back to this small town and our five houses. Most had a whole load of shocked GIs.

By nightfall we were lined up bumper to bumper with eight or nine tanks, two halftracks, one M-90 and three jeeps. We had set charges in the tanks and other vehicles that were disabled and set them off.

I was next to the last in line to the west of the houses when Jerry started to move in. The first notice I had was a head peering over a hedge 15 or 20 feet from where I stood at the .50-caliber on the M-90.

I fired five rounds and I had to hand operate after this or I'd get a jam.

I went up to the captain in the lead house and asked him our intentions. He said if we had to move out on foot to head north and we'd run into paratroopers.

I started back and noticed two Sherman tanks with no security and buttoned up. I jumped on the first and banged with my grease gun on the turret.

A head popped out and said, "We have room for two more in here, how about it, Sergeant?" I didn't get a chance to tell him I didn't like tanks, I'm claustrophobic, when two dogfaces jumped out of nowhere and hopped in. Down went the hatch.

I jumped up on the second one and did the same banging. About that time I found myself on the ground and saw the Shermans belch flame. I hopped up to the bogey wheel of the first tank again. There was an explosion and I was laying over a barbed wire fence with a burning sensation in my left heel and my butt (Five lives to go).

The screams of the boys in the tank still live with me.

A second loud explosion and they stopped.

By this time a mass migration of men were heading across an open field for the woods.

We gathered short of the woods and found there were close to 150 men and four officers in our group. I couldn't see anyone I knew from my outfit but I knew the action was so fast and I wasn't sure how long I had lain on the barbed wire fence before my reflexes made my legs move.

The four officers told us to put security out and wait as they would try to make contact with our boys.

We waited for six hours; still no return of the officers.

We sent four men out to see if we could contact any outfit, myself and three other sergeants.

I started across a barbed wire fence when I heard a loud yell in German. I hit the ground and lay still; so did the others. We suddenly heard a flare and in its glare two machine guns opened up and sprayed all around us for close to five minutes. As they stopped, we did a slow backward retreat till our legs could do the most good.

Back to the challenge of the boys in the woods. Still no officers.

We decided to head north in three split patrols.

I had used up my pills but still didn't have time to see how bad I was hit. (Two days later I got to see about ten or twelve small pieces and one fairly big piece in my left heel, which I dug out with my knife. The others less one are still traveling in me as one showed up in my chest five years ago and came out. It was the size of a large bee bee.)

I buddied up with a Corporal Smith from an antitank outfit. He'd seen a lot of action in Africa and had returned on rotation to the States and here he'd come back to get stuck in this deal.

We fought everyone and anyone in this heavy pine forest for the balance of the night, and also part of the next day.

Ran into a lot of Jerries and all were paratroops. I guess these were the boys we were told we'd meet if we headed north.

Smith and I decided to try to go behind the Jerries and back out in a less busy place. I had a compass and we headed northeast. Got to cut telephone lines in two or three places. Missed patrol of 10 men by 10 feet and some high bushes.

Had a grease gun and one clip of ammo. Smith had a carbine and 10 rounds. Both were loaded with dirt from crawling and laying on the ground.

Screaming meemies were all around us both back and front.

Smith said he'd had it and was going to give up. I tried to talk him out of it, but he headed to an open field and the artillery outfit set up there. I stayed put in woods.

He waved a handkerchief to two soldiers and they ran to grab him. He turned quite nonchalantly to where I was watching and waved me in. I was covered before

I had time to do anything.

I said, "Smith, I think we're going to get the business."

To my surprise we were treated with respect.

We were taken to a farmhouse for questioning and here I saw a cripple I believe to have been Goebbels. He was at the center of a group of officers and had a few questions by an interpreter as to our outfits and condition of same. The boys showed him how rough they were as we gave only name, rank and serial number.

From here we started a slow march with about 500 more GIs. We passed 9th Armored tanks that had been blown with shape charges lined up like so many ten pins. They must have had 25 to 50 vehicles and also alongside the road I saw our Christmas packages opened and looted.

All the troops we passed looked older than the boys we tackled elsewhere. But all had ideas this was to be our end in the ETO [European Theater of Operation], at least all the Jerries that spoke English tried to convince us.

Marched all day till just short of dark. Ended up in burnt-out factory where we had our first food – oatmeal eaten out of our steel helmets. Didn't like the idea but it sure tasted good.

Spent part of night unloading about six-inch shells. Tried to mention Geneva treaty but was told to shut up while I still had a choice.

Got so disgusted near morning that we were throwing shells onto piles. Jerry guard gave us a safe distance but still let us know he didn't like our crazy working methods.

Could see things begin to change as we marched into Germany. Guards were very young and rough on us.

Had a Catholic chaplain from 101st Airborne from Midwest with us. He was to have given midnight Mass on Christmas in England. Here he was trying to get Jerries to give us something to eat. Water was supplied by fresh fallen snow.

Stopped in old factory with blown out windows for the night of Dec. 24.

Father suggested we cover windows best we could as there wasn't any heat inside.

We found a candle and Father suggested we have services to welcome Christmas. The services were nonsectarian, but there wasn't a dry eye as we attempted to sing a carol.

We now heard airplanes overhead and the Jerries came running in to tell us if we wanted to continue breathing to put out the candle and stay put.

Guard told Father, "Put those candles out or I'll kill you."

He said, "If you have to kill me on this night, kill me. My name will still be here, and my soul will be up in heaven. You do what you want."

Planes hit all around us and Jerries were really teed off. Hit an oil supply other side of railroad yard. Sure looked good.

Dec. 25, '44: Were told to get out and start to move. We must have had 700 to 800. Still nothing to eat.

Father really told the Krauts his feelings. Finally got them to get a few burlap bags of frozen turnips. We each got a slice with coarse salt on. Tasted as good as any turkey dinner I've ever had.

Marched all of 25th and into 26th. Entered town of Gerolstein just after their first air raid. People really wanted to kill all of us. Guards had to hold them off. Seems our Forts hit a children's home and there must have been 50 to 60 boys and girls laying side by side near the road. Really felt sorry here. All were between two years and eleven years.

Marched into town just as B-24s came over for followup raid.

They really had fires going all over. We were put into a former factory building roughly 50 by 150 feet long. All the walls were covered by wooden racks for storage of parts. The racks were about two feet high and two feet wide by two feet deep. These were about six high to the ceiling. We were to sleep in these for the next few months.

We heard planes or at least we thought they were planes flying low over our factory all day. Came to find out all the surrounding hills here had launching ramps for V-1s including a major railroad yard. This was really a major target area for all our bombers, as we sure found out for the next few months.

We had a collection of sometimes 2,000 prisoners in this place at one time. I've seen times when we were stuck on work details that you'd not have room even to sit down no less lay down.

The way they got their volunteers for work details was very simple. Just throw all our wounded and sick out in the yard and let them lay till they got their 50- or 100-man details.

We were allowed in the way of rations all the water that ran through the streets above camp and into a brook behind our factory and anywhere from 10 to 15 men on a loaf of black bread. Once I had the detail of making soup for 2,000 men and I was given a horse's head for flavor. I had to knock the teeth out of it and put the head in the soup, eyes and everything. I'll admit I ate some and was very happy to get it. I've seen people eat dead rats.

One time they called two of us in to this place where the soldiers ate, and they had an officer from the SS. They had this little stinker, what the heck was that German? The small guy that was a bastard as far as the way he treated everybody, in the upper echelon of the Nazis ... Himmler. Nobody told me, but just by this guy's looks, if he wasn't Himmler he was a dead ringer. He came into that camp just before we got moved out, because we could hear and see artillery flashes and we knew they were getting pretty close.

They brought two of us in; they knew we were sergeants. We'd pulled the rank off but they still knew that because the threads were on the sleeve. And they asked us, would we make an announcement that they could record? They told us what to say, and they wanted it in writing. They had food there, and they said, "If you say that, you can have that food."

I said, "I love my country. I won't say anything against it."

The other guy said the same thing.

They spat in the food. It was really the tail end of what they had on the table, the fatty meat and all, but it was food. They spat on it and threw it in the garbage. They said, "Go ahead. Kill yourself. Die. Do what you want."

We got out of there. And when they left, other POWs came up and they took the food out of the garbage that he spit on, and they ate it.


We had quite a few wounded die and on two or three occasions I was chosen to dig a plain grave for them. This with our lack of food sure was a rough deal.

We had a Sergeant Eisenhower for our camp boss. He was really a rough bird. I saw him sic dogs on a GI that had stolen a potato.

He came in one night for a 100-man detail for a sled carrying job up to the launching platforms.

I was up in the sixth level cubbyhole. Had a sick GI in the next hole. Sgt. Eisenhower put a light up, saw his eyes, and pulled his P-38 – I yelled that the man was sick but he fired one shot into the hole and one into the GI as he fell. I hit floor on one bounce and was out into night before he knew who was there. The soldier was dead before he hit floor.

Sgt. Eisenhower tried for a week to find out who was in next hole, but nobody knew. Even tried to bribe boys to find out. I know I'd be among the missing if he'd found out.

He always reminded us that we weren't registered with the Red Cross and we sure wouldn't be missed.

P-47s were chasing us all over, strafing anything that moved. The Jerries took to air raid shelters and left the door open to look at us. Told us to make break if we thought we could. Never had the strength to go anywhere. Had GIs [diarrhea] really bad and also was losing weight fast.

Weighed 155 when taken, now must be close to 135 pounds.

Lots of tanks heading up to front being pulled or on trailers.

Had detail to dig out dead on two or three occasions. Dug out two old people side by side with an SS trooper. They never made cellar air raid shelter. They both were dead about five feet from safety. SS trooper said in perfect English, "Let's eat, compadres. This is what your Luftwaff did to my mother and father." I expected to end up with them, but he spared us for future work. (Four lives to go.)

While at Limberg a certain GI made a habit of stealing from the stretcher cases and sold the food and other items to other prisoners for good old U.S. cash. He was warned by a master sergeant First Ranger Battalion survivor – he was high ranking man at Anzio when he was ordered by our command to give up, as they were cut off in front of our lines and badly shot up by both the Jerries and our own snafu. They captured a town and also some Kraut tanks. Our artillery opened up on the town and nearly wiped them out.

The thief was caught doing the same thing again one night and the master sergeant/Ranger took him out bodily to a latrine trench and put him head first into the mess.

He didn't know that it was freshly limed and the GI thief was blinded. He tried when released to have the sergeant brought up on charges but we signed a statement clearing him (almost 1,000 POWs signed).

He later got to be the go-between man between us and the Swiss Red Cross. His name was Master Sergeant Chalmers.

He was a wonderful example of a brave and honorable soldier.

The Jerries really were afraid of him and tried later to get him out of camp on a detail when the Red Cross representative was known to be visiting.

This thieving POW when we got to Camp 11-A had close to $3,000 in American money taken off him at a sudden personal search.

He really cried out loud at this turn of events.

A number of times some of the boys would be out cleaning fat off the horses' guts to use for a tin can fire grill to fry their ration of black bread.

Really got to see the hold cigarettes have on chain smokers. Seen men get their only ration of bread for the day and trade a buddy that stole some cigarettes on a bomb clearing raid for one cigarette.

Getting to hear more and more of the V2s going over us each day. Also hear more and more that run wild and crash. What a mean explosion they made when they hit near us.

One night late in January of 1945 we were all rushed out into the night and on that particular night we had a roaring snowstorm going. All our stretcher cases were piled and thrown into the snow.

Sgt. Eisenhower needed a 100-man detail to pull supplies and ammo to a mountain anti-aircraft unit. This unit was located about 20 miles up into the mountains.

He was ranting and raving because he couldn't get the detail fast enough. It must have been 10 degrees and damp. One severely wounded stretcher case died while laying there.

Seemed like death at this stage was cheaper than the 40 odd cents our bodies were supposed to be worth in mineral value.

I like quite a few of the regular volunteers ended up pulling a sled loaded with antiaircraft shells.

It was a trip almost all the way uphill. We had four men to a sled and we drew a real goldbrick. He waited till we were about ten miles out and faked a passout so he rode the 15 miles while three of us pulled.

I ended up in a fight with this guy at a later date (incidentally, I won, which in my physical shape was a miracle).

About dawn we were stopped for a breather near a row of houses. I noticed a door open and saw a few fellows lean in and come back out with a drink. I ran up too as all we drank was snow on the whole trip.

Here was a beautiful young woman about 20 or so and she was handing out full glasses of real milk.

I got there in time to get one glass and hurried away as a guard headed up to us.

The girl quickly closed the door in his face and ended up waving to us from the window.

I tried to fix this place in my mind if I ever got another chance to escape.

We made it to the antiaircraft camp in time to see them eating breakfast. We even got a cup of their imitation coffee. Which tasted like the best we ever had.

On the way down to Gerolstein all the boys who had milk had a super case of the runs. We were a very sad, sick group when we got back to camp.

We again got stuck with an air raid digging out job, although we tried to tell Sgt. Eisenhower we had just gotten back.

I had such a bad case of runs that night that I stood and looked up to heaven and asked God, "Why? Why?"

I knew this was the worst day of my whole ordeal.

February '45: One day while caught in the open by one of our P-47s, six of us on an air raid digging project were strafed for about three good runs. Lucky none of us were hit. The pilot came in to strafe us near one of the guided missile launching pads, and he changed missions.

On his second run at the ground missile personnel he was caught in a crossfire, and as he headed up for altitude we could see he was hit and bad.

He flipped over at about 4,000 feet and came out like a shot.

His chute opened pretty close to the ground and he came down near the launching pads. He was quickly captured, although we got close to him with our curious guards.

We could hear he was really telling them off but good.

We were shocked to see a Chinese American flyer.

When he heard us speak to him in American, he almost flipped with joy.

He was loaded into a command car and amid cheers and wishes of good luck he disappeared.

We expected him to turn up at camp, but he never did.


Had a job to steal coal for a railroad conductor that lived near camp.

Got caught in an air raid and spent 15 minutes huddled with four other PWs near an air raid shelter. One PW made a break for the woods.

When the raid was over the corporal of the guard counted heads and threatened to blow our heads off if we didn't tell him where he went.

I honestly told him I didn't care. I said if he lived to be a hundred in Germany he couldn't have enjoyed life equal to fifteen years in our USA. I meant no flag waving here but sincere from the heart truth.

An officer listening nearby said in perfect English that he had to take his hat off to me, as he had spent ten years in Chicago and hoped someday to return.

Where were more like this guy hiding out?

They finally told us that the corporal's report to Sergeant Eisenhower at camp would be that the missing GI was the victim of a direct bomb hit. Seemed to go over OK. Don't know if this PW ever made it back or not.

Finally got notice that we were being marched out to another camp.

One morning we were told to get ready and we were given five days' rations, which consisted of: one-quarter loaf brown bread; two slices horse meat; one hunk cheese (about a quarter pound). All were told if they ate it now they were out of luck.

Four of us – all ex-paratroops or glider troops – decided to make a try at escape again.

We could see the sky to the east light up at night with artillery blasts. Our lines must be 20 or 25 miles to the east.

About 1,500 to 2,000 were being marched through Gerolstein west, destination unknown. While turning a corner in town, we noticed a house with barn connected about 150 yards off the main road. As we checked the front and back guard, we had approximately 50 yards distance between the first guard being able to see the farm and the back guard getting up to the corner.

So off we went. One sergeant had a severe cold and had to be helped into the barn (later found out he had pneumonia).

We no sooner got into the barn when we could hear soldiers talking in the farmhouse next door. We weren't sure they didn't hear or see us, but we had to find a better spot to hide. In the darkness we located by feel a ladder leading to an upper hayloft. So we went as quietly as we could.

We watched through a small crack as the tail end of the walking PWs passed. So far so good.

We must have been here four hours as quiet as we could be (the sergeant with the cold was having a harder and harder time covering up his cough), when one of the soldiers in the house came in to pick up some clothes he had hanging to dry. He had a lamp with him but we didn't think he'd seen anything suspicious. All at once he yelled to two soldiers inside and out they came running into the barn.

We made a quick, whispered decision, and myself and two buddies dropped on them. I know we'd have been more than a match in top shape, but we were in rough, weakened shape and we were quickly subdued. I had an old temple scar reopened and most of the fight was out of us when the sergeant with pneumonia yelled in German that we had it. I didn't know my name for a day and a half. We were shoved into the house and a hurried call was made to our old friend Sgt. Eisenhower. While waiting for a guard to pick us up we decided if they were taking us back we'd better go with a satisfied stomach, so we munched down our five days' march rations. Our stomachs almost turned flips with all this food at one time.

In about an hour our very special two guards came for the swine that had the nerve to try and escape the German elite.

Sgt. Eisenhower wasted no time greeting us as we returned.

"Well," says he, "if it isn't my old friends back again. You sure must really like it here. And I see you've eaten up your rations. So for the next week you'll cost our government no money for food." (Our conception of cost for food would be about three cents a day).

We were put into our pig pen and double guarded that night and every night we stayed thereafter.

I think we had a better deal for the next week than at any time we were there. We were sent to a field bakery to chop wood and keep the fires going under the ovens.

In the old camp we had three Russian women, PW's taken on the Eastern front. They were really husky and healthy looking, and they were cooks for the German soldiers and also morale builders for them, too.

They always gave us looks of pity before but now they managed to slip us a can of soup nearly every day. This sure helped out.

We also were allowed to eat a piece of broken loaves of bread at the field kitchen.

We managed to get into the bread storehouse one day and we each had a loaf of bread under our coat to take back with us, when into the storehouse came two soldiers. We were sure this was to be our end, when to our surprise they grabbed two loaves each and ran like the devil was after them. (Three lives to go.)

Shows the average German soldier's feeling the pangs of hunger too.

We come to find out from an English speaking Pole that two blocks over from this camp there are Americans being held prisoner in a private house. They were mostly stretcher cases. And they had an American lieutenant doctor for their care. They were going to let them be retaken by our advancing GIs, but now with four more witnesses to their treatment of 'our PWs,' they're a little undecided.

Said he heard Sgt. Eisenhower would like to see us disappear real quiet like. (Bang, bang, bang, bang!) But all of the other boys are afraid of the consequences. (Two lives to go).

Now they decide we'll go with the wounded by boxcar. One day we're all moved down to the railroad yards and loaded in two boxcars. One little window in a corner with steel bars. Window is about one foot by 18 inches wide.

Just as we're loaded into the cars and waiting for the engine to back out of its tunnel hiding place, a flight of four P-47s made a bombing and strafing run over and into the yards. Our car was strafed but no casualties. The car ahead had one man hit and one killed outright (he stayed in the car for the five days and nights it took to get to the Limberg registered PW camp.)

We had about 35 men each in our cars and a pail for latrine purposes. What a picnic.

When we finally got to the Limberg camp we were a sorry and smelly lot.

Here we were to be registered as a PW (families all had us missing in action. No other news) and given a delousing and straw ticks to sleep on the floor. But the British saw a light from one of the barracks one night and dropped some 500-pounders on both the barracks and the delousing hut which was blown to bits. I think from reports that 35 to 50 of our own PWs were killed here.

We managed here to see some soup from a kitchen that was getting Red Cross parcels. It had a piece of meat the size of a bean once in a while.

Some camp GIs that were here a year or so later were brought up on charges of feeding German soldiers and civilians with our food.

We were here about two days when a call came for all NCOs to form a line on one side of the camp. Us four para buddies didn't like the looks of this so we stayed with the bucks (Later we found out how wise this move was). They marched all the NCOs out amid a razzing from us of "You'll be sorry."

We managed to make friends with some British Hindus that were the neatest, healthiest PWs we'd ever seen. They were in the next compound to us. Also the Italians had the bordering compound.

The Hindus wanted good old Uncle Sam's gold, silver or paper money to supply us with our own Red Cross parcels.

I traded a watch I had for some bread and cheese but first the jeweler's eyepiece had to come out to check the jewels.

Some horse traders these boys were.

The Italians were a little less jewelers and a little more swindlers.

They'd show you a rotten dried apple over the fence and say it was an onion (very much in demand) and trade for clothes that had to be put in their hands first. Then if they even bothered they'd throw over the rotten "onions."

After a week or so of watching diplomatic relations get worse and worse, we were given the job of unloading two boxcars of U.S. Red Cross parcels. We broke our backs carrying these from the railroad yard to a storehouse, only to be told to march down to the loading platform for departure in the 40-x-8's again.

Here we were given a South American parcel, a half to each man, two PWs buddied up. We were loaded here about 45 to 50 in each car and shut in.

After two nights and days of running from our bombers we were halted one night and half of the men were taken out of our car, including my glider trooper pal Ken Ripple. He tried to express that he had to get his half of the package I had but the guard wouldn't listen. Instead he shoved some evil smelling Russian soldiers in with us. They were covered with dirt, filth, beards and lice! Oh, how I grew to hate this beast.

My body grew covered with scabs and they were festering as fast as they were scratched.

I hid the biggest remain of Rip's and my package as we were concerned how long it would be before we ate again if we ate it up. I had it wrapped in a burlap bag and I sat and held it between my knees. Some of the boys that had eaten their packages as soon as they got them knew I had the biggest part left, and one dark night I fought off five different attempts to take it from me. The man turns beast when starvation sets in.

We went for three or four days and nights before we pulled into a station and were told this is it. All the time we were on the move we only got water once a night and sometimes the boys would start a fight over a drink and the guard would throw the whole pail on the floor and we had to wait till the next night if we were lucky. Once I waited three days for a drink.

I didn't touch any of the package I was holding for Ken and myself in the three days we were separated. And when I got to see him at the station he was in tears when he heard and saw this. He also had a very bad case of pneumonia, and I and another GI had to carry him fifteen miles from the station to camp.

We had a constant alert and air raid every day about 12 p.m.

A double flight of B-17s crisscrossed over the railroad and launching sites and let the big ones go.

The civilians would head for the big community shelters early in the morning and it was after dark before they came back to town. A lot of times they didn't have a home left. Then they'd love to have killed all the PWs.

The SS troopers would slap them and tell them to show no signs of breaking in front of us swine.

Three of us – two former glider troopers and myself – made plans for escape. We saved a little bread and some dried horse meat. The night we were to make our break the doors were locked and we were forced to stay in all night.

This sure made for a sweet smelling mess, as there must have been 2,000 men in the building and more than half had the GIs and nothing to use but the floor and at times there wasn't even room on the floor.

Once in a while the Jerries would break down and give us a treat in the form of imitation jelly on our ration of bread.

And twice more within a two-week period we got the horse's head for soup. What a day when the lucky guy turned up with a pea size piece of meat in his soup.

We were getting to know the ropes of organized prisoner of war ways and means. The Canadian boys that were in the commandos at Dieppe and were prisoners for three or so years had the Germans figured to a tee. They had radios hidden from them. These they managed to get by barter with the French prisoners that worked the neighborhood farms.

They had the German guards asking how the war was going.

The officers made many a search but they never did turn up anything worthwhile.

Once one of the guards was searching for a civilian in one of the attics and he fell through the roof and broke his leg.

The Canadian PWs even set up a monetary system, telling all of us fairly new PWs the bartering price of cigarettes against all items of food such as two cigarettes for a fresh egg. All these items were stolen from farms either by guards or prison workers.

They even had a barter store set up to sell items for cigarettes, etc.

The Canadian PWs had gotten cigarettes by the thousands before D-Day. They even filled their mattresses with cigarettes to hold down inflation. Our boys tried a few times to outbid them and they learned this the hard way. But now that things were rough in transportation they and we couldn't get much of anything, although we did get a Red Cross parcel a week.

We even had situation maps set up in each 50-man room that were brought up to date by the Canadian PW with the radio for two cigarettes charge each room.

Never in all my days as a PW did I hear mention by anyone of women or sex with anything but respect, but little by little as our stomachs were partly filled, you'd hear reference to women in a more sexual reference.

We had Mass every day in this camp as the French PWs had built a beautiful chapel from all scrap wood. It would be a beautiful chapel even in freedom anywhere in the world.

We now heard through the BBC radio that the Allies were moving up to and near our camp.

One time we were told we'd be unable to visit the other compounds. The reason came out one morning when we saw the Polish compound empty and reloaded with the most pitiful bunch of humans I've ever had the misfortune to see. They turned out to be Jewish prisoners and also political prisoners. They all looked like small frail girls. They were all dressed in black and white striped suits.

They had sunken eyeballs and rotten teeth and also shaved heads. There were women, men and children and we had a tough time telling them apart. I knew we were not in the best of physical or mental shape, but we weighed in the neighborhood of 110 or so while their weight must have averaged 75 or 80 pounds.

When we marched out of this camp we saw the prisoners carrying out their overnight dead, stark naked, and they must have had 20 dead piled like cords of wood.

They got a bulldozer out and made a mass burial ditch and covered it up as we were being issued a package of Red Cross food.

But I saw those people go into that pit, and I said, "God have mercy on every one of them."

We also got a marching package of food, and we passed a steady line of the same type prisoners being marched into camp. They had their knapsacks if they were lucky and that was all they had.

They begged for a bite to eat and I'll admit we did start to throw them a piece of candy or a cigarette but they killed each other trying to get them, and the guards were busy cursing us and cracking their skulls with clubs. We passed three dead laying on the road in roughly a quarter mile. Before they hit the ground their clothes were stripped off and their knapsacks were fought over.

This sight lives with me even today. I've never been more sincere when I say for years I wouldn't even talk to anyone about some of these sights because they'd call me a liar and I'm afraid I'd really get mad.

I found out later that the reason the Jerries wanted to get them in camp was so the Allies wouldn't get to see them sleeping and dying in the open. They were afraid of the consequences.

We were told that our new camp was only 15 miles away but by later comparisons I'd say we marched closer to 50 miles.

We went two days and two nights. The old escape buddies – less the one with pneumonia, who stayed in the camp hospital, later to be released by Patton's rescue team – and myself were getting the urge to try again but we couldn't get the opportunity as they always found enough guards to secure ranks.

We moved into the new camp (Westertinke, near Bremen and Hanover), which consisted of Polish, English and Russian PWs. And also English civilians that were torpedoed and held here.

This was by far the best prepared camp we hit. It had mess halls, movies, dining rooms, community kitchens and playing fields.

They would send the prisoners that were to be exchanged with the British here and get them fat and healthy and happy so the good German lords within the Geneva treaty would be spread all around. Yes, yes!

We managed to get laundry soap and we also got showers. Our poor bodies were a mess. Recall hearing English GI say to buddy, "Look at the poor Russians. They sure look half dead."

We were covered by big lice bites and our scalps were infested.

I know here if we hadn't gotten all our shots before capture we never would have survived.

The fighting could be seen at night to the west of us. One night a group of German tanks went past the camp and a rumor was spread to the guards that they were British and all the guards took off from their posts. The British GIs climbed up the guard towers and stole the machine guns they left in their rush to leave.

The boys wanted to set up a battle zone in the compound but the camp senior officer said we'd be slaughtered, so the four machine guns were dismantled and parts hidden all over camp.

When the news spread that the guards had left the boys wanted to head out for open country. I almost went myself, but I decided against it when the shooting began to sound closer.

The guards finally came back quite sheepishly now and spent three days trying to find their guns. They threatened to cut off our rations, but as small arms fire could be heard they changed their minds.

One day a convoy of German tanks backed up to our camp and for two more days the British were forced to use smoke to get the Germans under control. The British were afraid to fire on the Germans as they knew we were there.

The boys painted big signs on the roof of the barracks to show the Royal Air Force who and how many PWs were in this camp.

One night the Polish compound left a fire burning and a bomber dropped a load of bombs that killed quite a few in their compound.

By now all the civilians slept in trenches they had dug to protect themselves from small arms fire and bombs.

Mostly all the GIs did too but myself and a few others would rather have a roof for protection from the rain and weather than catch cold outside.

By now quite a few trench sleepers had real deep coughs, and yellow jaundice was the fashion of the day. I was one of the fortunate ones. I never did get jaundice.

After being liberated by the British, they lined all the former guards of the camp up and had prisoners look them all over and decide who was decent and who was rotten.

They let the decent ones off with easy jobs and sent the rats on all the rotten jobs.

We were treated too good by the liberators. They force fed us everything we wanted to eat and our poor mistreated stomachs just couldn't stand the kindness. Some boys were so sick from overeating that they had to be hospitalized before we were able to leave the camp.

Our Army boys that were sent to get us ready for return were really swell Joes.

They got us set to leave in a matter of two days.

Meanwhile, we were nearly overjoyed to hear that the Germans had surrendered.

We had a close call before the end of our prison stay when Hitler passed the word down to kill all POWs. We knew from the way the guards wanted to get on the good side of us that things weren't going good, and we also doubted that they would attempt to carry out the last orders of Hitler.

The BBC was really giving us a lot of good news and the Jerry guards were very interested to find out just how things stood.

We finally got up one morning to find that we were to be taken by truck to an old bombed out German airport to be flown out in B-17s. The British came in Lancasters and cracked up two ships.

They only had minor clearance but it gave us something to think about as our forts took more space to land and take off.

Twelve planes came in all in one piece. We were loaded into the bomb bays, 25 men to a plane. They had a plywood cover over the bomb bay, and here we stayed till we got off.

We landed two hours later at Raye, France. Here the 11th Airborne had been waiting for action over the Rhine. When Patton took off over the Remagen Bridge it loused up their jump plans.

They hated the thought of going to Japan.

One British plane made a crash landing here and killed most all the ex-POWs and the crew. Some had been prisoners four or five years.

We also heard rumors that one Lancaster hit the runway in England and blew up, killing all 20-some ex-POWs right in front of a reception committee of Britishers. Some fate.

We were at Raye, France, for almost a week when we got a load of C-46s in and they took us to Camp Lucky Strike, France. Here we landed right in the camp airfield.

This was an embarkation point. We had 10,000 or more ex-POWs. Here was Ken Ripple, who also was liberated before the war's end. He was liberated by the American Third Army. He looked good after his siege of pneumonia.

We also met some other fellows we had been with at both Limberg and Gerolstein.

One day in came an Army C-46 plane. In it was General Eisenhower. He had a question and answer session right at the plane's side.

He asked us if we wanted to wait for single trips back on a boat or did we want to double deck. Of course we said double deck.

He told us we'd be on our way home within two weeks, and he was right.

We loaded ship at Le Havre, France, for a 12-day uneventful trip to Newport News, Virginia. From here we trained into Camp Patrick Henry, Va.

From here we were sent home for a 90-day furlough before returning to camp.

I was home three days and I ended up in a hospital for a 30-day visit to check a nervous and bad stomach condition.

My father was a manager for the A&P. He had a wonderful disposition, and he had a heart. He was making $35 a week. So what they would do with him, with the disposition he had, they'd send him and build up a store. When it got to a certain point, one of the bosses would take a friend and put him in, and send my father to another store and build that up.

They sent him down the last time to Roselle, New Jersey, and he built that store up in Roselle on Amsterdam Avenue, and what he did – he had $5,000 worth of insurance – and they must have told him that they were sending him to another store, because he shot himself.

He set an example for me to realize, because you ask yourself for the rest of your life, did I do anything to cause him to do what he did? After the war was over, when I first came home – my brother was still in the Pacific – I had a gun up to my head twice. Because I was so confused, and so sick, and you don't realize when you're so hepped up. I've walked away from arguments sometimes, but then I got my prayer. It was found in the wallet of Dr. Tom Dooley shortly after his death in 1961. It goes:

"Your Cross. The everlasting God in His wisdom foreseen from eternity the cross that He now presents you as a gift from His inmost heart. The cross He now sends you He has considered with His all-knowing eyes, understood with His divine mind, tested with His wise justice, warmed with loving arms, and weighed with His loving hands to see that it be not one inch too large and not one ounce too heavy for you. He has blessed it with His holy name, anointed it with His grace, perfumed it with His consolation, taken one last glance at you and your courage, and then sent it to you from heaven, a special greeting from God to you and alms of the all merciful love of God. – St. Francis de Sales."

I've given that to so many people; I've made so many copies. I don't care what religion you are, if you have a totem pole and you have respect for it, you have respect for my rights and I have respect for your rights, I'll accept it. I never argue religion. But when I saw that prayer, it really calmed me down.

When I came back, I had a guy who owned a gin mill who was a gambler, too. He wanted to send me up to New York State to Whitey Bimstein to make a fighter out of me. He wanted to give me $50 a week – $50 a week and I'd learn to box under the best trainer in the business. I said, "You'd be wasting your money." Because I know with that gut I'd never take it. I've got an irritable colon. Many a time I've wished I could dig Hitler up and shove it to him, and then I read my prayer and I calm down.

Once, I questioned God. That night when I was in the slave labor camp and I escaped and got recaptured, they had snow outside, and I had the runs so bad that I crapped my pants. They had taken my shoes, and I had that heavy underwear which they didn't take, that was the only thing I had, they took my jacket, and I stood out in the snow, about 1 o'clock in the morning, and I washed myself down, and I looked up to God. And I said, "Why me?"

I didn't hear any rustling, and I didn't see anything in the clouds, but now, when I see my four kids, and I see my ten grandchildren and my wife, and I see what I've made of myself as far as financially I'm not poor, I said, He's answered me. He's blessed me in a lot of ways.

He's answered me a thousand times.

*"The English crew had a galley, and one of our guys, I don't know how he did it but he convinced the bakery people to give him some loaves of bread. We were there two nights. Each night he'd come into our quarters with two or three big loaves of bread. No butter. But the hot, baked bread, it's just like cake. That was the high point of those particular days. At midnight we'd get a big chew of bread. Nobody ever asked him how he did it. And nobody ever found out because he was killed on D-Day."*

**Chuck Hurlbut**
**299th Engineer**
**Combat Battalion**
**D-Day veteran of**
**Omaha Beach**
**Interviewed in**
**Ithaca, N.Y.,**
**Sept. 26, 1998**

I was born in New York City. I lived there until I was seven. Then my mother died. My dad got laid off and he couldn't find work, so he thought he would come back to upstate New York where he was from. But the Depression was everyplace. He had two very demanding kids, and he was frustrated. So his parents suggested that we go out and live with them.

They had a farm not far from Auburn, New York, and that's where I lived until I graduated from high school. But I knew I could never be a farmer. It was beautiful and I loved the greenery, but something told me that was not my thing.

When I graduated from high school, I made the big decision that I had to go find something else. So I left the farm, with a lot of sadness, but they condoned it. My grandparents wished me well.

I went to Auburn and got a job. I was only 16. I played the clarinet and joined the Auburn community band. I was on a bowling team and a softball team. I met a few girls. Everything was going great. Then all of a sudden Pearl Harbor hit.

Ever since high school I had heard about Hitler and all this stuff in Europe, but I never realized how deeply it was going to affect me. Hitler and Europe, that was their war, don't get involved. Pearl Harbor turned everyone around. I don't think there'll ever be a time again when this country is so unified.

I never wanted to be a soldier; that was the farthest thing from my mind. But when something like Pearl Harbor happens, you get a feeling. "I'm supposed to do something." I couldn't wait to become 18 so I could be drafted. I wanted to do my part. So when I hit 18, within days I was down at the draft board, and registered. In three months I was called, went for my physical, and passed. Then I got the announcement: "You are to report to the Greyhound bus station in Auburn on such and such a date."

I went down there, and here's 60 or 70 guys, all in this draft group. It was the largest draft contingent ever to come out of Auburn. And the mothers and fathers and sweethearts, brothers and sisters were there. It was quite a congregation.

Finally they put us on a bus and sent us to Fort Niagara. And most of us guys knew each other. We had gone to school together, worked together, dated the same girls; there was a real strong camaraderie. And we said, "This can't last. You're gonna go here, I'm gonna go there. We're all going to be split up."

When the announcement came, about 90 percent of us stayed together. We couldn't believe it. We were going to be combat engineers. We couldn't care less. The idea we're all together was the big point. We don't care what we're going to be.

They put us on a train and sent us to Camp White, Oregon, where they activated the 299th Engineer Combat Battalion. We are the original members of the 299th. And we went through basic training.

The first few weeks were basic military skills: close order drills, marches, hikes, how to clean a rifle, what is a machine gun. And then you were introduced to the specialties of an engineer: bridge building, mine detection. Engineers are always thought of as building these enormous bridges. The combat engineers do the same thing on a minor scale in a quicker fashion, under fire. We learned how to throw a treadway or a pathway across a river. How to ford a river. How to blow up a bridge. How to build a Bailey bridge. We became pretty good at it.

After basic training, they sent us out on maneuvers to the desert. I never knew such a desert existed in eastern Oregon. It had scorpions, rattlesnakes, jackrabbits. Burning hot all day, then you freeze to death all night. And you're on maneuvers, it's like combat conditions, so you can't have a fire. It was pretty rough, but we survived that. Then they took us to Fort Lewis, Washington, which is one of the Army's oldest camps and one of the most beautiful. It was so good to have a hot shower, a change of clothes and a bed.

We were issued furloughs, so I got on the train, all the way back to New York State. It took about four days. But it was worth it. A funny thing – when I was home, everywhere I'd go, I couldn't buy a drink. It was always on the house.

I returned to Fort Lewis, and now we had a hectic schedule. They were getting us all ready. And we thought we were going to Japan. All through it, I always wanted to go to Europe. I said I'm probably going to combat someplace, and if I had my say, I'd rather go to Europe. I couldn't see going to the Pacific. The jungle. The malaria. The savagery of the Japanese. So of the two I preferred Europe. I thought at least they've got houses. At least they look like me. I think I'll get a better deal in Europe. I think they'll obey the Geneva Convention. These lunatics in the Pacific, kamikazes, savages, they don't obey anything. My preference was to go to Europe. And it looks like we're all set to go to Japan.

Then all of a sudden, we're off to Florida. We had been selected to take amphibious training. Underwater demolition. Very few units were chosen; we felt pretty good, because hey, we were chosen out of all of those units to go for this training.

We went to Fort Pierce, which is a Naval training station for underwater demolition, assault boats, they were the leaders of this particular stuff. Army units would be assigned to them, but it's a Navy base. We're the only Army unit on it. And we get the feeling that they resent us. No Army man can do what they can do. A sailor vs. soldier type of thing. But they told us what we had to do, all the drills, and we did pretty good. Before long we were doing what they did, and in a lot of cases we were surpassing them. Their animosity lessened and they accepted us.

We went out in the ocean and came in on rubber rafts, learned demolition, hand to hand combat, the whole business. A lot of the big brass – this was in December 1943 – came down to watch us, and we put on a big show. I guess right then they decided, "We can use this unit in an invasion."

And we realized that we're no longer just a combat engineer unit, we're a specialized group now. We're specialists in invasion techniques, beach assault techniques. And some of the guys thought, "Hey, piece of cake, we're so good."

But a lot of guys thought, "Wherever we go, it's going to be a suicide mission."

I was in the group that thought "piece of cake." I know all this stuff, and we're so good. I had just turned 18, and when you're 18, nothing bothers you. You're gung-ho. I'm on top of the world. That was a big attitude, but a lot of the guys were more serious than I was. They had these feelings. A lot of guys went AWOL. I think it was because of what they saw coming. But they were picked up and returned, and our commanding officer made damn sure that they were part of the invasion.

We knew we were going to hit a beachhead someplace. We didn't know where.

We went up to Camp Pickett, Virginia. We took some more infantry tests. And that's where I saw my first prisoners of war. All KP was done by German POWs. And I never saw a happier group of guys. They had it made. As you went through the line, they always had a big smile. They would ask, "Do you want more?"

We saw a lot – thousands and thousands more – later on, but of them all I never saw a happier group than that group at Camp Pickett.

We weren't there very long. Then we went up to Camp Kilmer, New Jersey, and by then we knew things were getting serious. We were getting ready to leave. They gave us some more drills, and a lot of paperwork, who's your beneficiary and all this gobbledygook.

We'd kid about the insurance. "Well, at least somebody's gonna get ten thousand."

At Camp Kilmer, we were quarantined; we couldn't go anywhere. Very restricted. From Camp Kilmer we go into New York, on the Hudson River, on the piers, and here's this big ugly boat waiting. We get on the dock, we all line up, and we go up the gangplank. Each of us has a great big barracks bag. Just prior to that, the Red Cross was there, and they gave us all a little sewing kit. Free. It's the last thing I ever got free from the Red Cross. From then on everything they charged for. They gave me a free sewing kit, a needle, a thimble, and a little ball of thread. Then we went up the gangplank, and there was a band there that played. The S.S. Exchequer was the name of the boat.

When we leave, the band's playing, the Red Cross girls are waving goodbye, we trudge up the gangplank, get on this boat. We stayed at the pier overnight, and in the morning we took off. We saw the Statue of Liberty. We go out a ways, then we meet a lot of other ships converging to make a convoy.

On the ship it seemed like one continuous chow line. You never had a great appetite; the seasickness and nausea affected everybody. But you'd go down in the galley – the fumes were unbelievable. You'd get some breakfast; then you'd go back up on deck. By the time you got on deck it was time to get back on line for lunch.

Lunch was usually an apple, a sandwich, something cold. Then it was time for evening chow. It was one continuous chow line. But there were times you could read books, play cards, poker. Some of the guys had crap games going. And we had a limited amount of calisthenics. The officers would get us together and we'd do plane identification. The greatest part of the day was watching the gun crews practice for antiaircraft. Our boat would go off, and this boat would go off, then that boat. Jesus, the noise. And the Navy gun crews were good. They were so synchronized and coordinated, it was something to watch.

About halfway over, we get a submarine alert. That's scary. You're out in the middle of the Atlantic. Everybody puts on a life jacket. You all get up on deck, and it's dark as hell. There was no moon that night. And you just wait. But pretty soon we heard that some of our destroyers found the sub and depth bombed it. That felt pretty good. But during that submarine alert one of our guys had an appendicitis attack, and had to be treated immediately. So during all that the doctor is down there operating on this guy. But he was tough. He was from Auburn, New York. He made it. That was quite a night.

Then Easter Sunday came, and the chaplains got together and put on an interfaith service up on deck. The Navy guys, the Army guys, they all were together. It was a simple service. But the setting: The ocean. The ships. A beautiful day. It's the most memorable, meaningful religious service I've ever attended.

When we got to the Irish Sea the convoy broke up, and we proceeded toward the Bristol Channel in northern Wales. British planes came out to greet us. They escorted us up to Cardiff, which is where we disembarked. It felt so good just to walk on land again, after ten days.

We had to go from the dock to a railroad station. We're marching through the city, and all along the way there's English people, they've got little flags and they're waving them, "Hi, Americans!" If you had chewing gum you'd throw it.

And I thought, gee, this is our first public appearance. We never had a parade before. That made you feel pretty good.

Then we get on the train and we head to Ilfracombe, which is on the western shore. It was the first time we ever saw quonset huts, and the first thing you noticed was charcoal. It permeated the air because all their little stoves were fed by charcoal, and it almost knocked you out. But we had hot showers, nice beds, all warm, a safe place to be.

At Ilfracombe we went right back into training. Within a day or two we were back in the English Channel, repeating our Fort Pierce exercises. We would practice our assault landing in rubber boats. Just practice, practice, practice.

Then we were sent south, to Dorchester, to a camp called D-2. We knew there was going to be an invasion but we didn't know where or when. They assembled us all, and a lot of big wheel officers were up front, and they told us about the invasion. "We've waited so long. We wanted to make sure everything was right. We had to have the equipment. We had to have the logistics. We had to have the plans. Most of all, we had to have the men trained to do this job. We now feel we have achieved that. We're ready to go. And we want you to know that the 299th has been selected to be one of the forces to be in the invasion."

In fact, they told us we were going to be right in the front row.

There were a lot of mixed reactions. We knew we were scheduled to hit a beachhead, so it was no big surprise. It was a great relief to know at least it's coming soon. We still didn't know when or where.

We went back to Camp D-2, and we were restricted. No passes. Nobody left the camp. But they treated us like royalty. Continuous movies, first-rate movies. Unbelievable food. Ice cream. Candy. Cigarettes. Whatever you wanted was there. We were treated like they were fattening us up for the kill. We knew why we were getting all this special treatment; hey, it's the least we could do for you. You're going on a suicide mission. And a lot of guys thought it was suicide. A lot of guys had deep anxiety feelings, because they knew what a beach assault could be. I felt that way too. But I went around trying to cheer up my depressed comrades. I said, "Hey, it's not that bad. Come on!"

Some of them would get dejected; they wouldn't sleep. You could tell by looking at them, that they had a hopeless feeling. I went around trying to show some bravado, but I think what I was doing was relieving my own anxieties. I was just as scared and anxious as they were.

Soon we leave that camp and go down to Weymouth. On the way down, there were acres and acres of every piece of military equipment you could describe: tanks, gasoline cans, guns. Everything was stockpiled all over, mile after mile. And we thought, do you realize that 98 percent of this came from the United States, came across the Atlantic Ocean? It was unbelievable.

We got into Weymouth and it was a madhouse. The port was full of boats going this way and that way, big boats, little boats, every kind of boat. And the whole village was packed. It was one big traffic jam. There were guys trying to march to their boats, there were tanks, there were trucks all lined up waiting to get on a certain boat. The boat had to come in, be assigned, and you had to be directed. MPs all over the place. It was total confusion. But it was organized confusion. Somehow they sorted it all out and they got to the right place. And we ended up on an old English channel steamer, the Princess Maude. We laughed and laughed at the name, the Princess Maude, this was our boat. It was a small boat. By the time we got on it, with all of our gear, there was no place to move. There was no room for calisthenics. You just found a space and sat down and read a book. You hated to go to your sleeping quarters because they were so cramped and dingy, and the boat kept rocking. It's in the harbor now and it's rocking, rocking, rocking. And all the guys who got seasick coming over, it all came back.

We were told in our final briefing that D-Day would be June 5th. So we're all geared up for it. We've got our attitude all set. Then we get to Weymouth and we're on our boat and we're ready to go. And all of a sudden they announce it's been delayed 24 hours because of a storm. That means we've got to spend another day on this rocking, crazy boat. And the guys are getting sicker and sicker.

The English crew had a galley, and one of our guys, I don't know how he did it but he convinced the bakery people to give him some loaves of bread. We were there two nights. Each night he'd come into our quarters with two or three big loaves of bread. No butter. But the hot, baked bread, it's just like cake. That was the high point of those particular days. At midnight we'd get a big chew of bread. Nobody ever asked him how he did it. And nobody ever found out because he was killed on D-Day.

Back at Camp D-2 we were shown models of the beach area. And the planes would take photographs, develop and rush them right to the invasion fleet, so we saw photographs of the whole beach that were only hours old. And it looked pretty bad, what we had to do. Our battalion had eight assault teams, and we were to cut pathways through the obstacles, the tetrahedrons, the hedgehogs, the Belgian gates, the poles, that were all along the beach.

Our mission was to clear paths through those so the rest of the troops could get in. And we felt pretty confident, because that's what we had trained for.

We leave Weymouth, and we get way out in the English Channel, and all of a sudden thousands of ships are all around us. We're at what they call Piccadilly Circus; that was the big congregation point. I can't describe the numbers, the sizes, the shapes – every type of boat was out there milling about. And finally they were directed to go their various ways.

We arrived at a rendezvous point probably 10 or 12 miles off of Omaha Beach, around 12 o'clock at night, and we stopped.

All the way over it was very choppy, and the guys who were sick were getting sicker; guys who hadn't been sick were now getting sick. The officers said, "Get some sleep." You couldn't sleep. You'd go to your bunk and all you could think about was what was going to happen tomorrow.

The British crew gave us a hell of a good breakfast. Whatever you wanted they would do. Eggs sunnyside up, down, omelets. Tons of coffee. A bunch of us went into a little room off to the side; we were sitting there talking about everything when two or three officers walked by, and they looked in. "Can we join you?" These were officers. We're all enlisted men. The officers joined us, and you would never know they were officers. We talked about movies. Automobiles. Sweethearts. Kids at home. Anything but war. We spent a good hour just bullshitting there, back and forth. And I left there with the feeling that those guys have got to lead us tomorrow, and they needed this little session as much as we did. It relieved a lot of tension on their part.

Then, of course, we were supposed to go to sleep, but you couldn't. We went up on deck and tried to look around but it was so dark and choppy, and there were thousands of boats all around us. We could see the big battleships off on the horizon. And I heard somebody playing a guitar out there someplace; it came across the water so clear. We tried to go to our bunks and sleep a little bit. You couldn't sleep. We lay there and we thought of home. And we heard the airplanes going over to drop the guys in the 82$^{nd}$ and 101$^{st}$ Airborne divisions. Go get them! We wished them well.

At two or three in the morning, they got us up and around. And we went to breakfast. This is where they made whatever you wanted. I ate two orders of custard pudding. I ate very well. But a lot of guys didn't show up. I've always thought, maybe they felt this was the Last Supper, and they didn't want to be part of it.

Then it's time to get ready. The first thing you do is hit the head. It's called a head on a ship, the bathroom. And guys start shaving, combing their hair. One guy's putting on cologne. You'd think we were going on a weekend pass. I and a lot of my buddies had goatees, so we spent several minutes making sure that that was just right. Shaving. Washing under our arms.

Then you put your stuff on. We all had new olive-drabs. I think we had long johns. We had a field jacket. And then they gave us these impregnated coveralls. They were so stiff and unwieldy they could almost stand up by themselves. They had been specially treated with some solution that would withstand gas. You put those on. And on top of that, you had your belt, your gas mask, a bandolier of bullets. And your cartridge belt had a bayonet, a canteen, a first aid packet, and more bullets. Your helmet. I made sure the chinstrap was down. And your rifle. And your backpack, which had your mess kit, your shovel, and your incidentals.

There's 50 or 60 pounds of stuff. And you're supposed to go in there and be agile.

I'm sitting there thinking; I've got a few minutes. I pull out some photographs of my family, and I'm looking at them. And I've got Eisenhower's letter that he sent out to all the kids, I read that again. I'm looking at this stuff and my buddy comes up behind me. He was a good buddy. We'd been through a lot together. He opens his jacket. And he had on the ugliest, gaudiest, most outlandish necktie I ever saw in my life. I guess a friend back home had sent it to him, and he was going to wear it on D-Day. What the hell, they couldn't stop him now. We laughed about that, and we thought about all the things we went through, and what we're gonna go through together. We talked about what we were going to do when we hit Paris.

Then we get an order to get on deck. So we throw our arms around each other. You can't walk with all this stuff, so we waddle up to the deck. We get up there, and all the guys are assembled, we're going over the side.

And we're saying things like, "Make sure you tell my mother this," or "If I don't see you again...."

Then we go over the railing and we go down the cargo net. The water's real choppy. And the LCVP, our assault craft, which we're getting into, is having a hell of a time staying close to the ship, because the net goes from the ship down into that boat. I'm halfway down, and the goddamn net goes up, I'm laying spreadeagled, and I'm looking at all this angry water down below. But I make it down. Everybody makes it down okay, and we get into our assault craft.

Right in the middle of the craft is a rubber raft full of explosives. And the guys line up around the raft.

I'm pretty sure the coxswain and his assistant were Coast Guard guys. We take off and go to another rendezvous point, and he circles and circles, waiting for other craft so they can all go at once. And all the time boats are zipping in and out.

Pretty soon they had a bunch of boats lined up. And timing was crucial, so they had to wait. We're about 12 miles out, and these are not fast boats, so I guess it took about two hours from this point to reach the beach. We had to hit at 6:33. So I'm guessing it's about 4 o'clock in the morning.

All of a sudden, "Vroom! Vroom!" We take off in a big line. On either side of us are similar boats to mine. We try to look and see, because we know our buddies are in these boats. You just can't make them out. You holler at each other, but you can't hear anything. And it's a very choppy sea. These LCVPs are not huge boats. But the speed of the boat seemed to lessen the rockiness of it. The waves just washed all over; within ten minutes, the water's just below your knees, the boat is full of water. Guys have started to vomit. That's floating all over the water inside the boat. And on the way in, you realize that half of these guys have already been sick back at Weymouth, this is not helping their condition. Here they are about to meet the biggest challenge of their life and physically they're just not up to par for what they've got to do. But somehow I felt pretty good through it, I was all right. And my buddy, Tom Legacy from Niagara Falls, was up ahead of me. He turned around, he flashed the necktie again, and I gave him a thumbs-up.

As we started going toward the beach, all the battleships opened up with their big guns. You never heard noise like that in your life. Prior to that, we had heard the bombers. They're supposed to bomb the beach. And as we get closer we can see the fighter planes strafing the beach. Then we pass a rocket ship, a big flat affair loaded with rockets, "Phshoo! Phshoo! Phshoo! Phshoo! Phshoo!" And as you go in, you see the rockets, the Naval guns, the planes. How could anything live through what they're getting? It's going to be a piece of cake. There'll be nothing alive there. That made you feel pretty good. And we'd been promised way back in England, there'll be so many craters on this beach, and all you've got to do is jump into a crater, you'll be protected.

We also passed an LCMP, the one that carries tanks, loaded with tanks. These were the tanks with the big canvas collar around them. They were a British idea. When they hit the water, these canvas things would allow them to float until they could reach land. And this thing started letting these tanks off. One went off. "Blooop!" Straight down. You'd think they'd know something was wrong. Second one. "Blooop!" Three or four went down like that. And we're right alongside of it. All of a sudden the guys come bobbing up, fighting for breath and air, they're like corks in the water. You'd think we could stop and pick them up. Nope. We had a mission. They're yelling and screaming. We had to go right by them. I hope they were rescued. I thought, "I guess this is war. There's no time for compassion. We've got a mission, and nothing can interfere." Boy, that hurt.

Now we're getting close to the beach. The officer up front is going crazy. He's looking at his map, then looking out, looking at his map, he's swearing like hell, and we could hear the rumors come back, "We're in the wrong place." This was true of almost every craft in the whole operation. They didn't estimate how strong a tidal current there was, and everybody went left of where they were supposed to land, and there were none of the landmarks that they expected to see. We were supposed to land on Easy Red, and I think we landed on Fox, which was the next sector over.

Everything's nice and quiet, then all of a sudden, ping, ping, ping, ping, brrrrrr, we could hear the machine guns hitting the ramp. We dropped the ramp. To my knowledge, we all got off the craft okay. But thereafter it was devastation. Guys started dropping and screaming all around you.

The first thing I did after getting off the boat was to take my rifle and aim it at a pillbox. "Pow!" I still don't know why I did that. It was an impulse.

That's the only shot I fired all day.

Then I grabbed the tow rope for the rubber raft full of explosives, which was right behind me. I threw the rope over my shoulder and I started pulling.

All of a sudden I feel it get heavier. I look around, and there's three bodies that were thrown in. Two are face down; I don't who they were. One is face up. I knew who he was.

I kept pulling. And all of a sudden, BOOM! A mortar came over and it hit the raft, and it blew all our explosives. I was knocked head over heels, and I blacked out. When I came to, I was on my hands and knees, I was spitting blood, and I had the worst headache you can imagine.

It took me a few moments to realize what happened. I sat back down, and I pulled my rope in, and all I got was a big piece of tattered rubber. That was the raft. The three guys, gone.

The one who had been face up was Charles Burt. I forget where he was from; somewhere in New York State. I'm pretty sure I know who the other two were, but I'll never be able to prove it. But in my heart I think I know who they were. I think they were my good buddies from Auburn, Johnny Spinelli and Vince DeAngelis. They were never found. They're on the Wall of the Missing. And it ties in to this, their whole bodies would have been destroyed. That's my gut feeling.

I saw a bunch of my guys down a ways, so I hollered to them. One of them was an officer. He said, "We've lost our explosives. We don't have any men. It's every man for himself. Try to get to shore the best you can."

I tried to stay with them but we were soon separated, and I was all by myself. And I start running from one obstacle to another. On the way I come across this guy laying and moaning in the water. The full tide isn't in yet; he's just being washed with the waves. I look at him. Jesus Christ, it's one of my pals, Joe Milkovic of Buffalo. On one of his legs I could see the raw bone through the flesh.

If I left him there he was gonna drown. I'm a little guy, and he was a pretty big guy. I knew I could never lift him and carry him in. So I got down behind him, I got my hands under his armpits, and I planted my feet in the sand and pushed with my feet and pulled him with my arms. It was slow, torturous, but we were making progress, very slowly, and I was exhausted. That was a hell of a lot of work. And I hoped and prayed that some German up there, some sniper or machine gunner would see us and take pity, here's a guy trying to save another, maybe he'll let us go. And it worked, because nobody shot at us.

But all of a sudden, here comes a tank. From where, I don't know. A small tank. The guy up in the turret, he looks down, I didn't even have to say anything. He saw my predicament. He dropped down. He said, "You're in trouble, buddy." He grabbed an arm and I grabbed an arm, and we dragged him up to the dune. And then the tanker said "Good luck," and he rushed back to the tank. I don't know his name. I don't even know what tank outfit he was in.

Now I was at the dune line. I looked around. I said this guy needs a medic. We all had a sulfa pack. I gave him what I could, and I didn't know where to put it. I just dumped the sulfa all over the place. I finally was able to attract a medic. The medic looked at him and gave him an injection of morphine. He said, "There's not much I can do, but leave him here, because we're going to have an aid station and we're going to send these guys out to the ship very soon."

The wounded man survived, although I heard he lost the leg. Evidently the medic was able to get him to a ship.

But I've made the dune now. I'm in one piece. And then you sit there and you look at all the chaos and the devastation. Guys floating in the surf, dead, wounded. The wounded screaming. And you're sitting in the dune and you're looking back at it, out into the water, and there are ships burning, smoking. This must be the day of doom. Armageddon. If this is war, I don't like it. All the beautiful plans we had made and practiced, all for naught. All confused, chaos.

I was numb. This was not the way it was supposed to be, and you had no way of coping with it. You had no leaders. Just pure chaos. And then you see all these dead guys, buddies. That's hard to cope with, the first time, to see death. And when you're a close personal friend, it hurts. You thought you were tough, brave and gung-ho. It gets you.

I said to myself, "I'm all alone now," where I brought Joe up to the dune. We may have been the first ones to have reached that far; there was nobody around. I had a hell of a time getting a medic for him; they were all out in the distance.

A lot of guys would be okay, then they'd see a wounded buddy, they'd run down in the tide and they'd get hit. So once I got the medic and I felt Joe was taken care of, I said this is no good, I've got to try to find some of my people. We've got to get organized here. I'm sure we're going to go back out and remove those obstacles when the tide goes out.

While I'm sitting there, about 60 yards away comes a guy staggering along the beach, staggering, foundering. His backpack is tattered; his clothes are in shreds. One arm is dangling. He turns and half his head is blown away. And something told me I know that guy, something about his stature, his walk. And he turned toward me and looked at me, and through all that gore and all that tattered clothing, I saw the tie.

I don't think he knew who I was. I wanted to cry out to him; I couldn't. I didn't have any voice. I was frozen. I couldn't move. He just staggered away.

Aw, Jesus. I never wanted to be a soldier. It was the last thing in my life I would have wanted to be. But Pearl Harbor changed my opinion. It was a lot of fun, these exercises, these hikes. Hey, a great bunch of guys, having fun. I didn't know what being a soldier was until that day.

I looked down to the east, and there was a Red Cross flag, and there seemed to be a lot of people moving around. So I said, "I'll try for there. Maybe I'll find some people."

There was a tank not too far away. I ran and made it to the tank. It's all burned out, smoke coming out of it. I hope those guys weren't inside. I stayed by the tank awhile, had a cigarette. And it gave me another chance to look out at all this confusion, chaos, devastation. I said, okay, now I'm going to try … as you went east, the sand dune got less and less, and ran out to nothing. There was a big open stretch I had to get across. So I weave, duck. There's a shingle on the beach, which is where, through the centuries, all the pebbles and stones that have been washed up have gathered. It's only high enough that you can lay down behind it. So I stuck with the shingle. I'd run, then I'd drop down, run a little more.

Finally I reached the aid station, which was behind some pretty good cliffs at the far east end of the beach. And hundreds of guys were there. Confused, disarrayed, disorganized. They'd lost their leaders. They were wounded. Down in the flat area were stretchers, stretchers, stretchers. Wounded guys that had been collected so far. The medics were trying their best, and a lot of the GI s were helping them. There was a hospital ship not far out. They were carrying the stretchers piggyback, under their arms, any way to get them out. I went in among these stretchers. It seemed like every third guy was one of my buddies. Now I know why I hadn't found any of my pals back there; they're all here. And every one took my hand – some of them didn't know what they were doing but some of them did – "You tell my wife," "You tell my mother."

As far as I know all of those guys made it back to England. The guys that we lost were killed instantly. These guys that were wounded, they suffered, but I think they made it.

Now I started looking for a rifle. The thought in my mind was, "I'm going to catch hell. I lost my rifle." Army discipline. And I thought, every rifle has a serial number, yours is assigned, how am I going to fudge that? I didn't worry. I'll just get a rifle. So I found one. There were hundreds of them, laying all over. I found one that looked pretty good. It was all full of sand. So I spent a few minutes disassembling and cleaning it. Then I spotted some of my buddies, and I went over and got together with them. We all agreed that things had gone crazy. But we were engineers, and sure enough, we're gonna have to go out there in the afternoon and do the job that we'd failed to do in the morning, so we stuck around. And that's what we did. Later that afternoon some engineer officers came by and said, "Any engineers here?" By that time they had a couple of bulldozers. We would remove some mines, but the bulldozers did most of the job. And we'd blow up the obstacles. We'd build a fire in the hole, we'd send up a flare to let the troops know. We cleared a big stretch of the beach.

There were still snipers firing at the beach. Machine guns. Mortars. Because this area had the Red Cross flag, it didn't receive a lot of shelling. They were acknowledging that it's a medical station. But once in a while one would come in.

We think that what really saved us – one of my buddies wrote an article on this – was that the destroyers came in so close, we wondered how they weren't stranded on the sand. They made several passes with their guns blazing at the pillboxes that were raising hell. A tank on shore would fire at a pillbox, and that would give the ship its coordinates, and he could fire. And the guns on the boat, they knocked out those critical pillboxes that were devastating the beach. My friend – and I agree with him – wrote that if it wasn't for the destroyers, we may never have made it. They played such a vital part eliminating that resistance. Because at 11 o'clock, we heard later that General Bradley's out on the command ship, they were going to call off the invasion on Omaha Beach and go down to Utah Beach where things were going much better. They were going to leave us like Dunkirk. And I envisioned a hundred Panzer tanks coming over the bluffs with a thousand screaming SS troopers right behind them, and we're annihilated. Where could we go, into the water?

But all of a sudden, a guy here, a guy there, a sergeant here, "Come on guys, let's go get them." They started up. They got these snipers along the way. They blew out a pillbox. About 1 o'clock, 1:30, up on a hill, way up on the horizon, I saw some Yankees, waving, "Come on up! Come on up!" And whoever those guys were, they were the heroes. They lacked the leadership but they had that initiative, the soldier quality, that said, "We're not gonna die here. Let's go get these guys!"

And then things got better. But there was a traffic jam on the beach. The tide was coming in, and that restricted the beach area. At one time they stopped all the landings until we could clear space for them. Nothing was moving. Everything was restricted right to the beach area. We weren't moving up the bluffs like we were supposed to. They didn't make it until these little squads here and there got together, this group and that group. And then we were able to get some tanks in. We filled in the ditches and the tank traps. Then we just overwhelmed them with equipment. But thank God Hitler was asleep. All their stuff was way up at Calais. He thought this was a ploy. Thank God for that.

In the afternoon, we went back out and we blew the obstacles. There were two or three of us from the same outfit; we said, "We've got to get with our own people. Let's start looking for them." We started down the beach, and we ran into a couple of our buddies. One of them said the whole outfit was assembling up on the bluff. So we made our way through the barbed wire; never thought about mines. And soon there was a pretty big group of our guys assembling up there with some officers.

They told us, "We've taken a pretty bad beating. We'll talk about it in the morning. Tonight just try to dig in up here. Stay close." So we went and dug a foxhole or you found a ravine, whatever you could, and tried to grit the night out. You'd lay down, but you couldn't sleep, because the infantry was still moving up. Tanks were moving up. There was a lot of commotion. Down on the beach, they were still unloading stuff. You were so excited and revved up that you couldn't sleep.

Later that evening, a couple of German planes came over. I don't think they strafed; they were reconnaissance more or less. Well, out in the harbor there were ten thousand boats, and every one of them opened up. It looked like the Fourth of July. I don't think they got either one of them, but it was a lot of noise. And a lot of guys took their rifle, I saw officers with .45s trying to shoot a plane down! And during the evening somebody hollered, "Gas!" Well, that shook everybody up. I still had my gas mask, but I heard guys crying, "I don't have a gas mask!" A lot of them went down to the beach; they thought if they got in the water that would save them. It was crazy. And it was a false alarm. If we ever found the SOB who shouted that, he wouldn't be around today. It was bad for 15 or 20 minutes. Finally, the infantry's coming up this trail not far away from us, they're looking at us with all our gas masks, and they're laughing. And you felt like a goddamn fool.

You learned an awful lot in those hours. You changed a lot of your opinions, attitudes, and you realized that hey, this is not a game. A lot of the craziness, the gung-ho attitude disappeared. It hit you that so many of your buddies were no longer with you.

The next morning we were assembled and the colonel told us how many men we'd lost, and we realized how much we had paid. Then we were given cleaning details. We were sent down to the beach to help clear up the debris; certain groups were sent to clear up mines. The place was full of mines, so certain sections were sent to clear roadways through these minefields. Thankfully I didn't get that. That's the worst detail in the world, mines.

None of our men were killed clearing mines, but three or four were wounded. One guy lost his fingers. That's what mines do. They might not kill you, but they maim you. Horrible. They're trying to outlaw them now. And the Germans were experts at mines. They came up with a plastic mine. We had mine detectors to detect metal. Now they're plastic; the mine detector's no good. And they had trick wires. This'll be a dead mine. If you detonate this, you set off that. And boobytraps. Because GIs seem to want to get souvenirs – loot – that's an American instinct, and they forget to be cautious. We lost a lot of guys because of that. They'll boobytrap their own dead. You want his helmet? It could be boobytrapped.

And they were so good at it. They had a mine called the bouncing Betty, you would step on it and it would jump up and get you right in the groin.

One day I'm going along, and there's a shoe. I kicked it out of the way. There's a foot in it.

I can't tell you what war is. You wouldn't believe how men; we're supposed to be human beings, civilized. On the beach, it was unbelievable. You'd see bodies crushed by tanks. The tanker can't see, and he's literally running right over guys. I hope they were dead when he did it. You walk along, there's two big tank tracks, and the guy's embedded right in the sand. Maybe the guy was wounded, he couldn't move. I don't blame the tank. They're up there, they can't see, they've got to maneuver, but that happened so many times. That's a pretty gruesome sight the next day.

I've seen guys with arms full of arms, arms filled with legs, carrying them off to a collection point. And I understand they made one great big trench and just dumped everything in there. Then a year or so later, after the war, they reclaimed and went through it, and they're all up in the cemetery.

And it always remains in your mind; any veteran who has seen combat wonders, wonders, why me? Why was he killed, why did I survive? It's a question you can't answer. But it bothers you. Why did they shoot him and I was spared? I've tried to appreciate it that I made it okay, and I've tried to say, well, I'll do my best to memorialize those guys.

Maybe that's why I was spared.

*"That morning, in the mess hall, I'd seen a guy. I'd seen him before. I never knew who he was; he was in a different squadron. He was a big, rough-faced guy, and I thought, 'Who is that guy?' I don't know why I noticed him.*

*"We came across this plane that's crashed, and in the co-pilot's seat, here's a guy sheared in two. From his waist down is in the co-pilot's seat. The rest of him is missing. We look up ahead and about a hundred yards away, here's the upper part of his torso butted into a tree. When I rolled him over, it was the guy I'd seen in the mess hall that morning."*

**George Collar**
**Bombardier**
**445th**
**Bomb Group**
**Interviewed**
**in Tiffin, Ohio**
**April 12, 1999**

I was brought up in the aftermath of World War I, and we were always taught that that was the war to end all wars. All of us kids were steeped in the heroics of Raoul Lufberry and Eddie Rickenbacker and Frank Luke, and we were a little bit sad there weren't going to be any more wars; we wouldn't be able to get to fight. Boy, we were really wrong about that! I think the draft came out in 1940, and I had a pretty high number, 319 or something like that. Back in the summer of 1941 I had a cousin who was in the 75th Toronto Scottish Regiment, which was sort of like a National Guard outfit. In 1939 he was called to active duty and went overseas. He was gone for six years. He was at Dieppe, he was down in Italy and he was all over with the Canadian army.

I had an uncle who was killed in the battle of the Somme in World War I when he was fighting with the British army. We kind of had a military background and we were eager to go, especially when everybody else was going. So one day another fellow and I drove over to Windsor, Ontario, and when we went across the bridge the customs man said, "What are you going to Canada for?"

We said, "We've got business."

He hollered down, "Two more!"

There were over 10,000 Americans who crossed the Ambassador Bridge to get into the Canadian army.

But when we got down to the headquarters, they said, "We want to see a birth certificate. Go home and get it and we'll take you."

When we got home, we heard that a local garage was recruiting for a special unit in Illinois that would train you and give you a staff sergeant rating and send you to Egypt to be attached to the British 8th Army to repair those old tanks that went over on lend-lease. So another fellow named Deed and I went down and signed up. We quit our jobs. They gave us a paper and said we had to take it over to the induction center on Monday morning. They didn't say what time. He took an early bus and I took a later bus, and I got there at 20 minutes after 12. When I went in, there was a great big master sergeant in this office.

"What can I do for you?"

I gave him the paper. He looked at it and said, "You're 20 minutes too late."

"What do you mean?"

"They filled that quota and cut off everything at noon."

I said, "What else have you got?"

He said, "We need a lot of people in the infantry."

I said, "Is there anything else?"

He said, "If you can pass the mental and the physical, you can get in the Air Cadets."

I said, "How do I do that?"

He said, "There's a traveling Cadet Board coming to your town next week. You go down, and they've got all their own physicians and test people."

It was like a big trailer, by the courthouse. You took this four-hour written exam, and if you passed that, they gave you a physical. And if you passed that, they swore you in on the spot.

Before I did that, I got on the phone and I called Canada. I said, "Can I still get in the Royal Canadian Air Force and be an American citizen?"

They said, "Since Pearl Harbor we can't take anybody."

So I went down to the Cadet Board and there were 60 of us. Out of the 60, about 25 passed the written test. It had a lot of mechanics. I did well on it. Then they gave us the physical. I passed that, and was sworn in as a private in the Reserves on the spot.

Then they told me to go home and wait to hear from them. They didn't have enough training facilities. I got notified to report to duty on the 5th of January, 1943. And this fellow Deed who went into that outfit that was supposed to go to Egypt, he ended up in the 9th Armored Division. The fellow I went to Canada with originally ended up in the Seabees in the South Pacific.

I reported to duty in Detroit. There were about 250 of us. They marched us in a body down to the station. They had a band there, but it was 25 below zero and the horns froze up and they couldn't play.

I went to Nashville, and they gave us all kinds of tests. I passed, and was told I could either go to pilot training or to bombardier school. I didn't do so well on the navigation. I said, "I want to be a pilot." Everybody wanted to be a pilot.

They sent me to Maxwell Field, Alabama. I went through pre-flight there, and I ended up at Carlston Field in Florida for primary training. And I washed out on a check ride. They washed them out like mad, because they had more people who wanted to be pilots than they could use. But they didn't have enough going to bombardier school.

I was disgusted when I washed out. I knew I could fly the plane but I screwed up a couple of things. On an S-turn I lost 50 feet. I didn't do too good on a forced landing. I did pretty good on the spins and stalls, and I felt in my own mind I could have passed.

That's neither here nor there; I flunked out. And that was one of the lowest points in my life, because everybody at home thinks you're going to be a pilot and all of a sudden you're letting everybody down. Including yourself.

Everybody who washes out has to go before a board, and they ask you: "What would you like to do?"

I said, "I want to go to ordnance OCS."

"Well, you can have that for second choice; we're sending you to bombardier school."

That's how I became a bombardier.

I went out to Texas to Ellington Field and went through pre-flight again. Then I went to flexible gunnery school at Laredo, and eventually to advanced bombardier school at Big Spring, Texas.

One of my partners in Ellington Field was Art Devlin, the famous skier. He later became a bombardier and he didn't go to Laredo; he went to Harlingen and I lost track of him, but he was on the Olympic team after the war. I visit him up in Lake Placid; he runs a motel up there.

We graduated just before Christmas of '43 and came home on a 10-day delay en route. Then we went to Salt Lake City where they made up the crews, and I was assigned to Reg Miner's crew.

We went to Casper, Wyoming, for phase training; then the weather got so bad that they sent us down to Pueblo, Colorado, and we finished our phase training there.

They gave us a new plane when we were up at Casper. We flew it to Topeka, Kansas, for alterations. Then we went on another plane to Lincoln, Nebraska, and we waited around Lincoln about a week. Finally our plane showed up and we got our orders. The orders were sealed. We had to get all our stuff together and report to the flight line. We got on the plane, and Reg Miner couldn't open that sealed order until he got aloft.

When we were in the air, we found we were going to Bangor, Maine. So we knew we were going to Europe. You either went to the Pacific or the Atlantic. There were two ways to go to Europe, the southern route and the northern. Bangor was the northern route; the southern route went down through Puerto Rico and Brazil and across to Africa.

From Bangor we flew up to Goose Bay, and the weather was pretty bad; there were still a lot of icebergs out in the ocean. Eventually we flew to Iceland. We spent the night in Iceland, and the next day we took off and made landfall at Stornaway on the island of Lewis. Then we went down across the Scottish Highlands and across the North Sea and part of the Irish Sea and landed on the island of Anglesea in Wales, in a place called Valley.

They'd issued the navigator and myself and some of the waist gunners big powerful binoculars that were supposed to spot any kind of ship. We didn't even see the ocean most of the time because of the clouds.

That was the last time we ever saw that brand-new plane. A lot of guys had spent money having nice logos put on, and then they lost their planes. We hadn't put any nose art on ours. Miner didn't go for logos much. It didn't make much difference. We flew with a lot of planes that had logos when we got to England. About the nicest plane I ever flew in – one of the best-kept on the ground – was one called Win With Paige. The crew chief's name was Paige, and the original pilot's name was Wynn. That Paige was a wonderful mechanic, and he kept that plane in tip top shape. We flew quite a few missions on it. To give you an idea of what a good crew chief does, he not only keeps the engine in good shape and everything top-notch, but he looks after the little things. Like one of the problems a guy getting in a nose turret has is those big clodhopper shoes we had; you couldn't get your heel between the gun saddle and the seat. So he cut the clearance of the seat. And another thing that was bad, when the Consolidated B-24 was first built, it didn't have a front turret. It had a big greenhouse and it had an old machine gun sticking out through the Plexiglas, and it wasn't too satisfactory. So they decided to put a turret in. What they did at Consolidated was take a hydraulic Consolidated tail turret and mount it up in the front. It was a cobbled-up job and it was a mess, because they had two sets of doors, and you had trouble getting in and you had trouble getting out. And you don't want to have trouble getting out, I can tell you that.

What they did in our group – I don't know whether they did it in all the groups, but we had good engineering in our group – the later planes were coming in with electrical nose turrets. They were beautiful turrets made by Emerson Electric. They only had a single door and it was easy to get in and out. One of the problems with a hydraulic turret is they get to leaking, and then they just don't operate right. With an electrical turret; you've got a lot better control.

We arrived in Valley, Wales, sometime in May and we stayed overnight at a little base there. The next day we went on trucks and got on a train and we went up through North Wales and over into Staffordshire. There was a staging area called Stone in Staffordshire. We were there for several days, and then we got orders to pack our stuff and get down to the train depot, and they took us up to a place called Warrington, I think it's in Cheshire. It's not too far from the old Ringway Airport; I think that's now Manchester International Airport but at that time it was a small military airport. And as we pulled into the station at Warrington, it was June the 6th, 1944, because the stationmaster came running out, and he said, "They've landed in Normandy!" Everybody cheered.

We got off the train and they put us on trucks and took us over to Ringway, and they loaded us on some old B-17s and took us to a place called Clontow in Northern Ireland; it's probably about 40 miles west of Belfast in County Tyrone. The purpose of the base at Clontow was to train the new pilots in formation procedure. Formation flying is one of the toughest things they had to do because here's all these thousands of airplanes at all these bases clustered into an area probably about the size of northwestern Ohio. When you're going on say a thousand plane raid, you've got to form. And forming is a tough job, because you've got to be at a certain altitude in a certain spot at a certain time. That's easy to say, but when there are all these bees flying around, that's not too easy. What they did was they had radio signals coming up from the ground called bunchers and splashers, and they homed in on those at a certain time and a certain altitude. And the first guy up there was called a zebra ship. Each group had a zebra ship; ours was an old B-24-B called Lucky Gordon, kind of an orange dappled looking thing. He'd be up there and he'd be firing certain color flares; each formation had to have a different colored flare, so you had two or three things going, you had the radio signal plus the zebra ship firing these flares, and you circled around and circled around until you finally got in formation.

At Clontow, there was a crew that had trained with us in Casper and I knew the bombardier. His name was Freddie Crockett. They had a  co-pilot by the name of

Olsen. He was from Long Island. A big, tall, blond-haired, Swedish looking guy. Had a good voice. Used to sing in the light opera. He was down at this lake – this lake, mind you, is 15 miles across. It's a huge lake. And Olsen was down there monkeying around and he fell in. An eel fisherman by the name of Peter Coyle fished him out. And he took him up to the house to dry him out and give him some hot tea and whatnot. So he got acquainted with the family. Peter Coyle was a bachelor but he lived with his sister and her husband and his mother in this old stone cottage. Their family lived in that cottage for over 250 years. And he's a guy about 40. So the next night, Olsen said, "I'm going over to Peter Coyle's. I'm taking my tobacco ration for the grown-ups and some candy for the kids. Do you want to go along?" I forked over my tobacco ration and some candy, and we went over to Peter Coyle's cottage, and he treated us like we were long-lost brothers. They didn't have much. They had a stone floor and the chickens came in and out the door. They didn't have a fireplace; they had a raised stone hearth. And the smoke was peat smoke; it went right up the side of the wall and out a hole in the roof. They had an iron hook, and they brewed their tea on that. They made us tea and eggs.

After we were done, Peter Coyle had four little nieces up to about 10 years old, and they started to sing. Boy, could they sing. They were just like larks. It seemed like everybody in Ireland could sing. First they sang Irish songs, and then they sang "The Yellow Rose of Texas." I'll never forget, they sang, "The yellow rose of Texas beats the belles of Tennen-see."

Then we all started to sing, and Olsen was really a good singer. When we got done, we felt like we were their own relations. Peter Coyle took us down to an old barn, and there were a lot of bicycles and horses and wagons outside. There was a traveling theatrical group that was putting on a show. Between acts, one guy got up who used to sing songs in rhyme about people in the audience.

Well, they must have given him our name, because this guy sang a big song about Olsen and me and about Olsen dropping in the lake. I'd give anything if I had a tape recorder. I can't remember the words, but it was all in rhyme and it was all in tune, and it was really an honor.

When we got done, Peter Coyle gave his rosary to Olsen, and he gave me a little religious medal. I don't think I'm superstitious but I really am. I didn't have that the day I went down. And I didn't have a roll of tape. I always carried a roll of tape because one of the first things that happened was an evadee came to give us a talk. He was someone who had been shot down and was helped by the Underground, and he eventually crossed the Pyrenees Mountains on foot. And he said, "One thing you've got to do is protect your feet. And the best thing you can have when you're walking is a roll of tape, so you won't get blisters." I always carried a roll of tape, but the day I went down I didn't have my roll of tape with me. I didn't think I was going to fly that day. And I didn't have my GI shoes, which I normally carried. The tape wouldn't have done me any good anyway, because I got captured as soon as I landed.

After we were assigned to the 445th Bomb Group, we were assigned to a nissen hut. There were only two people in my hut when I arrived. One of them was a Lieutenant Reed, who was a bombardier from Alliance, Kansas. He'd been in a terrible crash in England coming back from a mission, and he was the only survivor. He was about half flak-happy. He'd been in the hospital and was recovering, and he was just about finished with his missions. He might have made a mission or two more, but boy, he was jumpy. He played the cornet. And his hero was Mugsy Spanier. He had a little windup phonograph with all of Mugsy Spanier's 78 records; he'd play them and he'd tune in with his cornet. He'd played a lot of jazz gigs in Kansas City.

The other guy in our hut was a fellow named Captain Steinbacher. Captain Steinbacher was from Williamsport, Pennsylvania. He was one of the original pilots that flew overseas with the group. He had finished up. He had played football for Penn State. Good looking, big, burly, and a heck of a nice guy. He and another pilot named Neil Johnson had finished their missions, and they prevailed upon Colonel Terrill, who was the commanding officer at that time, to put in a word for them. They wanted to stay in England and get into fighter planes. In the meantime they volunteered – in those days they could get done with 25 missions, but they volunteered to do five more while they're waiting. He'd just finished up his five more, and he didn't have much to do, so he always used to come down to breakfast at 3 o'clock in the morning with the guys who were scheduled to fly because that was the only time you could get fresh eggs. I got acquainted with him because he had the bunk right across the aisle from me. He lent me books.

He came down to breakfast the day we were going on our first mission. We didn't fly with our own crew. They always broke you up a little bit and flew you with another, experienced crew. In fact, they may have flown Miner one ahead of us. I know first the day I flew, I flew with a Lieutenant Schreck, and Miner was flying as co-pilot off our wing.

When we got down to breakfast, Steinbacher was eating fresh eggs. All us rookies were kind of antsy. We're starting to ask him about this flak and everything. And Steinbacher says, "Oh, you don't have to worry about that flak. You see those black powder puffs out there, they're not going to hurt you. They've already gone off. Fact is, you're never going to see the one that hits you, so there's no use worrying about it." Well, that made you feel a little better. Not much. Oh, he did say one thing. He said, "When they start getting yellow centers, they're getting a little close."

So we went down to briefing and Metro Moe – that's what they called the weatherman – gave a rosy picture about the weather: "It's a little cloudy on takeoff; it's just ground fog. It'll be burned off by the time you get back. Maybe."

Then the intelligence officer came on. He had this map of Europe, and it showed where there were flak places. He had us going over the Netherlands. He said, "We've got you going through a flak gap, so you shouldn't see any flak until you get on the bomb run." We were going to a place called Kothen, which is south of Berlin. It was quite a long mission. We were supposed to bomb a Junckers engine factory. And the instructions were, "If you can't see the target don't bomb. Go to a secondary target at a place called Stendal." And the same thing applied there.

So we're flying across the North Sea and we no more than made landfall when up came the flak. We're supposed to be going through a "flak gap." Up came the flak and it had big yellow centers.

Luckily, we got through that all right. But then we got on the bomb run, and we were on that damn bomb run for 12 minutes. That's a long time. And the flak was thick as hair on a dog; you're going right into it, bomm, bomm, bomm, bomm, bomm, bomm, all over. It looked just like a whole poppy field full of black flak. All of a sudden, BANG! It sounded just like a sledgehammer hit the plane, and a piece of flak came in the side of the nose and went right between the navigator and me and out the other side. Miner was flying off our left wing and I looked over and saw a burst underneath his plane and I saw them feather an engine and they started going down and oh God Almighty, I thought, I'll never get to fly with Miner. But they made it back on three engines.

We were on that bomb run for 12 minutes, and the worst part of it was they didn't drop the bombs. Then we go over to Stendal. Same thing over there only the flak wasn't quite as bad, but we still didn't drop the bombs. So on the way back we had to hit a target of opportunity because you can't drop the bombs in Belgium or France or the Netherlands unless you've got a specific target. We came across some marshaling yards about halfway between Hanover and Berlin on the main railway line, and we plastered them pretty good.

That first mission was a pretty good foretaste of what was to come. The next mission we had, we went to a buzz bomb site. It was a short mission, over in the Pas de Calais. These buzz bomb sites were in the forest, and were camouflaged so that you couldn't see them from the air. The only way you could bomb one was from Underground reports. And we were lucky that day. We hit what we were supposed to; at least that's what they said. But I went on another one in the same area, and we couldn't find it. We circled around and around until I thought we were going to run out of gas, and we finally had to come back without bombing. We had to drop our bombs in the North Sea at a jettison point because they were RDX bombs, and they weren't too stable on landing. General purpose bombs you could land with.

The RDX was a high explosive. The GP bombs you could roll off a truck and it wouldn't hurt them, but the RDX was unstable. One day we were at Tibenham and there was the damnedest explosion I ever heard in my life. It must have been 30 miles away. The depot blew up; I don't know how many people were killed. Blew a whole bomb dump up. You could hear it all over East Anglia. There was very little news about it because they kept it quiet. But I heard later that some guys were unloading RDX bombs and they rolled them off a truck, and one of them went off and blew right in this bomb dump.

I was taken off of Miner's crew. Miner was scheduled to become a lead pilot. He was a good pilot. And [Frank] Bertram was a good navigator. They replaced me with a radar guy; that's all I know. They put two guys on his crew and they took me off. They called me in the office one day and the old man, Major Martin, said he's going to put me in the pool. And he said, "Don't worry. You're going to get plenty of action." When I went down I was on my 29$^{th}$ mission. Miner's crew was on about their 19$^{th}$ mission. I flew so many missions. Day after day after day I'd be on a mission. All you could think of was getting up and getting down and going to bed.

I always thought I flew with seven different crews. I came to find out I flew with 10 different pilots. In one period I flew with two different pilots, Jerome Bernstein and Lieutenant Klein. I flew with Schreck the first mission. I flew seven missions with Miner. Then I flew four with Jerome Bernstein. I flew one with Wren, who had been Bernstein's co-pilot. And I'll never forget that mission. That was my 13$^{th}$ mission. Whenever you fly a mission with a co-pilot you're always a little leery because he didn't have the training a pilot had. But we thought Wren was good. We had a guy with us that mission; I'm not going to mention his name. This guy had been flying AT-6s at gunnery school at Laredo, and he was a chickenshit guy from the word go. Normally pilots are pretty nice guys. But this guy thought he was the king of the world. When he came overseas he was a first lieutenant, and Wren was only a second lieutenant. When this guy arrived, he had his own crew, and as soon as that plane landed, he went into the operations office and wanted to fire his whole crew. So Major Martin interviewed each guy one at a time. Instead of firing the crew, he put this guy in the pool and gave them another pilot.

Here we are flying with a pilot with whom we'd never been on a mission before except as a co-pilot. And the first lieutenant is flying as co-pilot. I was the bombardier. And from the minute we took off, this first lieutenant is crabbing about the way Wren's flying the plane. This gets irritating after a while, because you're worried about the guy anyway and then this guy is barking at him all the time. You don't like that over the intercom. You want peace and quiet.

Finally, when we got on the bomb run, I got control of the plane. And he's still barking all the time. You're supposed to maintain radio silence on the bomb run so that the bombardier can concentrate. Finally, I let him have it. I said, "Get the heck off this intercom! We're on a bomb run."

Now he's going to have me court-martialed.

When we got back down, they took him off the crew again. Last I knew he was still sitting in the pool. I don't know what ever happened to him. He may be alive yet. He may have a nice family, he may be a nice guy, I don't know, but he sure irritated me. Anyway, I didn't get court-martialed.

I flew with Jack Knox and J.R. Lemons and Howard Boldt. Poor old Bernstein was a good pilot. He was from New York City. He's got Alzheimer's now, lives out in Oregon. I flew with Donald. He got killed on the Kassel raid. Bob Russell, I still correspond with him, he's a good guy, lives out in San Diego. Brett, he got killed on the Kassel raid. [Jim] Schaen got killed on the Kassel raid.

On the 16th of August I went on the Dessau raid. I always thought I was flying with Bernstein but I was flying with Klein that day. That was a tough target. It was not far from Magdeburg; it had a lot of flak. And we had supercharger trouble; the pilot couldn't keep it in formation. He couldn't control the plane. So before we got to the target he had to get permission to leave the formation and head back for England. He called me up and said, "Get on the bomb sight and pick out a target of opportunity before we get to the Dutch border."

I said, "Okay."

In the meantime, we had a guy by the name of Frederick Jacoby who lives in New York City; he's retired from Columbia University. Lives on Central Park West. Frederick Jacoby was an intelligence officer. Donald S. Klopfer was our intelligence leader; he was a major. He was a partner with Bennett Cerf and Alfred Knopf and they started Random House. He died in his eighties a few years ago. He was a good friend of Jacoby, and after the war Jacoby worked for him for a while in the publishing company, then he eventually went into television. He was one of the original guys who ran the Howdy Doody show. He eventually became a publicity man for Columbia University.

Jacoby always was pushing to try to get on a mission, so they finally let him go, and he was riding up in the nose turret that day. When we started back for England we called for some fighter escort. It didn't show up right away, but here we are stooging across Germany all alone in real good weather, and I had to get on a target. I see the Dortmund-Ens Canal coming up, and I'm going to hit a bridge on it. I pick a bridge out, and I'm on the bomb run. I've got control of the plane. Everybody's supposed to keep their face out of the intercom. Old Jacoby's real excited because he thought fighters were coming after us. "Oh my God!" he says, "There's an airfield!"

He screwed me up and I knew I was never gonna hit that bridge. I thought, "I've got to do something quick because the Dutch border isn't very far away." So I hurried up, and you've got to remember, on this autopilot – it was a Sperry that you've got on a B-24; you can rack that baby clear over to 45 degrees back and you won't tumble the gyro. A B-17 had the Norden autopilot; it'd only go about 18 degrees back and it would tumble the gyro, then you're really screwed. I racked that baby – I tilted everybody about 45 degrees. I went down and I got on that bomb run on that airfield that he's pointing out down there. I've got the course killed with the one knob, and I'm trying to kill rate, and I knew I wasn't going to get it killed in time and sure enough the bombs went over the top of the target and hit in a woods. And I was mad at Jacoby. "You dirty bum. My chance for being a hero here, and you screwed it up." I thought if I could have only got that bridge. I kind of barked at old Jacoby a little bit. We got back to the base, and he rushed right into the intelligence office. He came running out, all smiles, and he had a folder full of maps. He said, "You know what that was? That was a night fighter base, and they had their planes stashed in hardstands in the woods!"

We had a party at the officers club one night, and Jimmy Stewart came in with General Timberlake [Stewart had been a squadron leader in the 445th] . Of course, being a second lieutenant I'm not about to go up and start talking to Jimmy Stewart. He was a lieutenant colonel then. He and General Timberlake were standing at the bar, and all the girls – there were a lot of nurses and English girls there – they circled around him like flies around a horse biscuit. You couldn't get close to him. He was a good friend of Captain Steinbacher. Eventually Captain Steinbacher and Neil Johnson both went into P-51s. And the night that Jimmy Stewart was there, Steinbacher came back from a raid to Munich, and he had shot down his first FW-190. He was celebrating that. Later on – I found this out afterwards from Major Martin – after the Kassel raid, one night he came back from a raid, and he did a buzz job over Tibenham. He damn near took the rooftop off, and he pulled up and went into a high-speed stall and crashed. It killed him. I talked to a guy that was in the medics that went out and dug him out of the plane. Terrible. He was a big guy, old

Steinbacher. When I got back home and I got my belongings back – they would go in the hut and take all the belongings that they thought were yours, and they would go through everything, and they censored everything, threw your address books away – among the things they sent to my home was a pair of Brazil boots that were too big for me, and I think they belonged to Captain Steinbacher. They used to buy them down in Natal, Brazil, on the way over on the southern route.

The day before the Kassel raid we bombed the railroad yards at Hamm. They had been hit quite a few times, but the Germans always were able to get them running again in a couple of days. They had big trainloads of Russian prisoners whose sole job was to fix those railroads. I flew with Bob Russell. It turned out to be his last mission. And Krobach was the co-pilot. He was the operations officer. There was flak but we didn't see any fighters. We got back over the North Sea – this was Russell's last mission – and he got permission to leave the formation and he just put that baby in a dive, and he flew so low we had to come up to clear the top of a church steeple.

The next day, I was scheduled to go on a three-day pass. I even had the pass. And normally, you'd go the night before. The pass didn't start till midnight. You'd go down to Tibenham station and catch the train the night before. But I didn't do that. I thought, I'll go down there and take my time. I had it coming, too. I hadn't had a three-day pass for about 17 missions.

About 3 o'clock in the morning, there was a jeep that the guy who woke the crews up used. He was a sergeant from the 702nd Squadron headquarters; he had a jeep and it had a squeaky brake. In the middle of the night you'd be sleeping and all of a sudden you'd hear a jeep coming, you'd kind of get about halfway up, and you'd listen. If you didn't hear any squeaky brake you knew you're okay, you could go back to sleep. But if you heard a squeaky brake out in front, oh my God, he's coming in our hut!

He'd come in and you'd just lay there hoping he wouldn't come over to your bunk. Or he'd grab you and shake you, "Come on, Lieutenant, you've got to get up! You're going on the mission." And hey, he woke me up.

I said, "I'm not going. I'm going on a three-day pass."

"No," he said, "I've got your name here on the list. You're going to take a guy's place."

I knew whose place it was. It was Lieutenant Aarvig on Schaen's crew. Schaen and Aarvig and his co-pilot, Bobby McGough, and his navigator, Corman Bean, were all in our hut. Aarvig hadn't come back from London on his three-day pass. So I'm taking his place.

I was mad. I didn't want to go. I had my heart set on going to London. Well, okay. So I went down. And I remember distinctly, I think that was the morning that Major General Kempner came to the briefing. I think it was that morning, but sometimes I get mornings mixed up. It seems like he was there and he came to the bombardiers' briefing.

As I recall that briefing, we were supposed to hit primarily the railyards. Now everybody says we were supposed to hit the Henschel engine works, but as I recall it, we were to hit the railyards and right adjacent to the railyards was the Henschel engine factory and we were supposed to hit both of them. And I remember I was pretty honored that Kempner showed up at our bombardiers' briefing.

Then I went out and got in the plane and we took off.

As I remember, we came in – you always tried to go on a target downwind because it's faster; you don't want to go upwind, because you're sitting there like a bird waiting for somebody to shoot at you. They always tried to get you downwind and as I remember we had a westerly-northwesterly wind that day. We came in and hit the initial point, and we were supposed to take a little turn to the east. We took a big turn to the east. We wound up going north of Kassel, and straight west towards Goettingen. And as soon as we made that turn, our navigator was on the intercom. He said, "Somebody screwed up. We're not supposed to be turning this much." Somebody goofed. Probably the "Mickey" man. The radar man. I think that's exactly what happened. I think the radar guy screwed up, and that was it.

It turned out later, that radar guy happened to be at the same barracks [in Stalag Luft 1] as Miner and Bertram. I was in a different compound. They told me they questioned him about that. He swore up and down that he hit Kassel. Everybody knew that was wrong. Even the dumbest guy, if he looked out the window, he could see the Kassel flak over there, and you're coming down here.

The radar man wouldn't have been looking out the window; he was looking through some type of a scope. But if somebody else were looking out the window, they should have known. It was ridiculous. Maybe by the time they found out it was too late. In my humble opinion, once we made the mistake, you couldn't just come back because you'd be flying through the group. It would be a disaster. But why couldn't he have made a 360-degree turn and gotten behind the rest of the group? He [the command pilot, Major Donald McKoy] made a split-second decision. He looked at the map and saw Goettingen. So he decides in a split-second [to bomb Goettingen]. They screwed that up, too. The only thing it killed is a cow. We hit the fields. It was a fiasco all the way around.

You've got to chalk it up to an error. You can't chalk it up to somebody having an ulterior motive. The only thing that's really bad about it was that somebody failed to notify our fighter escort.

We dropped the bombs at Goettingen and then instead of turning around and getting the heck out of there they made the same pattern they originally had for Kassel, only about fifty miles too far west. We made a right turn, and in the vicinity of Eisenach we made another right turn, and at that point we got hit by about 150 FW-190s and ME-109s. They came in on a broad front, in three waves, and were totally unexpected.

The first inkling I had that anything was wrong was when I heard something hitting the plane. It turned out to be .20-millimeter shells. Before we got hit, I saw these small flak bursts in front of us, and I'd never seen flak like that; it seemed like brown basketballs right in front of us. And they were very close. I thought, "I never saw flak like that." It didn't dawn on me that it was fighter cannons coming from behind.

Then I started feeling jolts hitting the plane. There was one underneath the turret and there were some on the left wing, and the next thing I knew the left wing was on fire.

About that time this fighter plane came over the top of the plane. It couldn't have been more than ten or fifteen feet above us. I tried to get the turret trained on him but nothing worked. The turret was dead. The only thing I could think of was that the hydraulics were shot.

I wasn't wearing a flak suit at the time. We had them, but I never could wear one in the turret; an average-size guy couldn't get into the nose turret with a flak suit on. Maybe a little guy could. I never wore a flak suit. I didn't even wear a flak helmet. I was just in there with my uniform and my heated flying suit.

Shortly after that fighter plane went over, I looked out and saw the wing on fire and we started nosing down. At the same time I looked over toward the lead squadron and I could see at least two planes flying along on fire, and finally they dropped off.

The flying suit I was wearing was a brand new model that the British had come up with. It was tan, and instead of having a liner with little wires in it, the wires were in the jacket itself, which was sort of padded, and you had your little boots that you wore underneath your regular flying boots. It was a much more comfortable jacket, and also it served as a piece of outerwear. The only thing that was bad was that I forgot my GI shoes. I should have had them with me because I lost my flying boots when I bailed out. They took off when my parachute opened, and there I was in my stocking feet.

You also couldn't wear your parachute in the front turret, so I had it sitting someplace near where you got out of the turret. When I got out it wasn't there.

Corman Bean, the navigator,  had it in his hand. He had his on already and he snapped mine on me. Then he bent down and  opened the nose wheel door, and then he hesitated. I thought he didn't want to jump, so I kind of gave him a little boost, and he gave me heck about that later. He said, "I was looking up to see what the pilot was doing."

I just kind of nudged him a little bit and then he went out. I went out right after him, and I thought, "I'd better make sure this chute's gonna work," so I hadn't fallen very far when I pulled the ripcord and Boom! My boots took off.

I'd estimate we were at 18 or 20,000 feet when I bailed out. A lot of guys decided to delay their chute, but I didn't. I'd never been in a parachute before. We'd had instructions, but it wasn't much. All they told you was a chest pack is like jumping off a 12-foot wall, so you know you're going to hit pretty hard. Especially when I didn't have my boots on, it kind of scared me.

When I bailed out, it was just like the battle in "Wings." You'd hear those guns shooting and you could hear stuff blowing up and planes blowing up and you could see bomb bay doors come floating by, and the fighters sailing in on these guys. It was just like the movies. Better than the movies. More realistic.

Everything happened so quick. It seemed that there had to be about 40 chutes in the air, and there was bedlam. But gradually, as you went down, the battle faded away. Pretty soon you could hardly hear it, and when I got into the clouds it was deathly silent. I could see nothing and hear nothing. It was the eeriest feeling. It seemed ethereal.

When I broke through the clouds at about 3,000 feet, I could see everything on the ground. There was a panoramic view. A beautiful scene. Little village. Ruined castle on a hill and a little river. I couldn't make out anybody on the ground yet.

About that time I heard a plane coming. I looked up and here came a fighter plane about my level, right toward me. When he saw me, he banked around, about the length of a football field away. And I could see it was a P-51 with a yellow nose. He saw me with my Mae West, and he knew I was American. He waved at me and I waved at him. And then he went on and his prop wash hit me, and I swung as high as the Eiffel Tower both ways.

When that settled down, I began to see more clearly on the ground. I was coming down with the wind behind my back. They told you to land facing away from the wind. Then you can see what's coming up. And they also told us when we're going to hit the ground to relax like a tumbler.

Before that happened, though, I could see a guy coming up a lane on a bicycle. He was looking up at me. And I was stretching things but I thought, "He's probably a Polish slave laborer, and I can talk him into hiding me out."

When I landed I twisted my left ankle and I fell on my left shoulder. It knocked the wind out of me, and the chute was dragging me across this field. Luckily it was a plowed field. I reached out and pulled the shrouds and collapsed the chute.

I was laying there trying to get my breath when the guy on the bicycle came up and pointed a luger at my head. I thought, "That's the end of that Polish slave laborer theory."

He was jabbering away at me in German and two other farmers came across the fence with pitchforks, and they made me pick up that huge, bulky chute. I was in my stocking feet and they prodded me along, and we headed toward the village. As we came into the village, the people came out of the houses and they lined the streets like a gauntlet, and all I could think of was old Daniel Boone and Simon Kenton running the gauntlet in the old days. And they were hostile. They were hurling epithets at me in German which I couldn't understand, but I knew that it wasn't praise. All of a sudden a kid about 15 years old came out and he had a big rubber boot on and he kicked me right in the rear end.

Then they took me down to this barn in the back of the burgomeister's house. Outside there was a courtyard with a wall around it and a big gate.

They started to search me. They made me loosen my pants and they were hanging down around my ankles, and I was standing in my stocking feet. They were looking for a pistol. I think they were disappointed because I didn't have one.

About that time I heard a commotion and a guy came through the crowd and he was really angry. He let me have one right between the eyes with his big old horny fist. I almost went down but I didn't. He swung two or three times more, but I ducked. I was trying to get my pants back on with one hand and fend him off with the other. Finally I got my pants buckled up and then I had two hands to work with, and he cut off the fight and he went over and picked up a long-handled spade. Normally a spade has a short handle. This one had a long handle and had a square nose. And he came at me with that spade. I saw him swing and I ducked and I felt it whistle over the top of my head. I thought, "I've got to get in close on this guy." I closed in on him, and I got hold of the spade and he got hold of it and we were wrestling for the spade, and about that time there was an old man in the crowd with a big white walrus mustache and he had a green felt hat on, and he came out and started to help me. He realized that they shouldn't be killing this guy, even if he is the enemy. Then the burgomeister and the village cop came to my aid and they disarmed this guy.

They took my escape kit away from me and whatever else I had. They had a bunch of stuff they had collected from the planes, and there were two big old felt boots. I pointed at my feet and the burgomeister gave them to me. I put them on, but they were about two sizes too big and my feet sloshed around in them.

Then they marched me up the street to the church, and they put me in this little jailhouse underneath the church tower. I was the first one captured, so I was alone. They locked the door, and all there was was a little shaft of light coming through a small window, with straw on the floor.

I just sat there trying to figure out what's going to happen next. That's when they threw Sergeant Eppley in, who was our top gunner. He told me he saw the planes coming in and he started shooting at them, and he watched those tracers coming up the fuselage of the plane right towards his turret. He didn't get wounded, but he didn't hear the bailout bell, and he was still in the turret when he saw the co-pilot go by and then the pilot, so he dropped right down behind them. He got down into the bomb bay – all of the people from the flight deck are supposed to go out the bomb bay. But evidently the radio man had already gone up towards the nose. And when Eppley got to the bomb bay, the other two guys are going up to the nose. So he reached out automatically and he pulled the handle on the bomb bay doors and they opened. The only thing he could think of is that they had pushed instead of pulled or vice-versa, and they didn't open so they thought it was jammed and they were going up to the nose. I think that's what killed the pilot, because when Eppley bailed out he said the plane blew up shortly afterwards, and the pilot must not have gotten out. His body was found right near the wreck.

The tail gunner and the two waist gunners were killed, too. Whether they were killed in the battle or blew up in the plane we'll never know.

In the next few minutes, every time you turned around they're opening the door and throwing another guy in. We must have had 14 guys in that room before long. One of them was Red Dowling [Jim Dowling is one of the veterans profiled in Tom Brokaw's "The Greatest Generation"]. Red was hurt, and he was also sick, because he threw up in the corner. That's one reason I remembered him, that and his violent red hair.

When I first wrote to him years later, I said, "I think you're the redheaded guy that was in that little cell with me." He wrote back and said, "I'm the redheaded guy."

Pretty soon they opened the door and told us, "Raus!" We all stood up in a line outside the door, and they came down the line and picked three of us out. They picked me and Eppley and this guy whose name I thought was Summers. I know he was a lieutenant, and he said he was a navigator. They loaded the rest of the fellows on a Wehrmacht truck and away they went. And they took us three and marched us down the street, and up the street came two haywagons. Each wagon was drawn by a team of horses. And there were a whole bunch of men and boys – they were either older men or younger boys – and they all were armed to some extent. There was one guy – he was an older guy but he was short; his name was Hans. He had black hair. And he had an old Mauser pistol with a wooden holster. The wooden holster serves as a shoulder piece. It was a World War I Mauser with a big broom handle. Then there was an aristocratic looking guy on a horse, and he had a fine shotgun. He was riding around through the hills and fields and he'd come back and report where there were bodies and where there were  wrecks. None of these people were military. They were all civilians.

We marched up the street. I still had no idea what they were going to do with us. We're marching alongside the wagon and we got up to a little orchard with a fence around it. We went through the fence, and lying there on the ground, face down, was one of our fliers with no chute.  And then I found out what they wanted us for.

We had to pick the bodies up.

When we picked this flier up, he was still warm, and every bone in his body was broken. He was limp. One of the Germans had an envelope, and we took one dogtag off and he put it in this envelope, which they sent to the Red Cross. And I remember reading that guy's dogtag. His name was Bateman, and he turned out to be a navigator on Johnson's crew which Dowling was the bombardier on. We picked him up and put him in the haywagon. Then we marched around up and down the hills and fields all day long, till almost dark, and we picked up a dozen or more bodies. Parts of bodies. We went in one little cow pasture and we found two legs, and this guy must have been big because his thigh was big and heavy, and he still had his flying boots on. And it was an officer because he had forest green pants on. We picked those legs up and put them in the haywagon. We went up on a hill and we found this plane crashed up there, and there was a turret, and there was a guy in there and the top of his head was sheared right off. You could see his brains.

We found another guy who came down in his chute and he must have been killed in the fall. He was lying with his feet in a little creek. We came across a meadow and there was a guy laying in a pool of blood, and it turned out to be Joe Gilfoil. He was tossed out over the static line by the guys on Miner's crew after he got hit in the leg by a 20-millimeter shell. And it happened that Gilfoil had been on Schaen's plane before, and Eppley was a good friend of his. When we rolled him over and he saw who it was, he almost passed out. Gilfoil's skin was a bluish-pale color because he had been drained of blood. There was blood all over the meadow.

That morning, in the mess hall, I'd seen a guy. I'd seen him before. I never knew who he was; he was in a different squadron. He was a big, rough-faced guy, and I thought, "Who is that guy?" I don't know why I noticed him.

We came across this plane that's crashed, and in the co-pilot's seat, here's a guy sheared in two. From his waist down is in the co-pilot's seat. The rest of him is missing. We look up ahead and about a hundred yards away, here's the upper part of his torso butted into a tree. When I rolled him over, it was the guy I'd seen in the mess hall that morning.

I paid particular attention to his name. His name was Geiszler. Martin Geiszler Jr. Everybody on that plane was killed with the exception of the pilot. The pilot's now dead, but I had a little article he wrote one time, and he said that after they got hit, he must have been blown out because he doesn't remember a thing until he came to in the hospital.

When I was in Stalag Luft 1, there was a fellow from Los Angeles by the name of Oscar McMahon in the same room I was in. This Geiszler was from Bell, California, which is in the Los Angeles area, and after the war I got a phone call one day. It must have been the summer of '45. I got a long-distance call from Bell, California, and it was Mr. Geiszler, this guy's dad. He said he wanted to know who I was, and if I was the same guy that was on the Kassel mission.

I said, "Yes."

He said, "We were at a Red Cross meeting and we met a fellow named Lieutenant McMahon and we asked if anybody knew of anybody that was on the Kassel mission and he said, 'I knew a fellow who was a prisoner with me.' " He said, "My son, Martin Geiszler Jr., is missing and we don't know what happened to him. All we know is he went down on the Kassel mission."

I said, "Look, I've got to tell you right now. Your son is dead."

You could have heard a pin drop.

I hated to tell him, but what are you going to do? You aren't going to tell him he's alive. I could have said, "Oh, I don't know anything about it," but I didn't want to do that.

Then he said, "Can we come to Michigan and see you?"

I said, "Sure."

By God, if they didn't come to Michigan; the war was still on in the Pacific and it was hard to travel. They came clear to Michigan, he and the Mrs.

I didn't tell them tell them all the details. They never did know that he was torn in two. But I said, "I can definitely tell you that your son is dead because I was one of the guys that picked his body up. I hate to tell you that." But they thanked me for telling them because they didn't know.

It was only a couple of weeks later that the Red Cross notified them that he was dead. But those people, they used to send our kids presents – books and clothes – he offered me a job; he owned a factory in Bell and wanted me to come to work for him. They had one more son that was still alive.

One other guy on this plane that I picked up was Berquist; he was their radio man. Nobody on that plane lived except the pilot. And Mrs. Geiszler, when she found out the pilot was alive, she was bitter. I don't think it was his fault. She thought, "He shouldn't be alive if my son's dead."

We came back after going all day long, up hill, down dale, picking up dead bodies. We had two haywagon loads of bodies and parts of bodies. We came into the cemetery at Lauschroden. We unhitched the horses and left the two wagons standing next to a stone building. Then they marched us into town and we went up to the village pump, and we drank water until we thought we were going to die because we hadn't had a drink of water all day. All we'd had to eat all day was a couple of apples that some kid gave us.

Then they marched us over to the little jailhouse again, and pretty soon – this must have been a little after dark – they brought us a big mug of ersatz coffee and some white bread. That's the last white bread I ever saw until I got back to the United States.

A little later, we'd just gone to sleep when they rousted us out again. There was a Wehrmacht truck outside, and it was full of wounded men.

We got in this truck, and we drove all around the countryside until about 3 a.m. We'd stop in a village and they'd take us up into an old mill or an old barn and there'd be a wounded guy laying there. Sometimes they'd tried to help him and sometimes they hadn't. We'd bring them out, lay them in the truck – one guy had a 20-millimeter hole right through his thigh. How he was alive I don't know. We brought him back, and all these guys are in there, and Jerry Cathol was laying near the tailgate. He thought his back was broken. It wasn't, but his hip was dislocated.

Jerry Cathol was a big guy. He played end for the University of Nebraska. And I carried that big guy up two flights of steps. Three o'clock in the morning in Eisenach at the hospital. And after we got all these wounded people unloaded and in the hospital, they took us three guys that weren't wounded over to the Wehrmacht base. They took us downstairs and there was a guardroom down there. It had rows of wooden shelves, about six feet deep, and they had a raised end like a pillow made out of wood. About 25 of our guys were laying on these shelves. One of them was Ira Weinstein. One was McGregor. And there were two guys that were wounded; they were laying on stretchers on the floor. They should have been in a hospital. One guy had a leg wound and it was bad. The other guy couldn't walk either. We had to carry them.

We stayed there for a couple of days. I don't know exactly how long we were there. You couldn't tell whether it was daylight or dark because you were down in the basement. In the morning they'd bring us a bowl of barley and at night they brought us some black bread and ersatz coffee. They took us one by one and the guy tried to quiz us, and he took our wristwatch. If it was a private watch he gave it back. If it was a government issue watch he kept it. But he gave you a receipt for it. They took mine, because mine was a government watch. I've still got the receipt.

Eventually, two guys showed up from the Luftwaffe. They were feldwebels; high-class sergeants. Spoke English, and they had Walther submachine guns. They told us, "We've been delegated to move you to an air base at Erfurt. We're going to go by civilian train. We'll protect you, but keep a low profile. Don't say anything or do anything that would stir things up." Also, when we picked these wounded guys up, they put a bunch of loaves of bread underneath the blankets. That was supposed to be our food on the trip. They said, "Under no circumstances show that bread to the civilians."

We marched down the street and we got on a civilian train. We had a whole car to ourselves. We went through Gotha and we got up to Erfurt. And Erfurt at that time had never been bombed; it was quite a picturesque town. That's one of Martin Luther's old hangouts, quite a historic place. We got off the train and marched up the streets. We had these two guards. And it was hot. We weren't in too good shape, and you get tired carrying these stretchers, so we had to keep changing off all the time. It was uphill almost all the way. We got up to the top of that hill, and we just about died. We set the stretchers down in the street and we all sat down. One of the guards stayed there and guarded us; the other one went over to a beer joint and had a beer. And about that time a lady came out from a house and she had a big can full of cold water. Boy, did we drink that water!

Then the guards scrounged around, and pretty soon somebody showed up with a two-wheel pushcart. It had rubber tires. We put those stretchers on there and we pushed them and pulled; it was nice. We just about got out of town, and we blew a tire. Then we had to start carrying them again.

About suppertime we came dragging onto that Luftwaffe base; I mean we were dead. We came in carrying the stretchers and went right in this barracks. We all flopped right down on the wooden floor and went right sound asleep. That was an awful day.

We were there a couple of days, and then they ordered us all out into the street, and there was a big truck waiting for us. A staff car drove up and a German colonel got out. He called the roll, and when he called the roll he said, "Veinshtein."

There's little old Weinstein, about five feet tall.

"Veinshtein," the guy says. "Das ist Jude."

I thought, "Uh-oh, they're gonna kill Weinstein."

Weinstein thought that, too, I think. But the colonel didn't say any more. All he said was, "Das ist Jude." And the next thing you know we're on a truck heading for the Erfurt station. We get to the station, we unload, and we're standing in a column of twos on the sidewalk, and a couple of SS guys come out with black uniforms. Meaner than hell. And they start in on us when they find out we were "terrorfliegers." They were ranting and raving and a crowd started gathering, and they were getting the crowd all worked up. About that time the staff car drove up with this colonel. He stood up in the back seat and he read the riot act to those two guys. You should have seen them scram. He was a Luftwaffe colonel.

We got on the train, and at about midnight we arrived at Frankfurt am Main. The railroad station looked like a skeleton. All the glass was laying in pieces all over the floor. But the trains were all running in and out. They pulled our car onto one of the tracks, and we're all sitting in there, and away goes the engine. It left us sitting there.

Pretty soon somebody in the crowd discovered there was a POW train over here with a bunch of Amerikanisch terrorfliegers. So they came over and they started getting hostile. They started picking up paving bricks and they were threatening the guards. The guards told us to lay down on the floor, and they held their burp guns on these guys. All it would have taken is a rock hitting one of the guards' heads and we'd have been dead. You know what saved us? The air raid siren went off, and everybody skedaddled for the air raid shelter except us; we're sitting there. Soon we heard a plane coming; it was a Mosquito, and he dropped a great big bomb about two blocks up the street. Man, did that shake things up.

By the time the all clear sounded, an engine came in and hooked onto us and pulled us out of there. And they took us to the little town of Oberrussel, which is a suburb of Frankfurt. It was what they called an interrogation center. They marched us up the street. It was dark; it must have been one or two o'clock in the morning. We marched up these dark streets, and the guys that were leading us didn't know where they were going. They had to stop and ask people.

Finally we came to this camp. They took us in the courtyard, and the courtyard was full of Polish, Canadian and British paratroopers that had been captured at Arnhem. I was right next to a Polish colonel, and I was hungry. I saw they had a garden plot, and there was a cabbage. I reached down. I couldn't get the whole head but I got a few of the leaves. They weren't very good eating; they were the outer leaves.

Finally, they took several of us to a basement room and several to another room.

And the next morning they came along with a big canister of Purple Passion – that's what we called it – it was cabbage soup. Boy, that tasted good. Then they said, "We're going to take you one by one for interrogation." I had a little compass. I hid it underneath the window in a crack. It's still there because we never came back to that room.

They took me down to this room and there was a guy sitting there. He had an Afrika Korp uniform on. It was a light summer uniform. He looked like a captain. He spoke perfect English.

"Here, have a cigarette."

"No thanks."

"Have a seat."

He starts talking real friendly. And then he starts quizzing you a little bit.

"What group are you in?"

"Can't tell you."

"What kind of plane were you flying?"

"Can't tell you. Not supposed to do that."

He kept doing that, asking this and asking that. Finally he says to me, "You don't need to answer any more, right now anyway. But I can tell you a few things."

He said, "You're from the 445th Bomb Group." He knew all about our group. For crying out loud, he knew more about it than I did. "Now," he said, "if you want to go to a permanent camp and be with your friends, you're going to have to answer a few questions. Otherwise you may be here for a long, long time."

I said, "I'm just supposed to give name, rank and serial number."

"You do as you please," he said. Then he dismissed me and they took me out. They put me in solitary confinement in a room on the second floor. It had a single bunk there, with a mattress filled with excelsir. Excelsir is like fine wood shavings. That was a standard bed in Germany for prisoners. I stuffed some of the excelsir into my boots because they were too large, only I didn't know it but the excelsir was full of fleas.

While I was in solitary there, if you had to go to the toilet, there was a rope; you pulled that rope and it dropped a signal down in the hall. And the guard, when he got around to it, he'd lead you down to the toilet. You weren't supposed to talk to anybody in there. And then he'd bring you back. I've heard of guys that were in there for twenty or thirty days. I wouldn't have lasted that long. It was so hot, it was like an oven, they must have had steam heat. There wasn't any air. I went down to the toilet once and there was a Royal Air Force guy there, and he spoke out of the corner of his mouth. He'd been there about thirty days. I thought, Jeez, this is going to be awful.

The next morning, they rousted me out and I got out in the hall; there must have been 200 guys in the hall. Most of the guys from the Kassel mission were there, and there were some from the 15th Air Force. They took us out into a courtyard and there was a barracks by itself out there. We went in there, and there were British paratroopers. Polish paratroopers. Paratroopers are taken care of by the Luftwaffe, because paratroopers are part of the Luftwaffe in the German army. We're all in this room, and they took our shoes off. They tied the laces together, threw them in a pile on a blanket and away they went. That's so we couldn't escape. I was kind of hoping I'd get a better pair but I didn't.

Boy, were these paratroopers rough guys. They held out two weeks up at Arnhem and they were only supposed to hold out for seven days, and they got captured. And this one British guy, tougher than hell, he says, "Wait till we start winning the war. We're gonna bollix all the men and shag all the tarts."

The next day, they came along with that big blanket full of shoes. We all fished out our own shoes and put them on. Then they marched us up to the railroad station, put us on a train, and we're heading for Wetzler, that's what they called Dulag Luft. Wetzler was the hometown of Zeiss Camera Company. Also they had a 20-millimeter antiaircraft gun factory there. On the way up, there were planes strafing so they backed us into a tunnel. We got up to Wetzler late in the afternoon. We'd just gotten out of the train, and we're all standing there, 250 of us, and the guards have burp guns on us. At about that time the air raid siren sounded and along came a flight of P-51s, and I thought, "If they see this" – we're standing right next to this old steam engine – "that's a good target." We were sweating blood. The guards went over in the entrance to the air raid shelter and held their guns on us and made us stand next to the engine. The planes circled around and they came back, and I thought, "This is gonna be it." They made one circle and they took off. The only thing I can think is they knew there was a prison camp there, or it's possible it could have said POW on top of the train.

Then they marched us up the hill into the camp.

That's where we first encountered Red Cross parcels. They got Red Cross parcels and made meals out of them. It was pretty good food for a day or so. Then eventually we were put into contingents and went up to Barth. We went through Berlin – what a shambles that was.

At Barth, we were in Stalag Luft 1. We didn't do too bad until the first of the year of 1945. Right after Christmas. We used to get a Red Cross parcel a week per man, and eking that out along with your German rations you just about had a square meal a day. It would keep you alive. But when they cut back on the Red Cross parcels, we lived on 800 calories a day till Easter. Longer than Easter. I went from

170 pounds down to 135. And you don't have much ambition and pep when you get hungry.

Sometime in 1945, they rounded up all the Jewish guys and took them over to the North 1 compound and put them in a single barracks. There was a funny thing about that. They never got Weinstein. But yet they took an Irish guy.

Around the end of April, things got really hairy. We could hear the Russians' guns. They were approaching Stetin; that was 60 miles away. The Germans gave us permission to dig slit trenches, which we did.

We knew where the lines were because there was a secret radio in camp and everybody got the news every night – the real news, not what the Germans were telling you. Colonel Hubert Zemke was our senior Allied officer. He was head of the 56th Fighter Group. Colonel Zemke was approached by the German colonel, and he said, "We may have to move this camp." In other words, we'd have to march to the west, towards Hanover. And Zemke said to Colonel Warnstedt [the German commandant], "We are not in any kind of shape to be marching. We've got people here that have practically been on a starvation diet for four months. We can't march very far. What are you going to do if I give the order, and everybody sits down in the middle of the compound? Are you going to kill us all? Besides that," he said, "you know and I know the war's pretty near over." Warnstedt did know that, too.

So Warnstedt said, "I don't want to see any bloodshed, so I'll tell you what I'll do. When we get ready to evacuate, I'll let you know and you can take command of the camp."

This is all going on unbeknownst to us guys because this is high-level stuff. So on the evening of the 30th of April, 1945 – we got locked in every night; the lights went out. The power was shut off about 10 o'clock. We could open up the blackout shutters and get some air. We're laying there; some of us are sleeping. About 2 o'clock in the morning, the word got around. "Take a look at the guard towers, they're all empty! And the dogs aren't in the compound." They had dog patrols every night.

Somebody broke the doors open and we got out and sure as hell, the Germans had left. So Colonel Zemke sent word, "Everybody stay put in his compound. Don't move." Because we didn't know where the Russians were.

At 6 o'clock that morning the first Russian guy showed up at the gate. He was some kind of an officer but he was drunk. He was on a white horse. And he was raising all kinds of hell. He said to Zemke something about, "What do you mean? Aren't you happy to see the glorious Red Army? I don't see anybody cheering. I don't see any towers being burned down."

Zemke thought, "I'd better give this guy a little show," so he passed the word,

"Burn down a couple of guard towers." Then they lit some guard towers and everybody took off over the hill. They all went to town, and Zemke was fit to be tied.

They came back the next day, and you should have seen what they brought with them. They had a full tracked vehicle, brand new. It drove in. And there were horses, there were sheep. Rabbits. They took everything. It was awful. And this guy Crotty, a friend of mine who was in our room, he was quite a drinker – we always told him the only thing that kept him alive was getting shot down – he went in town, the Russians were all drunk because it was May Day, that's a big celebration – and they'd uncovered a bargeload of Holland brandy in the harbor and everybody had bottles sticking out of every pocket. They were all drunk and they were making everybody else get drunk.

And old Crotty, they carried him home on a shutter.

The Russians had a policy of automatically killing the burgomeister and anybody that's connected with him. A bloodthirsty policy. So the burgomeister of Barth went out on the dike and took his family with him, and he shot them all and killed himself.

Warnstedt I think got away. There was another German major that wasn't a bad guy that was captured there, I imagine they killed him. But I'll tell you what they did. A couple of months before we were liberated a whole contingent of Ukrainian partisans came into town. They were fighting on the Germans' side, and they were like irregular troops. They had all horse-drawn vehicles. They were driven out of Poland, I guess, and they came into our town. The Germans let them come up on our peninsula inside the compound and they built a tent city there. And I heard that the Russians rounded those guys up and murdered every one of them. Stalin was the most ruthless, bloodthirsty sonofagun that ever lived. One of our guys would go to town, he'd liberate a bicycle from somebody and he'd be riding along; if a Russian saw him and he wanted the bicycle, you either gave it to him or he'd blow your head off. The Russians went in the jewelry store and they shot the jeweler. I saw Russians with wristwatches up and down both arms. We got sick of the Russians pretty quick. Some of them were all right. Some of them were just ordinary guys like anybody else, but some of them were real rabble-rousing communists if there ever was one.

Finally, they came in and got us on the 13th of May. We were liberated the First of May and on the 13th they flew in with B-17s to the Barth airfield and picked us up and took us to France.

A lot of guys ate too much right away and got sick. I heard one English guy died from eating a lead cake. That's a cake that's made without any risers, like it's made out of hardtack biscuits, heavy as lead. It lays heavy on your stomach.

First we went to Camp Lucky Strike in France. That had been a staging area for when the replacement troops came in, but they were making it a staging area for POWs. They only had rations for 9,000, and 20,000 showed up. You didn't have too much extra to eat. I saw a donut line the length of the runway once.

Eisenhower finally came and gave a big speech. He said, "I don't understand why it is that we've got to take care of 20,000 in this place that doesn't have the facilities, and we've got all kinds of bases over in England with plenty of facilities." So I was the first guy to sign up to go to England, and they flew us out of there in a Liberator. It flew right over Tibenham. The personnel at Tibenham had already left for the States; there wasn't a plane on the hardstands. And they took me up to Horsham St. Faith. Treated me like a king up there. I finally got home about the middle of June.

*"The judge started the ceremony. His wife sat at a desk, and he's standing up there in front of us and reading off this rigamarole, and she's there filling out official papers. There were two kids on the floor under the desk playing Monopoly, and Jack got anxious and kissed me, and the judge said, 'Now if you'll wait just a few minutes, son, this will be all over.' "*

**Jeannie Roland**
**Widow of**
**Jack Roland,**
**712th Tank Battalion**
**Interviewed in**
**Bradenton, Fla.,**
**Jan. 26, 1995**

I met Jack when he was at Pine Camp, in New York State, and I was teaching school. One of my students was going with a soldier there. I had a car and I took her out there and I met Jack, and every time that we'd get in that car to head for Watertown, New York, the state troopers would stop us. I hadn't been driving very long and I was scared anyway, and the first time they stopped me, I thought, "Oh my God, what have I done?" They wanted to see my driver's license and the registration to be sure that I owned the car and that I wasn't some soldier's girlfriend that was just driving.

After it happened three or four times, when they'd stop me I'd laugh and they'd say, "Well, you've been stopped before," because they didn't think I looked old enough to be driving.

I was just out of college then. When Jack and I were in Georgia, I was walking down the street one day and this old lady was out sweeping her lawn. There was no grass, but she was out there with this whisk broom, and she said, "You'd better hurry, little girl, you'll be late for school." And I thought, "Little do you know. ..."

We were married in August of '42 in Phenix City, Alabama. I got off the train, which I'd been on for a day and a half, and Jack wouldn't wait till the next day. It was 9:30 at night, and we went over the bridge from Columbus, Georgia, to Phenix City. We went up on the hill to the judge's home. There were cabs lined up there; a lot of other young people were getting married, too.

Phenix City was also called Sin City. I'm sure the judge was busy during the day, downtown, but he lived way up on a hill; it looked down at night, and it was quite a beautiful sight. And people were lined up there, waiting to get married.

It cost two dollars. No blood test. They asked what my address was and Jack said 600 Broad Street, Columbus, Georgia, which was where we were going to live. So the judge started the ceremony, his wife sat at a desk, he's standing up there in front of us and reading off this rigamarole, she's filling out official papers, and there are two kids on the floor under the desk playing Monopoly, and Jack got anxious and kissed me, and the judge said, "Now if you'll wait just a few minutes, son, this will be all over. ..."

Ohh, I was thinking the other day how young and unsophisticated we were. There were so many things we didn't know that kindergartners could teach us today.

We were in Columbus for about a year, and then we were in Augusta, and then Columbia, South Carolina. Jack was in the intelligence department, and one of his friends was having a hard time convincing his wife, Millie, that she and I and all the other wives had to leave, because the men were going to go overseas. Millie said, "Oh, I've heard that story before. I'm not packing. They're not sending us anyplace." And Fred, her husband, said to her, "If Jack Roland said that the wives have to leave – he knows what you don't know – you have to leave."

The men left in February. Of course we kept hoping that war was going to end by Christmas [of 1944], and we waited, and waited, and waited, and it didn't. And it wasn't easy.

As a teacher in 1941, I was one of the people who had to sign people up for ration books for tires, for gasoline, for meat, for sugar, for coffee and so forth. I was a home economics teacher, and one of the things we did was I had the women in this small community get together to put on a meal for a large number of people, for practice, in case we had to have some kind of help for people. I hadn't thought about that in a long time. Those were some experiences.

I went to the University of Buffalo. When I was teaching, one of my students had a boyfriend in Pine Camp, which was probably ten miles from the little town where I lived, so I offered to take her out there. That's how I met Jack. I had a 1935 Ford. Four-door. I got that big salary, eleven hundred dollars a year. And about half of it went for the car payments and upkeep. But I got room and board with one of the local families for ten dollars a month. She even packed my lunch to take to school.

There were several of us girls from that little community who were going with soldiers. When Jack and some of the rest of them left to go to Fort Knox and then on to form the cadre at Fort Benning, I was playing the piano for church services, and I was very fond of the minister and his wife. She had a new baby and I went into Watertown to see her, and I was weeping and carrying on because my boyfriend had gone. Some of the other girls were confiding in the minister. Then one day, while I was in Columbus, Georgia, this man in civilian clothes came and showed me his identification, and wanted to talk to me about this minister in this little town up in the Adirondacks. He questioned me at great length, and then he said, "When is your husband going to be here?"

I said, "The bus brings him back about 7 o'clock at night."

So the man came back, and he and Jack went in the kitchen and shut the door. Oh, we had a fancy place, boy, it's a good thing there was rent control because we paid eight dollars a week and we were lucky to have a rotten bedroom and a kitchen we shared with people. But Jack and this fellow went in the kitchen and shut the door, and he was questioning Jack at great length, because of his intelligence work. And Jack would never tell me what was said, but do you know that a few months later I discovered that the minister was a German spy? I was just flabbergasted!

I had several miscarriages, but we have one child, a daughter. She has four children. She married in '72, this young man who got a job in Canada doing cancer research. They had the children, and then he decided that he wasn't making enough money, so he went to medical school. For five years we subsidized that, and he divorced her. Then for five years she was alone and took care of those four kids; they were from 2 to 9 or 10. And finally she met this young man; we were up there to visit her and the kids, and we met him one summer, and along in the spring of the next year he called us and said, "I'd like permission to marry your daughter." And I thought, now, there's a change! They've been married, it'll be five years this spring.

The two oldest grandchildren are a freshman and sophomore at university this year, and then there are two teens at home. Three girls and one boy. The boy's the youngest; he was born on our anniversary.

Jack and I were married in August, and boy, was it hot in Georgia! And I was never colder anyplace than I was that winter. The house was sitting up on blocks and the wind went howling underneath. But it was hot in the summer. There was one place in the city that was air conditioned, and that was the theater, and we didn't have money enough to go too frequently.

We were friendly with one couple, Fred and Millie Lemm. Fred and Millie were married three weeks after we got married, and we stood up with them at the ceremony. When the war was over, they lived in Cleveland, and Jack and I used to go out there, and then they'd come to New York to visit us. They had two girls, about the age of my daughter. And then Fred developed a kind of cancer, and for five years he was in and out of the hospital, and just going downhill. Millie would call us and say Fred was in the hospital, and Jack would be down in the basement of our big old Victorian house, which is where his darkroom was, and he'd hang up his phone down there and come upstairs and say, "Let's pack," and we would go out there. We went to their daughters' weddings; they came to New York to our daughter's weddings. We raised our kids together. Then finally, Millie called and said that Fred was very bad. So we dropped everything and went out there. Before the freeway was built, it took us about six hours to get there, but I tell you, I'd drive to the Cleveland Clinic, I could find that place in the dark with my eyes closed we went there so often to see him.

When the war was over, Jack came home and wanted to go to photography school, and he was accepted. We lived in western New York. So we got in the car and went to New York. When we got there, it was November, and they said the classes are all full, you'll have to wait until March. Jack was so upset; what will we do? And I said, "Let's go over to Long Island," because I had an aunt and uncle there. At that time, there was only one hotel, the Garden City Hotel; no motel, in fact there are not too many motels even now. So the next day I said, "Why don't we go over to Rockville Centre, to the employment office, and see if we can get something to keep us occupied and pay the rent until you can go to school?" There was an excellent photo studio in Rockville Centre that had just gone into the employment office and said they'd like an apprentice, and Jack got the job. And he got much better experience than he would have had he gone to school. Because he got the business aspect of it, and the whole thing.

After he'd been there a couple of years, we decided that we were going to go back to my hometown in western New York and start a studio.

What was it like when Jack was overseas? It was hell. I was teaching school, in another small town, over towards Elmira. When he came home, I hadn't heard from him for weeks. When the war ended, he was in Germany having his appendix taken out. The war in Europe ended in May, and he came home in September.

I weighed 104 pounds. I weighed 120 went he went overseas. I was so frantic, not knowing where he was. I boarded with a woman who was a volunteer for the Red Cross, and she came and called up the stairway one day and said, "Jean, how long has it been since you've had any word from Jack?"

And I said, "Eight weeks."

She said, "Would you like me to do something about it?"

I said, "Yes." A lot of mail was lost, there were all kinds of complications, but I was worried to death.

I had lost so much weight that Jack said when he got off that train, if he'd taken a good look at me, he'd have gone back. The bones in my hips were showing. But it was no worse for me than it was for anybody else. I'm sure.

Jack was wounded in the summertime. I was at my mother and father's house in Friendship, New York, when the letter came, and I opened it up, and he said, "I have been wounded and I'm in the hospital in England." Well, I got in my car and took off for my friend's house, I was so upset, and my father started looking for me all over town. In a few days I got a telegram from the War Department, but I'd already had the letter.

That was at the end of July and he was in the hospital until Thanksgiving. He had been hit in the front and the back with shrapnel. He went back in time for the Battle of the Bulge. Penicillin had just come out as a treatment and they used to put it in the shoulder. It was mixed with oil I guess and stung like mad, and he just about punched out the nurse one night, and finally he said, "Don't come in here and give me a shot until you know that I am thoroughly awake!" Because it hurts a lot. But I'm sure it saved a lot of lives, too.

When Jack came home he was not the same person that went overseas. And we didn't talk about it. He never did tell me a whole lot about what went on. He had nightmares. He'd get up out of bed in the middle of the night and get in the car and disappear.

But I don't think any of these men came home the same as they went.

Before he went away, we laughed and laughed and laughed. Everything was lovely. When he came home he was more serious, but also, he was just not himself.

After he got his photography training we went into business, and we had to struggle like everybody else, but we did it ourselves. He opened a photo studio over a store in the center of town. And then we found this big old Victorian house, three stories, fifteen rooms, full basement which we finished off, in Friendship. And he got a GI loan. We struggled awhile, and he worked himself to death. But we worked like mad, and when our daughter was five years old and started kindergarten, I went back to teaching, and I helped him in the studio.

I was just going to go back to teaching for a while, but I stayed 25 years. And Jack built up his business and his reputation so that he had all the carriage trade from western New York; he even went to Buffalo to take weddings, and as far west as Jamestown. In fact, he'd sometimes do three weddings on a Saturday. He worked, and as he worked and worked, he pushed himself, and he pushed the food. And he got heavier and heavier, which was not healthy, but nobody can diet for you, you have to do it yourself.

We stayed in business until the doctor told me that I had to retire, because of the climate, so Jack said, "If you're going to Florida, I am, too." So we sold the house and the business; it's not the easiest thing in the world to sell a great big house like that. But we found a buyer, and Jack trained a young fellow, and I was in Florida all of that winter. Then he said, "Come home and sell this furniture or I'll burn it." And so he finished training the young fellow and moved to Florida, and the place that I had been renting became available that fall to buy, so we bought it.

My parents were descendants of people who came from England and Scotland in the 1600s. One of my brothers who was a teacher did a genealogy, and he and his wife went to graveyards all over New York State and up into New England, and searched county historical groups and so on.

My maiden name was Dodson. Some of the family, way back, were named Dodgson.

Jack was born in Virginia and grew up in Kentucky. And then he went to Indiana. He was 15 years old when he went into the Army. He and his friend enlisted at the same time and signed each other's papers. He said that he wasn't heavy enough to be accepted, and the guy at the recruiting station said, "Go eat some bananas and drink some water, and come back," and he did. He said, "I gained two pounds."

Jack's father died before I met him, and his mother I'd rather not discuss. He had a painful childhood.

Was he younger than me? Before we were married, I said to him, "When is your birthday?"

"In January."

I said, "Well, you're three months older than I am," and he never cracked a smile or said a word. Later, he said, "I'm a child groom. I'm not even 21."

That was after we were married, yessss. Oh, he was a pistol.

*"It was not until four years after the war that they finally identified Newell and said he definitely was killed in action. They still called it 'killed in action.' They didn't call it murder."*

**Kay Brainard Hutchins**
**Red Cross girl**
**Sister of**
**Lt. Newell Brainard,**
**who was murdered**
**by slave labor camp**
**guards after**
**bailing out of his**
**B-24 on**
**the Kassel mission**
**of Sept. 27, 1944**
**Interviewed in**
**West Palm Beach, Fla.**
**April 16, 1999**

In 1941 our local Morrison Field was taken over by the government as an air base. Planes landed here before they flew on to Africa, in the early part of the war.

I worked at the base hospital as a secretary. Then, in 1942, the beautiful Breakers Hotel in Palm Beach was taken over and made into a hospital. I was transferred there to be secretary to the commanding officer. The military closed it two years later, and, after having spent millions to make it a hospital, more millions were spent to make it a hotel again. Seems politics were involved, and the local people couldn't do anything about it.

Anyway, that's one way I met so many GIs. I was the right age at the time, and not married as many of my close friends were. They had married at 22, or earlier. I was 23. The number of boys around here was unbelievable. In addition to 3,000 at Morrison Field, there was a Signal Corps base about 20 miles north of here, and in Fort Pierce there was a Navy training base for underwater demolition. Now they're called Seals. I dated one of the officers there. Oh, I couldn't go steady with anybody. I never had so much fun in my life!

I got a lot of proposals. Everybody wanted to get married before they went overseas. Fortunately, I didn't take them too seriously, and remained friends with a lot of them through the years. Most of them are dead now, I'm sorry to say. But I'm 80 years old now, so I've seen a lot of years. In 1980 I started attending my bomb group reunions. When I finally went overseas with the American Red Cross I was stationed with the 486th Bomb Group in East Anglia.

When I arrived in England I didn't know where Newell's base was. At that time he could only write "Somewhere in England" in his letters, and it wasn't until after VE Day that you could say where you were. Even my mother didn't know I was in Sudbury, Suffolk, until after VE Day.

When I came home I saw in the first 8th Air Force book they put out a list of all the various groups and where they were stationed. That's when I learned Newell had been in Tibenham.

After Ream General Hospital [The Breakers] closed, I worked a few months with Military Intelligence. Then a friend of mine told me she had seen an article in Parade magazine about young women going overseas to work for the American Red Cross. Furthermore, she said to me and two of my close friends, "Gee, if I were single and didn't have these two kids, that's what I'd be doing."

Virginia Claudon had also worked at Ream General, and Grace Frost was in her second year of teaching school. We thought it over and decided it was something we'd like to do, too. So we three got together and sent in applications. Virginia and Grace both had all the qualifications as far as the college education and everything went, but I had never gone to college. However, I had worked since I got out of high school at some very interesting jobs – a travel bureau, for a prestigious bank in Palm Beach, and my war work at Morrison Field and Ream General. So we each wrote our own letter. I was the first one to hear from the Red Cross. Grace soon got word, and so did Virginia.

We were called to Atlanta for physicals. Grace and I passed but Virginia had a physical problem, and was called later. We also had to send several letters of recommendation.

By this time, the war was well along, and both of my brothers were missing in action. Grace and I went to Washington, D.C., in November 1994 for training. Soon the Battle of the Bulge broke out, delaying our leaving for the ETO. It was more important that they get GIs over there, so there was no room on the ships for Red Cross girls until late in January. I always remember the date we left because you could write it 1-2-3-4-5. January 23, 1945. So we zig-zagged across the Atlantic on the Queen Mary, with 101 Red Cross girls and thousands of GIs aboard.

At the Red Cross headquarters in London I was first assigned to hospital work. I was disappointed, but they thought since I had worked at Ream General, that's what I wanted. However, they wanted us to be happy, so I asked to be changed to clubmobile work, or something like that. They were willing to change my assignment, and asked if I would like to be at an Aero Club on a bomber base. With two brothers in the Air Force, that suited me fine.


My father, Albert Brainard, graduated from Cornell as a civil engineer. He later went to Columbia and got a degree as a highway engineer, from the very first class of highway engineers. He was the first one in the country, I was told, because his name began with a B, and no one in his class had a name beginning with A.

He married my mother in 1915. He was 33; Mother was 28. And the First World War had started. He worked in Washington as the senior highway engineer. My sister and I were both born in D.C. I know from my mother talking about it that he was very involved in the camps they were hurriedly building to train soldiers.

But by the time they'd been married seven years, Mother had four children and my father had an illness that nobody could diagnose. He was working with Standard Oil of New Jersey, and we learned years later that he had multiple sclerosis. He never worked again.

It was 1925, and we were living in East Orange, New Jersey. Mother had a sister, 12 years younger, and she and her husband were down here in Palm Beach and making money hand over fist in what was called the Boom in South Florida. Of course they were in the real estate business. They had two small children, and they said it's so wonderful, the weather's so good – at this time we didn't know it was multiple sclerosis – why don't you come down here, this is probably a good place for Albert to get better. So we sold our house in New Jersey. We had moved to East Orange when he was with Standard Oil. Both my brothers, Newell and Bill, were born in Orange.

The whole family moved down to Florida. We brought all our furniture. I think we had a 13-room house, and we moved into a two-bedroom, one-bath house. The two-car garage was half-filled with furniture. Then Mother went into real estate too.

Those were the years of the flappers. Not Mother. She was too old for that, but Ruth was typical, with silk stockings rolled at the knee, cigarettes and martinis, and a Packard convertible. Then the Boom suddenly collapsed and they, along with many others, took off overnight for Havana. They probably had been selling lots out in the swamp. So Mother was left on her own, with an invalid husband, four kids and no money.

This was before the Wall Street crash in 1929. One Monday morning, *none* of the banks opened. Period! Everything fell apart. At least we had plenty of company – nobody had any money.

Betty and I missed the excitement of the times. We had already learned to do the Charleston! Ruth and her husband eventually returned to New York. He became an alcoholic and Ruth died of pneumonia when she was only 32. No sulfa and no penicillin then, of course.

We had an uncle in Connecticut (my mother and father were both from Hartford) who was 17 years younger than my father. Mother told us that my father was embarrassed when he was in college and came home and found his mother pregnant. But the much younger brother was now a doctor, and he wrote to Mother, "Send Albert up here. You can't handle four kids and an invalid." Today they can keep patients with multiple sclerosis living longer, but still there's no cure.

So my father went back to Hartford to live with my uncle and his wife and my grandmother, who was still living. And Mother went into business. She was already an RN, but she had four youngsters to think about. Who would care for them? It was different back then … and no one could afford a nanny, anyway.

Our church, Holy Trinity Episcopal Church, opened a small store. I forget what they called it, the Women's Exchange or something like that. If you could knit a sweater or bake a pie or paint a picture, whatever you did you could sell it there and make a little money, hopefully. A volunteer who worked at this store told Mother that they had a lot of people bringing in pies, but few brought in any cakes. She suggested Mother might try that.

Mother said, "I never considered myself a baker, but I guess I could bake a cake." So she did, but found people couldn't afford to buy a whole cake. So she came up with the idea, "Why don't I make cupcakes? Then they could just buy one, two, half a dozen, whatever." She switched to making cupcakes, and they were very popular. She became "the cupcake lady."

At that time all drugstores had soda fountains and office buildings had lunch-eonettes, so one or two of them said, "Mrs. Brainard, how about bringing us some of those cakes? We could use them at lunchtime." And she supported us for years with her popular cupcakes. Betty and I helped by icing cakes before we went to school. All this was done in our own little kitchen.

Mother did that for 12 years. Then she rented a house – a big, lovely old place – and put up a sign, "Guest House." There were no motels then. Some people returned year after year.

By this time Betty and I had graduated from high school, and Mother was able to support the family. We didn't live very high on the hog, but nobody else did either. It was the Great Depression and nobody had much money, but we had a hell of a good time around here. We had the beaches, where we'd meet friends on weekends, but Betty and I both worked and were able to contribute, and the Guest House was a big success, too.

Bill was the youngest of us, Newell came next – he and I were only 17 months apart – and Betty was the oldest child. Newell started at the community college, but then was offered a good job at a bank, so he dropped out and went to work. My first job was working for the city physician at $7 a week, which included half a day Saturday. It seems funny now. But later I worked at a bank and only got $60 a month. It was so completely different from today. But I bought all my own clothes and I managed to have a wonderful time. We got along without TV. I loved to read; all of us in our family loved to read. And, along with our many friends, we saw movies, attended dances, and spent a lot of time at the beach.

I was still 16 when I graduated, and that was because of the Depression. They divided our classes into those who were the slowest and those who were moderate, and then there were those who caught on quicker. They don't like to do that anymore. We took half the year for fourth grade and half the year for fifth, and that made us graduate a year earlier than we would have otherwise.

I used to go North on my two-week vacation each summer. We could take an extra week or two without pay if we wanted during our slow time of the year. I would visit relatives.

By this time my father had died. He spent his last year at the Masonic Home near Hartford. I've kept the letters he used to write me ... you can see how his ability to write diminished.

As soon as war was declared, Bill and Newell enlisted in the Air Corps. In late '42 they were called for training, but they didn't get overseas until later. Newell had married Lorraine Sproul as soon as he finished flight training, and they spent eight months together before he went overseas. Newell was a co-pilot, due to be made a pilot the next mission, I was told. His pilot, Ray Carrow, survived their being shot down over Germany. But Newell was not so lucky. Ray now lives in Miami and we have kept in touch over the years by phone and letters.

Lorraine married four times. The second one was a mistake. They moved out to the Everglades. He was big on farming, which was not her cup of tea. I think she was only married about a year. A year or two later she married a very nice guy, a veteran. She had two boys by him. Then he came down with leukemia, and when he was in the last stages of it, and hospitalized, he jumped out of the hospital window. Her father was the tax collector, and he owned the lot next to him and he built her a house. So she and the boys returned from Pittsburgh. She was still young and pretty, and soon married again, this time to a member of the Rybovitch family, who are known worldwide for the fishing boats they make.

I found some papers in my mother's desk after she died in 1957, and one of them was a newspaper article dated Sept. 28, 1944, about a bombing raid the day before. That was the day after the Kassel mission. Could she have sensed correctly that Newell was killed that day? She never knew he was killed, but she did say to my sister Betty, "I have a feeling Newell. ..." Stories had been told on the radio about some of the atrocities, dragging the prisoners through the town, and Mother said she had a feeling Newell was being mistreated. Makes you wonder about, what is it called, ESP? She didn't save any other clippings about bombing missions.

The letter I received from George Collar was the first I knew of what had possibly happened to Newell. I had written to the 8th Air Force newsletter seeking information about Newell, and George saw the letter and wrote to me:

"April 6, 1987. Dear Mrs. Hutchins, I noticed the article regarding the B-24 'Blasted Event' in the July 1983 issue of the 8th AF News, and a footnote saying that this ship was shot down on the Kassel raid of 27 Sept. 1944 with the loss of your brother, Newell White Brainard. I was quite interested since I also was shot down on that same raid in which we lost so many bombers. I did not know your brother Newell personally, since I was in the 702nd Squadron while he was in the 700th. I was on my 29th mission that day and was a bombardier on the crew of Lt. Jim Schaen of Pontatoc, Miss., who was killed. Although we lost 25 bombers that day, the Germans also lost the same number of FW-190s. I have been corresponding with a Mr. Walter Hassenpflug of Friedlos, West Germany. He was a boy of 12 years at the time of the air battle and since it made such an impression on him he has since made a considerable study of the events of that day and is probably the foremost authority on it. I sent him a copy of the article and am sending you a Xerox copy of his reply.

"As you can see, he is not exactly sure of your brother's fate but is constantly digging and may come up with more information. I obtained your address from the editor of the 8th Air Force News and hope that you will not consider this letter to be an invasion of your privacy. You may or may not care to delve further into this painful matter. In any case, I remain, Sincerely yours, George M. Collar."

Now, this is a copy of a document from the National Archives, that was sent to Walter Hassenpflug and which George Collar sent on to me:

"In reply to your letter of July 10, 1986, we searched the records of the office of the quartermaster general and located missing air crew reports. We also searched the records of, according to our files, Joseph A. Lemp, Paul Kolliger and others who were tried for their involvement in the shootings of 2$^{nd}$ Lieutenant Cowgill and Lt. Scala and others. [Newell was one of the 'others.'] "If you wish to order copies. ..."" Well, what they say is it costs money to get them.

This is a copy of a letter from Walter to George that George sent me:

"... I do not know where and how Newell Brainard died. It is possible that he landed with his chute near the village of Nentershausen and was one of the five airmen who were shot to death there. This, however, is merely an assumption. Therefore, I would like to know if his sister, Kay Brainard Hutchins, knows something about it. Do you know if she's still alive and if it's possible to contact her? A few weeks ago I met a lady from Lauschroden, 77 years old, who spent a few days here. ... She remembered that the prisoners were handed apples through the window in the prison. I think I'll be able to get more information this way."

That was the first I heard about five men being beaten and then shot – and that's March 5, 1987.

I got George Collar's phone number from information and I called him right away, and that's how we got started. I would write to Hassenpflug, he would respond, and I'd call George.

It was four years after the war that Newell was definitely identified and we were told that he was killed in action. They still called it killed in action. They didn't call it murder. Then they said, "We referred your letter to our military field branch for an examination," and then I heard from them something about a fire in Missouri. "This agency has made several attempts to retrieve the individual deceased personnel file of Newell Brainard from the National Records. Unfortunately, that center is unable to locate the file. However, a major fire at that center destroyed or severely damaged a lot of the military records ... etc." That's the only information I could get. But in 1990, I was working in New York for Douglas Fairbanks Jr, which I often did in the summer. I also worked for him in Palm beach during the winter months. He was off to London on business, so I decided to take a few days off and go to Washington. I had a cousin I could stay with and he took me to the National Archives, where I requested the files on the 445$^{th}$ Bomb Group.

They brought out a big box with all these files in it. I started first reading a little here and there, and I would occasionally see where Newell went on a mission. They'd have drawings of the formations, where each pilot's place was. I knew

Newell was Ray Carrow's co-pilot. I had spoken to Ray several times by phone, and he was sure Newell did not get out of the burning B-24.

When I got to the Kassel mission file, it was empty. There was a note inside which read: "This file has been missing since…" I think it was 1973. This was discouraging, but then the head of the Archives came along and asked if I was finding what I came for, and I told him about the file being empty. He said that's the way it was when the files were turned over to them. I told him why I wanted information on my brother's death. He was very helpful, and said, "What you really should have is his burial file." Then he took me to a phone and gave me a number to call. I asked for a copy of the burial file, and was told it would take a few weeks, but they would mail it to me.

They did. I was still in New York when this large package arrived. It was at least an inch thick. I started reading page after page of information. Some things I knew, but most of it I didn't know – and it was 80 pages before I learned that what Hassenpflug had said might have happened did happen. Newell and four others had been beaten, then shot in the head and killed. I also learned that the six people who were involved in the killing had been tried for "violation of the laws of war." They were found guilty and several were hanged, others jailed. This was Feb. 5, 1948, three years after the war.

These are some of the papers from the trial:

"List of offenses: The accused were tried on two charges and particulars. Both charges were based on the violation of the laws of war. The first particular alleged that the accused participated in the killing of four American prisoners of war. Also participated in assaulting two or more unknown POWs.

"Trial data: Tried by a general military government court appointed by the commanding general of the United States forces, European Theater. Findings were made and sentences imposed as follows: Josef Ehlen, first charge guilty, second charge guilty. Death by hanging. August Viehl, first charge guilty, second charge guilty. Death by hanging. Reinhart Beck, first charge not guilty, second charge guilty. Four years.

"Franz Muller, first charge not guilty, second charge guilty. Six years. Martin Baesse, first charge not guilty, second charge guilty. Six years. Paul Winkler, first charge guilty, second charge guilty. Sentence, death by hanging.

"Evidence: Prosecution – Four unknown American fliers parachuted to earth on 27 Sept. 1944, two in the vicinity of Nentershausen and two in the nearby village of Suess, Germany. The two fliers who landed in Nentershausen were taken to a labor camp in Nentershausen, beaten and then shot. The two fliers who landed in Suess were brought to the Nentershausen labor camp and there taken out and shot. All of the convicted accused except Beck participated in the beating or killing in one way or another.

"Defense – All of the accused denied active participation in the beating and shooting of the American fliers, although all except Beck witnessed at least one of the killings. Ehlen attempted to justify his illegal actions by stating that the Americans had attacked him and the other accused. Beck was involved in the incidents only to the extent that he went into the camp enclosure to collect a bill for bread at the time two of the fliers were being held prisoner.

"Discussion: Each of the accused except Beck was present at a killing, and although each denied that he killed or beat any flier, the court was justified in arriving at the findings of guilty to the respective charges since there was ample evidence to show that all of the accused except Beck were eager principals in the beatings or killings and not merely curious bystanders, as each accused contended he was. The evidence was sufficient to support the findings and sentences except as to accused Beck.

"Summation: The court had jurisdiction of the accused and of the offense. Examination of the entire record fails to disclose any error or omission which resulted in injustice to any of the accused except Beck."

This is the "Report of Burial." It says, "Murdered. Brainard, Newell, 700 Bomb Squad, Nentershausen, Germany, 27 Sept., 1947." This says 1947. Maybe it was a typographical error.

"1) Previously buried as unknown X-1535 at St. Avold. Identified through exact comparison of tooth chart obtained for X-1535 and that for Lieutenant Brainard.

"2) Estimated height and color of hair for X-1535 in agreement with that for Lieutenant Brainard.

"3) Clothing of X-1535 marked 'Brainard.'

"4) Estimated date and place of death for X-1535 in agreement with Missing Air Crew Report for Air Crew 42-110022 of which Lieutenant Brainard was a crew member, co-pilot.

5) German Dulag record KU-3079 indicates that Lieutenant Brainard was killed in the area from which X-1535 was disinterred."

They buried him first as an unknown, and then after they did all this investigating, they went and brought him back. Newell had had a head injury – I got all this information from Hassenpflug – evidently either he was injured by flak or hit his head when he jumped out of the plane or when he landed. [Ray Carrow, Newell's pilot, says the plane was on fire when Newell bailed out. Carrow jumped moments later, and the fire burned off all his hair.]

They first took Newell to somebody's house, and the lady of the house was concerned about his head injury and had a nurse sent in – a Red Cross nurse from the town – and she bandaged his head. But then he was taken away from that house. He was supposed to be turned over to the military authorities, but somehow or other this didn't happen. There were four at first and then one came in from another area; whether Newell was that one or not I don't think they ever knew. But the person that they turned him over to – I don't know who did or how they made the mistake, but he was running a slave labor camp, and they said that anybody who was in charge of slave laborers was a tough guy to begin with, and so rather than turn them over to the right military people, he just beat them up and killed them. Then, lacking all identification, all five were put in an unmarked grave, which was later located by our military.

Newell was then buried in France as "unknown." Later he was disinterred again, and in addition to finding his name on underclothing, the bandage was still around his head. That convinced Hassenpflug that they had found Newell. The military also used dental charts for identification. When I went over for the dedication of the monument, I would like to have talked with the German Red Cross woman who bandaged his head, but she was in a nursing home in another town.

Newell was always very responsible, and brother Bill just the opposite. Bill hoped to be a fighter pilot, but didn't make the grade, surprisingly, and was sent to gunnery school. He ended up a tech sergeant and gunner-radio operator on a B-17.

He, too, had to bail out of his plane over Germany, even before Newell. His plane went down July 26, 1944. Fortunately, he was turned over to the military and eventually became a POW.

Bill was full of life, but since World War II he has simmered down a lot. Growing up he was good looking, even voted the best looking boy in his graduating class. He was full of fun. He still has a good sense of humor, but uses it seldom. He and Newell used to double-date, mainly because we had one car between us. I used it during the day, and they'd put in a quarter's worth of gas to use the car at night. Sometimes I had to buy another gallon in order to get to work. All three of us had chipped in to buy this second-hand car.

The car was a Ford. There are so many things I could tell you that are interesting but not for your book. During the early years of the war – the war was going on in England, but not here yet; before Pearl Harbor in other words – a woman and her brother rented rooms from my mother, when she had the guest house. We had a room over our garage – a garage apartment they called it – one big room and bath is all it was. That's where they stayed. And they liked the Palm Beaches so much.

They were English and walking was nothing for them; they would walk everywhere. They didn't have a car, but Roland was an excellent mechanic; he knew all about automobiles, and this Ford would stop on us every once in a while and we couldn't get it started, and we would have to leave it where it was and go someplace and call Roland and say, "The car is on such and such a street; would you see if you can get it running?" And he could always do it. He was a young, tall, handsome kid, and he was eager to be at war.

And I know the story now. The end of the story is that they were not brother and sister. She was his mother. I guess they had come over here to see the United States, and I often wondered if the family looked down on the fact that she had gotten pregnant and had this boy ... but they passed as brother and sister for years. It wasn't until late in the war that he finally became an American citizen and got into the service, probably around the Battle of the Bulge. Because of his eyes he couldn't get into the Air Force but he was in the infantry. And he stepped on a land mine and was killed.

Eventually I met his mother in London. I spent a couple of days with her, and she told me that she was into spiritualism – I guess she had been so devastated when he was killed. She thought it was all her fault. But she said that the spiritualism had helped her a great deal. And incidentally, she told me that Roland had seen Newell and everything was fine up there. But the spiritualism brought her back to ordinary living, and I thought, "Well, whatever it takes."

My mother ended up taking her own life. Not immediately, but in 1957. I had two boys and I wanted a girl very badly, and I finally had a girl, and she was only three months old. My mother had angina, which I now have, but at that time they couldn't do anything about it. And she had very high blood pressure which I do not have. And she had eye trouble, probably cataracts, that they didn't know how to handle at the time. So she couldn't watch television. She couldn't read anymore. She couldn't drive a car. Life to her was over. And Jack and I had just built a house. We had the house but we had no furniture, and I've often wondered if she had this in mind, among other things that she was tired of living; she didn't think she was living actually. My sister was very good. Betty bought her a house. Betty bought the car. Betty bought the TV. She did everything. She had a job that she had worked at since she was right out of high school, and she became a buyer for this shop and ran a big business. She had more money than the rest of us. But I think that the whole business of Newell entered into it, and my father's illness; my mother never married again. She never had a date with anybody. Never seemed to object to that. She never longed for that.

She was just shy of 70. She had a gas stove, and she just closed herself in the kitchen and turned the gas on. I think she also planned that, because we had a colored girl, as we called them at that time, who came every Friday, and had been with her for years, and when she came the door was locked, so she looked in the kitchen window and she could see Mother on the floor. She called my sister, and Betty called me. It's a tragedy, but if you knew my mother, it was her way of handling things.

I married my first husband on the rebound, so to speak, after getting a Dear John letter from an officer I had dated overseas. I guess I was flak happy. I went out to California to visit Mary Jo, my dear Red Cross friend, who married one of the pilots on our base who I introduced her to. She and I both had to go to Germany when the war was over. She was one of the first Red Cross girls to be assigned to Berlin. We didn't get home until 1946, while almost everybody else came home in 1945. We hadn't done the two years we volunteered for, so we were assigned to American Red Cross clubs in occupied Germany.

When I came home, I had numerous job offers. I decided to work for a law firm that was very well known in Palm Beach, but I said before I start work I'd like to take a little time off. It was the middle of the summer, so  they said that was fine, why didn't I wait until September to start?

In July, Mary Jo called me from California, and we both felt out of place. All our friends were living it up and drinking and having fun, and we'd been living in these completely destroyed areas. Aschaffensburg, where I had been stationed, was 70 percent destroyed. Aschaffensburg is about 30 miles from Frankfurt. I was so depressed there that I asked for a transfer, and I was transferred to Erlangen, which was right outside of Nuremburg. Erlangen  was a hospital city so it wasn't as badly beat up. But then we came home and everybody was living it up. My friends would say, "I got a new car! Got a new Cadillac, $3,000!" Can you imagine? Then Mary Jo called me and she said, "Whit's going to come down and visit" – he lived in Northern California  –  "why don't you come out and visit at the same time? My brother's just gotten out of the Navy and I think you should meet him."

So I flew to California. Mary Jo lived in Santa Barbara, and they met me at the airport in Los Angeles.

The brother was a nice guy, but we didn't hit it off. Her cousin Jimmy came over, though, and the four of us – Mary Jo and Whit and Jimmy and I – we all had a wonderful time. We had so much in common. Jimmy had a sister a couple of years younger; she was going steady with a boy, and we just all had fun together. I ended up thinking I was in love with Jimmy and he was in love with me, and Mary Jo and Whit were going to get married. Sissy and her boyfriend were going to get married.

I had to come home after five weeks – but I'd already told Jimmy I would marry him. And my mother – that was the only time I ever saw her really unhappy about who I was going with. She didn't know Jimmy at all, but I guess she thought I was doing this on the rebound, and I didn't think of it as that. She knew me better than I knew myself.

We didn't get married until October, and the longer we were apart, the more I wasn't really too sure we should get married, but I thought, well, I told him I would and he's driving all the way across the country to get married, and my sister said, "You got yourself into this, now you'd better go ahead and get married." So I did. Jimmy and I moved back to Santa Barbara for a while, and then we moved to Los Angeles, and I thought when we got to Los Angeles I'd go to work. I was already sure I wasn't going to stay married. It wasn't his fault at all, it was my fault, the whole thing. And darned if I didn't learn the first week I was in Los Angeles, which was three months after we were married, that I was pregnant. So I knew I was going to have to stay longer, and I did. I lived with Jimmy for four years, and when Kim was three years old I decided I was coming back to Florida. Jimmy wasn't very happy about that, but he knew that I wasn't happy in California.

When I was in Paris on my way to Germany, I had met a captain who was a year younger than I. Some Red Cross girls were sightseeing the first day we were in Paris and as we walked past one of the outdoor cafés near the Opera House, these GIs were sitting at a table and they called out, "Parlez vous Francais?" and other silly remarks. They said, "Come have a drink with us." There were four or five of us girls and five of them, and I just happened to sit next to this Jack Hutchins. One of the guys in the group was from Jacksonville, Florida. They were in Paris on a three-day pass. They were headed home. We were headed to Germany.

Jack took an immediate liking to me. He was very attractive and nice, so I didn't mind when he said, "How about a date tonight? The whole group of us are going to go out."

I had already made a date on the train from Dover into Paris. I was in one of those old  clipper cars that held six people in a compartment. It seems to me there were two black officers, Air Force, I think, and this white officer and me, and one other Red Cross girl. One of them, a very nice guy, was with the military, OSS or something, and stationed in Paris. He didn't make any pretense of not being married, but he said, "How about having dinner with me tonight and I'll show you Paris from the roof garden." I guess I knew he was married but I thought that sounded nice; he was going to take me to dinner at the Maurice – in fact I think he lived at the Maurice. If you've ever been there, it's one of *the* top hotels in Paris.

And then I met Jack. So I did something we used to do at the University of

Florida when I visited up there. I said, "I'll have a 'late date' with you. I'll be back at the Red Cross hotel by 10 o'clock, because I'm just going to dinner with this very nice person."

Well, my date did take me to dinner, and then he took me up to the top of the Maurice – from there you could look out all over the city and it was beautiful – but I told him, "I've made some plans to go out with a group at 10 o'clock."

He said, "Okay, I'll get you back."

It was about 10 after 10 when we got back, and dammit, they'd been there and gone. I was mad as hell. Well, that's a fine thing, they couldn't wait ten minutes? There were GIs in the lobby, however, including one who played the piano, so we had a great sing-along, which was fun. And early the next morning I was called from downstairs and told someone was there to see me. And it was Jack Hutchins.

He told me they went to the Moulin Rouge and did things I would have enjoyed too, but from then on we were arm in arm and walked all over Paris. The boys stayed out so late with us that they couldn't find a place to stay. By midnight, all the beds were taken. They slept in the lobby of a Red Cross hotel one night. They had to go back to port before we left.

I had taken some pictures, and I mailed some to Jack, but he never responded. "Well, that's the way it goes, I guess."

After seven months doing Red Cross work in occupied Germany, Mary Jo and I arrived back in New York. We were there several days, then she left for California. I had a cousin living in Manhattan, so I spent another few days with him and his wife. I looked up a Navy friend I'd known for years, and he took me to lunch. When I returned to the apartment, I immediately left to catch a train for Hartford to see my relatives there. My uncle greeted me with, "You had a call from Jack Hutchins, but he said he'd call again."

I said, "Jack Hutchins???"

He said, "Yes. Don't you know him?"

So I told him about meeting him in Paris, but said I'd never heard from him again.

Well, Jack did call back and told me he was walking on the street in New York with his wife – which I didn't know he had – and saw me with my Navy friend on the other side of the street. He said they were headed for a hotel to have lunch and he had phoned me from the hotel. They lived in Pittsburgh.

In those days the long-distance operator would stay on the line with you as long as necessary. It's quite different today.

I had an easy address to remember: 25 Currie Crescent. Jack hadn't forgotten it, and told the operator he was making a person-to-person call to Kay Brainard. The operator called the only Brainard in the book, and my mother answered the phone.

Mother said to the operator, "I'm sorry, she's not here."

"Do you know where we can reach her?"

"She's at her cousin's apartment."

"What's her cousin's name?"

"Frank Brainard."

"Do you know his phone number?"

"No." So the operator found his number in the New York phone book. But when Jack reached my cousin, he was told I had just left to catch a train for Hartford. But Frank was able to give the operator my uncle's phone number. And that's how Jack tracked me down.

When he called again, he got me, and he wanted to know if I was returning to New York. I told him I wasn't, that I was going from Hartford to Washington, D.C., to check out of the Red Cross. Of course, since he was with his wife, I really didn't care one way or the other. After all, he'd never written to me.

But seven years later, he called Currie Crescent again and this time my brother answered the phone. Jack asked brother Bill if I was there, or living in Alaska, or where is she? And is she married?

Bill said, "Well, she was married but she's divorced, and she has her own apartment." Then he gave him my phone number and he called me and said he had a vacation coming up and would like to see me. He also said he was separated and getting a divorce.

I wasn't dating anyone specifically at the time. I remembered that he was nice and lots of fun, so I said, "Fine." He asked me to find him a place to stay, and I said I would. And a few days later I picked him up at the airport. He asked me to have dinner with him that evening, and while we were there he said, "You are going to marry me, aren't you?"

I didn't say yes or no, but that started the romance all over again. When I took him to the plane to return to Pittsburgh, I said, "You'd better write to me this time."

He said, "I'm not very good at writing letters."

And I said, "Then let's forget the whole thing."

Well, he started writing letters and pretty soon every day when I came home from work there would be a special delivery letter stuck in my screen door. That only took overnight and it cost 20 cents in those days.

After six months of his flying down whenever he had a holiday weekend, he gave up his banking job and moved down to Florida. And six months later we were married. It was 1953.

My five- or six-year old son Kim was living with me. He had just started school, but by the time he was seven, every summer he would fly to California and spend a month or more with his father. He told his classmates he had "two daddies." Jimmy and I stayed good friends. His sister and I still communicate, and I still correspond with neighbors we had when we later lived in Pasadena.

I had two more children, first William in 1954, and Carole two years later. Little by little, I learned that Jack was an alcoholic. He didn't drink at home, except socially, but would stop at a bar after work, and forget to come home for dinner. This got worse and worse, because he drank at expensive bars in Palm Beach, and bills were neglected. Then he would borrow money. By the time Carole was three and in day-school until noon, I started looking for a job.

I had a friend who was a social secretary in Palm Beach and she gave me the name of a woman who needed secretarial help, and that's how I met Mrs. George Blabon, of the Anheuser-Busch family. She was the first granddaughter of Augustus Busch, and was described to me as "hell on wheels, a real bitch."

I went to interview her anyway, and then to work for her. She had a staff of seven. Housekeeper, maid, cook, laundress, gardener, sometimes a butler, and me. She was difficult, but worse with those considered servants. Evidently I was considered on a higher level. I ended up working for her for 20 years. Once in a while I'd quit, then go back when it pleased me, not her.

She was well-known for her parties, and I was expected to be there, properly dressed. I had to greet each guest at the door, and give him or her a card telling them their table number. This was more fun than work, because as the years went by, they got to know me and I was treated like a guest myself.

I paid all the help, helped plan the daily as well as party meals, made numerous phone calls to her bridge-playing friends, learned to balance a checkbook – it wasn't all bad. And they were only in Palm Beach for five or six months, so I had summers off to be with my children. Then she started staying longer and longer in Palm Beach, and when she told me she had decided to stay year-round, I realized it was time to quit for good.

I didn't tell you about George and his fishing boat. He loved to go deep-sea fishing, and he and his boat captain were out in the Gulfstream and he had just caught a beautiful dolphin, so they sat down to have a beer – a Busch beer no doubt. Lily drank Scotch instead, and lots of it. Anyway, George suddenly had a heart attack, and even though the captain radioed the dock to have a doctor meet them, it was too late; George was dead.

Lily took the dolphin to a taxidermist and had it mounted in all its glory, and she hung it over the mantelpiece. Well, everyone thought it was a great catch, but her friends at parties would look at it and say, "There's the fish that killed George."

Mr. Blabon was too rich and prominent to go to a mortuary like most people did. He had to be laid out at home. Lily had him put in his casket in her bay window overlooking Tarpon Cove, where their beautiful Palm Beach home was. The funeral was put off until relatives and friends could arrive from St. Louis, and Lily had them all to dinner the night before. During dinner she went to take a look at George, and then her guests heard her scream. They rushed to the living room bay window where she stood beside the casket. Poor George had been sitting in the sun too long and all the things the mortician puts into the body had drained out or dried up, and George was a wrinkled mess. The funeral was to be at 11 the next morning, so the mortician had to come get him and do his work all over again that night.

Mrs. Blabon weighed 300 pounds, so all her clothes were made to order by an excellent seamstress, and she looked very well-dressed. There was a doctor in Palm Beach we called the "Society M.D." He was popular with his patients and didn't mind making house calls. In fact, he was invited to many of the social dinner parties. However, he overdid it, staying up all night with one of his patients who was dying, and he suddenly dropped dead himself. Mrs. Blabon was at the hairdresser when she heard the news. She returned home and was crying when she came in. I asked her why she was crying and she said, "Dr. Johannsen died." And with tears coming down her cheeks she added, "He always called me Old Fat Ass." She was really going to miss him.

I left Jack one summer. I took the kids and drove to Pennsylvania, where I had relatives I could stay with. Two weeks later Jack started going to Alcoholics Anonymous. Two months later we got back together … but it was never the same. He became so involved with AA, in addition to his job at PaineWebber, that he was difficult to live with. He began to slip off with a very wealthy woman who he met at AA, and when her husband (also in AA) died, he asked me for a divorce. I said, "Be my guest!" We had lived together for 20 years.

When our divorce was final they were married. Fortunately, he took out a good insurance policy for my benefit, as he died five years later of a heart attack – and his wife died of cancer several months later.

That's when I retired. Nine months later, I didn't have a baby, but I had a phone call from Caleb Gray, a gentleman who worked for a catering firm, who I knew from the Blabon parties.

Caleb, in addition to catering, also did part-time work for Douglas Fairbanks, Jr. He was helping him write his autobiography by doing the necessary typing. He told me he wasn't coming down to Palm Beach that winter, as he had written a book and wanted to stay in New York and work on having it published (it never was). He wondered if I had time to do some work for Mr. Fairbanks. He was delighted to learn

I no longer worked for Mrs. Blabon, and asked if I would work for Mr. Fairbanks.

I told him I was tired of being "retired," my kids were in college, and I would be very interested in possibly working again. Caleb said he was coming to Palm Beach soon and would call me.

Two days later I got a call from Mr. Fairbanks and he asked me if I could come over for an interview that afternoon. It was during the Christmas holidays, and I told him I was having my children over for dinner, but I could come the following day. That was all right with him.

I went to his Palm Beach home about 11 in the morning. When I arrived, his wife was talking on the phone. Mr. Fairbanks said, "Excuse her, she's talking to one of my daughters in England."

When she hung up she came to join us. So, just making conversation, I said, "Where in England does your daughter live?"

She said, "Oh, it's just a little town you've probably never heard of. It's Sudbury, Suffolk."

I said, "That happens to be just where I spent the war years. So right away we had something in common, and furthermore, Mr. Fairbanks and I got along fine. So he said, "Can you start work tomorrow?" I could, and I did. And it turned out to be a wonderful experience.

Douglas and I both had a chip on our shoulder because neither of us got to go to college. But he was tutored by a gentleman in France who was a history buff, and Douglas can tell you anything about the history of the world, but particularly England. And he knows everybody in royalty, historically and otherwise. He gets a Christmas card every year from Queen Elizabeth and the Queen Mother. Everywhere he went he made friends, and he and I became very close. He stood in for Jack, who was long dead, when my daughter Carole got married. We got an extra day off. We were traveling for American Movie Classics at the time, and between gigs in Portland, Oregon, and Palm Springs, California, we slipped in a trip to San Francisco for the wedding.

Douglas and Mary Lee were a devoted couple in a strange way. He traveled all the time, Frequently going to New York from Palm Beach or London or Los Angeles. His schedule was unbelievable, but every night he would call Mary Lee. In addition, before he left he always tucked a note under her pillow. And this went on year in and year out. They ended up being married for 49½ years.

I had only been working there a few days when Douglas handed me – well, it was obvious that I had become his confidant – he handed me a letter and said, "Will you make me six copies of this?"

It was a six-page handwritten letter, and eventually I found myself reading it.

I wasn't sure whether I was supposed to or not, but I wondered, why six copies?

It was from a woman he was breaking up with … someone he had known for a long time … and I was to send copies of the letter to several gentlemen I knew were important in his life. They must have known the woman, too. Many years later she started writing to him again … but she was living in France by then.

So that's how it started out – no secrets kept from me!

I knew his wife had never had any affairs. However, there was one man, the husband of one of their good friends – always on their guest list – and occasionally he came down to Palm Beach by himself. He would call the Fairbanks' and if Douglas was out of town, he would take Mary Lee out to dinner.

One time when he was in town, they went out to dinner and when they returned the two of them sat in the car parked in their circular driveway. The next morning she said to me: "I can't have any fun! Last night when we came home Joe and I were having an interesting conversation, when Giuseppe opened the door and yelled, 'When are you coming in? I want to close up the house!' " That's about the extent of her dillydallying.

Mary Lee died of cancer in September of 1988. And in 1991 Douglas married one of his old friends who he used to see in New York a lot. She was 30 years younger than he was. We still keep in touch and when I'm in New York I see them.


One morning I was watching the Today show on television, and they were interviewing the librarian of Radcliffe College, whose library specializes in collections of "women's work." She said she would like to hear more from women involved in World War II.

I wondered, "Would that include me?" Mother had saved all the letters I sent home while I was overseas with the Red Cross. They were handwritten, and I had spent one summer typing them into manuscript form – and ended up with 362 pages. So I selected a few of the letters and sent them to the librarian.

I received a note from her right away. "Yes, we are very interested. We would like your typescript, as well as the original letters." Now they have them, and I have an archive.

Then two years ago I received an invitation from Radcliffe to attend a luncheon in Palm Beach. I thought it was probably a fundraiser for the college and I was going to send my regrets, then I thought, it's at a beautiful home in Palm Beach … I'll go. So I went and it was lovely. Each guest was greeted with a glass of champagne and a chain to wear around your neck, and was given a name tag noting the year you graduated from Radcliffe. I was the only one there who had no graduation date!

Radcliffe was a girls' school, but some of the women had brought their husbands. They were a friendly group. Some even noticed that I had no graduation date, and I would confess I did not graduate or even go to Radcliffe, adding, "I'm just a guest."

The president of Radcliffe as well as the librarian were at the luncheon, and eventually I was standing near Mary Maples Dunn, the librarian, and she noted my name tag and said, "Oh, you're our Red Cross friend who sent us the letters you wrote your mother in World War II." Then she asked me if I had continued to work for the Red Cross after the war.

I told her I had at times done volunteer work, but not on a regular basis. Then I added, "The most interesting job I've had lately is to work with Douglas Fairbanks, Jr., as his assistant. I've worked for him for over 10 years."

She said, "Oh, that must have been fascinating!"

And I said, "Well, yes, it certainly was."

It was then that she said, "Why don't you write a memoir on what it was like to work for Mr. Fairbanks?"

So I did. I've left out a great deal that I could have put in there , but I wouldn't. He has written two books and says himself that they would have been more successful if they'd been, as they call it in Hollywood, kiss-and-tell books. His publishers were disappointed, I think, but he wasn't going to change his mind. And I wasn't going to do it either.

I knew both Mary Lee (his wife after a four-year marriage to Joan Crawford when he was 19) as well as Vera, who he married in 1991. But he and I had sort of a special bond.

We still keep in touch. If I'm in New York I see him; when I'm not, we chat on the telephone quite often.

In 1990 I worked all year in New York, sharing the Park Avenue apartment with Vera and Douglas. Had lots of fun. Saw numerous Broadway shows, and met many interesting people.

In addition to our office work, I accompanied him on trips all over the country when he was representing American Movie Classics – AMC on cable TV.

When I sent my "memoir" to Ms. Dunn at Radcliffe, she wrote me and said, and I quote: "I read your memoir with the greatest pleasure! Your tales of working with Douglas Fairbanks are very enjoyable – sad, gossipy, historical, all at once!

She also wrote that she would give my memoir to the manuscript department, so it would be catalogued in the Harvard computerized catalogue, where all their collections are catalogued. That's so students of Hollywood would no doubt find it and use it in the years to come, she said.

My brother Newell was in the same bomb group Jimmy Stewart was in. He wrote home that he had seen him, but had not met him yet.

My first son was born in 1947 and I named him after Newell. He's Newell White Neilson, but is called "Kim" – a contraction of Kay and Jim – and he is an artist. He also screen prints T-shirts and other things. … It's hard to make a living as an artist. His father was more a commercial artist, and specialized and won prizes as an interior designer. My father, although an engineer, did beautiful pencil sketches.

Who is the pilot in this picture with my name on a Spitfire? That's another story. I met him while standing in line to get a train ticket home from Washington, D.C., and he wanted a ticket to return to South Carolina. The train ran out of seats, so we had to settle for the next day. This was in 1942.

Sandy Sanborn had been home on leave to recuperate from burns he received when his plane had caught fire. He had been flying with the Royal Air Force since before Pearl Harbor. He asked me if I knew much about Washington. I told him I'd been born there but left when I was about two, so I didn't remember anything.

He suggested we hire a taxi to drive us around, and we could do some sight-seeing. We spent the day together, and met at the station the next morning. We sat together on the train, but he got off in South Carolina, and I went on to West Palm Beach. He returned to England, and from then on he named four Spitfires after me. We corresponded throughout the war, and I saw him once in New York briefly in 1944, shortly before I went overseas.

I've talked a lot about my family, and the interesting jobs I've had through the years, and the great people I've met, as well as the wonderful places I've been. But I must say, the American Red Cross work I did in World War II, both in England and Occupied Germany, are the times that meant the most to me. And hardly a day goes by that I don't think about my brother Newell. I had hoped to attend the 445th Bomb Group reunion this year in Savannah, but my angioplasty had to take precedence.

However, in spite of being 81 now [author's note: This is from a postscript, written in October of 1999] , I'm flying to Tucson, Arizona, next week for the 486th Bomb Group reunion, which I have attended for many years. We trade photos, pore over scrapbooks and albums, tell tall tales – if our memory doesn't give out.

And we're all very proud of the record of the Mighty 8th Air Force of World War II.

*"Someone called out, 'Here comes our fighter escort!'*

*"I looked out my little window, and there's a hell of a lot of commotion, and I saw these radial engine planes. I thought, 'Those are our P-47s.' All of a sudden they peeled off and there was the Swastika. And about that instant, they start flying through the ships."*

**Frank Bertram**
**Navigator**
**445th Bomb Group**
**Survivor,**
**Kassel mission**
**Sept. 27, 1944**

*Because it was not possible for me to interview Frank Bertram in person for this book, he dictated his story into a tape recorder, and sent me the tape. This narrative is derived from the transcript of that tape.*

The Kassel mission of Sept. 27, 1944, actually was percentage-wise the worst loss of any mission throughout the war. Of the 35 planes that went in to the target, I believe only five – to be completely accurate, you have to talk to George Collar or Bill Dewey – got back. Twenty-five of the bombers went down immediately around the target, or were crippled badly enough that they went down within a radius of maybe 15 miles of the point of combat.

You mentioned something the other day about post traumatic syndrome that apparently a lot of the veterans from Vietnam have had, which was not even heard of in Korea or in World War II. However, it must have been there to a certain extent. It is my opinion that nobody who went to war, particularly if they went overseas and more particularly if they got into combat, you came back, you were not the same person. For guys who were prisoners of war it was even worse, because you actually felt that you were looked down upon. It's very demeaning to be a prisoner in war. You're stomped on to a certain extent. Some people more than others. If you get the full stories of POWs; you talked to Mr. Levine [Bernie Levine, whose interview is on the World War II Oral History web site], I don't know how much you talked to him about it but I like his deal, that he's never gonna be cold or hungry again. Boy, those were bitter winters. Every once in a while something snaps you into it. You try to forget about it and then something snaps and bingo, you start thinking. Things like that happen to me where I actually relive every moment I was in that plane that day, after coming under attack.

In all the missions I was on we had never been attacked by fighters. The primary reason for that is our particular group, the 445th Bomb Group, was known exceptionally for their close formation. And when you have a close formation, usually enemy fighters are not going to attack you because you throw up such a concentrated cone of fire it was not feasible for them to try and penetrate it, whereas the groups that were spread around were sitting ducks. That's why it was such a shock when so many of our planes went down that day. But we were scattered. We were just getting back into position, into our close formation, when we were hit.

The day of that mission, my crew was not supposed to fly. We were a radar crew, so we alternated with another crew. They had their plane, we had ours. We had flown the day before and we actually led the mission; our squadron was deputy lead squadron and in the lead squadron both planes with radar were knocked out by flak, so we took over. That was going into the town of Hamm. We had no problem going in; we got out of there, came back and we landed safe. So it was a surprise when they asked us to fly the next day. We were looking forward to a little rest and recreation, to going into Norwich and raising a little hell. But fate intervened and here we are.

When the group flew in toward the target – the tactics of the Air Force were I won't say to zigzag but you'd go from one place to another to avoid areas of known flak guns. Because if the Germans could see you, they could hit you. They were that good. Even at 22,000 feet, they could come damn close, if they could see you clearly, with the great optics they had.

We did our usual deal till we came to what they called the initial point. The initial point in a bomb run is where control of the bomber is turned over to the bombardier. And from the initial point to the point of impact, which could be anywhere from 10 to 30 miles, the pilot has no control whatsoever. You're on a straight heading, no matter what comes through the formation, what kind of flak you get, you've just got to rough it out, straight ahead. As all the planes in back of you do.

This day we had to make a little left turn to hit the initial point. As we made the left turn, we went further left than we were supposed to. I immediately called the pilot, Reg Miner, and said, "Hey! We're going the wrong way! We're going too far left. Call the lead plane and find out what's going on."

And he came back and said, "They said, 'Hold it in. Hold it in.'" We kept turning farther left, and I thought, "We're going to miss the target completely."

The target was not visible from the air, but with the radar scope we had the target picked up, and with the little that we did see from the air to the ground, and the paperwork I was doing, we knew where we were exactly.

We were not the only one that caught the mistake. I think almost every plane in the formation that had a halfway good navigator called immediately and saw what was going on. You could actually look out the pilot's window and see the flak off to the right, which we were supposed to be going through. Why we kept going to the left we'll never know. We never did find out.

We released the bombs near the town of Goettingen. As it happened it was in an open field; probably killed a couple of cows. Then we followed our regular method to come out of the bomb run and head for home. That was a left turn off the target; a right turn, which took us on a southeast heading; another right turn, which took us on a southwest heading; then another turn to the right, which took us on a northwest heading.

While we were just getting back together after the fourth turn, someone in our plane called out, "There's a dogfight!" And all the time I'm thinking, "Oh boy, are we gonna catch it from headquarters when we get home," because we dropped the bombs uselessly.

Then our radio operator, Joe Gilfoil – who was mortally wounded that day – said, "There's a fire in the bomb bay!"

Right after he said that, all hell broke loose. I'm looking out my little window – I sat in back of the pilot and had a window about one foot square – and here's this flak, maybe three feet around when it explodes, a sort of a grayish black. And I'm thinking, "What the hell is this? We're at 22,000 feet, and these guys are shooting through the clouds and hitting us like this?" I couldn't believe the accuracy. And then someone called out, "Here comes our fighter escort!" I looked out my little window, and there's a hell of a lot of commotion, and I saw these radial engine planes. I thought, "Those are our P-47s." All of a sudden they peeled off and there was the Swastika. And about that instant, they start flying through the ships. There were shells, explosions and guns chattering, you puckered up immediately and the lead hit the stomach, words just cannot describe your feeling. It's absolute sheer terror for a while, panic for a while, and then anger.

At that point, all I saw was four planes. Apparently they were ten abreast, but I just saw the right side of our plane, and these planes shooting at us. And all of a sudden a big explosion hit the ship and the top turret gunner, who was right opposite me, came crashing to the ground. The turret got a direct hit from one of these planes, and it blew the Plexiglas out and smashed it right in this guy's face and he fell down right at my feet. His name was Mac Thornton. I looked down and I knew he was dead. His face was just frozen; the blood was solid. At that point in September it was very cold, I think it was 20 or 30 below zero at that altitude, so everything freezes instantly. And I panicked at that point. I could see explosions going through the ship into the bomb bay. The interphone was out. We knew we were going to have to bail out. So I went to the bomb bay door and I almost fell over poor Thornton; got my foot caught in his arm and almost panicked to get out of his way. Then I couldn't open the bomb bay; it was stuck. There were holes, and there was gasoline pouring in the bomb bay. To this day I swear the fact that the Germans blew that turret off saved us from exploding, because I think that sucked all the gasoline fumes from the bomb bay right out through the top. Otherwise I'm sure we'd have blown up, as many of our ships did that day.

I was wearing a chest pack chute. I crawled up to the nose wheel to check that and see how the guys up there were doing. The nose turret gunner was firing at the planes as they went by, because the attacks were from the rear. As they'd go by, the gunners up front would shoot at them.

I tried to open the nose wheel door and it was frozen shut. I thought, "Now we're doomed. We're trapped." So I thought, "I'll see if can kick it open."

All this time I'm nervous, I'm scared. I expect the ship to explode at any moment.

I kicked and kicked, and I got the nose wheel doors open. I damn near fell out because I kicked so hard. I pull myself back up and one leg is dangling. Now I'm sitting on the edge of the nose wheel looking down at nothing but clouds and once in a while they would clear a little bit but the clouds were pretty dense. I'm looking down, dangling in space, and the plane is starting to yaw – that is, going from side to side, and up and down a little bit. As I learned later the engine was on fire, and there were all kinds of things I didn't see because I'm inside the plane. I back up to get back in the plane, and I look behind me – all the guys are lined up with their parachutes ready and they're pointing to me to go out.

I went out feet first. I didn't free fall, like you're supposed to do – I probably counted to 10 or 15 and pulled the chute. The chest pack has a little pilot parachute which comes out first and grabs the air, and then that pulls the main chute out. There's always the possibility that wouldn't work and you'd have to claw your way through getting the main chute open, so the more time you've got the better it is. As it happened, mine took off and popped, and boy, it was a jolt. I thought my legs would fly off. We were lucky – we had brand new parachutes, brand new harnesses, brand new electric flying suits that day – it was the first time we wore them. A beautiful gabardine flying suit. And I went out with just my electric boots. I didn't have my shoes with me. Other fellows jumped out with shoes, they were luckier. I had grabbed my good luck charm, which was a little baseball mitt that my wife had given me, and I put that in my pocket. I had my prayer book, which I kept in my shirt pocket all the time. And we had an escape kit which I grabbed, and shoved that in one of my pockets before I went out. And I had a gun, too. We had .45s and we weren't supposed to take them, but some guys took them. I had taken the clip out, but I had the gun with me for some reason, which I got rid of on the ground.

After my chute popped open I looked around. Our plane was gone. I didn't see anybody else. I couldn't spot any other chutes in the area, but they all went out right after me; as a matter of fact, those in the waist undoubtedly went out first.

The pilot came through okay. He took the plane as far as he could, then bailed out. The co-pilot, we didn't know what happened to him but we presume he got killed. And it turned out that he was not found until the middle of November, which was almost two months later. Up on a hill in a big beech forest they found his body, what was left of him. So we never knew truly what happened.

The bombardier went out and broke his leg when he landed. Our radar operator, Branch Henard, went out and landed okay. I thought Mac Thornton was dead. As it turns out he was right in back of me going out, which I couldn't see; you had goggles on, you had an oxygen mask. I couldn't tell who was in back of me.

Our plane had three navigators because it was leading the squadron. One of them was a fellow named Jackson, he was the pilot's navigator. He went out okay. He landed okay and walked around for a couple of days before he got captured. Our engineer got out okay, and he didn't get injured. He was actually free for ten days, and he was probably the most nervous man on the ship. He was a very nervous individual; his name is Bob Ault, from Texas.

The radio operator, Joe Gilfoil, lost his leg – a shell just about ripped it off when it hit the ship. The two waist gunners threw him out, hoping that the blood would coagulate, but I understand that his leg just about snapped off, and when they found him on the ground he was dead.

Of the men in the waist, Alvis Kitchens – Cotton was his nickname – had a good section of his rear end taken off with some flak; not flak but the 35-millimeter.

He got hit in the butt, and so did Larry Bowers, although not as bad as Kitchens.

The tail gunner broke his ankle when he bailed out.

We really received no training for parachuting that I can recall. I tried to manipulate the chute when I was coming down; on the way down I saw a fighter plane in the distance coming closer. It turns out it was an FW-190 and he went by me – I couldn't judge the distance, but maybe a couple of hundred yards – and he waved to me. I could see his hand waving. I presume it was a wave. Maybe he was out of ammunition. But he didn't circle me; he just kept right on going east.

I was going east too, because the wind was very strong, west to east. I probably drifted four or five miles farther than if I'd held my pull string another five or six minutes, as some of the guys did.

As I came down I could see there was a lot of beautiful green and I saw some little villages, and I could see these woods. I thought, "I'm going to hit those trees just sure as hell." And I did. I tried to manipulate into a little meadow nearby, but I couldn't budge that chute. And I hit the trees. I would say they were 60 to 80 feet high. I tumbled straight down, right through the trees. And right now I can hear those branches snapping as I hit them. I hit the ground with such force that it knocked me out. I broke my wristwatch. And when I came to I couldn't move my legs or my back. Now I'm panicked again; here I am and there's branches all around me, the chute's around me, my feet are killing me, and then all of a sudden the feeling is starting to come back. I start moving and pretty soon I could feel everything and I thought, "I'll see if I can roll over and get up," which I did, and oh, my feet are sore. My knees are sore. My back hurts. But particularly the ankles and feet.

Fortunately, all the branches and stuff on the ground had probably saved me from bad damage.

I gathered up the chute as best I could; it was a struggle. I could hardly move my feet. I threw branches over the chute and I took off for the west. I hadn't gone 150 yards when I heard the damnedest noise. It sounded like a V-1 rocket, putt-putt-putt-putt, or a motorcycle. I could hear German voices real loud. I was walking down a forest road, and I ducked off the road and all of a sudden this old truck came by and it was blowing smoke; I think they had a coal burner running it. I dove behind something where they couldn't see me. There were a bunch of German soldiers and civilians in the truck. After they passed, I resumed marching, and I was just dragging. One time I heard a very guttural sound, like a sergeant directing troops, and I picked my way over through some trees and down in a little valley I saw an airplane. I couldn't tell if it was a Messerschmitt or a Focke-Wulf, and then further away there was a guy with horses plowing the ground, and he was yelling at the horses. I ignored that and went my merry way through the woods.

I came to a point where there was a big, broad autobahn. It was getting dark so it was probably around 4 or 4:30 in the evening. I had walked about three and a half hours at that point. Our combat was about 11 o'clock.

Now I'm really hurting. I don't know what I'm doing. I'm scared. I'm tired. In Germany they have these towers where hunters go up and they sit up there and they shoot the deer. I slept under one of those towers that night. I put a lot of branches over me and damn near froze to death.

I got up the next morning and started hiking. I found some pieces of our airplanes that I recognized. I found a motor embedded in the ground, the propeller all bent up. I wondered what happened to all the guys who were in that plane. And I'm going from forest to forest – some were birch, some were beech and some were aspen; they're beautiful forests over there – and I'm thirsty. All of a sudden I come across a pool of water and it's dirty, but I had this escape kit that had this little deal with the pills you mix with the water to make it drinkable. So I'm down there on my knees, and all of a sudden I hear a noise. At this point I still have my gun, and I think, "Oh, Jesus Christ, I'm caught with this," so I threw it away. It wouldn't have done any good anyway, since I had no bullets. I'm frozen. And I hear this noise getting closer and closer, and I'd just gotten the water in this little tube where you put the pills in – all of a sudden out of the woods comes the biggest stag I've ever seen. He had a big rack on him. He took one look at me and he split and I split. We both got out of each other's way!

I kept on walking. Some of the trees were so big and close together I had to go sideways to get through them. They weren't big in circumference, but they were close together. I'm going along, and as it turns out, I'm headed toward the Werra River.

As I go there, first I hear an airplane, then I hear an explosion. The whole ground shook, and I thought, "My God, what happened?" I figured that a B-17 got its bombs hung up after a mission and came by and just dropped them on the other side of the river. I thought, "My God, this is the most terrifying thing," although it was a mile away from me. I could have been over there. How can these people even survive a thing like this?

I'm near the river so I'm staying in the woods, still being able to look out and see the river. I continue to follow this river to see where it goes. I'm going through the woods and here's a field; a farmer had just plowed and it's full of potatoes, so I go out when nobody's looking and I grab a whole bunch of potatoes. I must have had between 15 and 20 potatoes in my pants pockets. Then I'm going along a little further, and I see what looks like men with pickaxes hitting something and my first thought is, "My God, they've got one of our men up there and they're beating him to death." It was actually our lead ship that went down right in that area, that blew up; this is the plane that led us to this debacle. I walked right by them. I presume that motor I found was off their ship. And I guess they were just chopping up the pieces that were left there. I went by the area and I went a little further and then I came to a beautiful valley. I'm looking down this valley and the river's over to my right, but a little creek comes off the river and goes to the left and there's a railroad track up there, and up the hill there's more woods. So I thought I'll lay low and go up through those woods, because I knew there was a town nearby.

While I'm looking out at this valley, I hear another airplane and I hear explosions, and I look up in the air and see all these pieces flying down. I thought, "My God, a bomber blew up!" And as these pieces floated down, I noticed they're a funny shape. It turned out they were propaganda letters sent in German. And counterfeit money. Great Britain and the United States decided if they couldn't ruin Germany with bombs they'd ruin their economy with phony money. So I laid low for a while before I went across this little meadow, and then I decided, well, I'd better do it. I went across. And I couldn't move very fast. Then out of the corner of my eye – I'm about two-thirds of the way across – I see a movement. All of a sudden here's a bunch of kids. There was a little bridge across the creek I was headed for and I knew I couldn't make that because I'd be out in the open, so I turned and went straight to the creek. And I got down behind a tree. Because of the injury to my leg, I had to have one leg straightened out, and it was hanging in the water.

I'm laying there the best I can behind this tree, and all of a sudden I look up and I see this one little kid. As it turns out it's Walter Hassenpflug. He looks down at me, and he doesn't know that I see him because I've got my eyes half-closed. He jumps up and runs back and he comes back with another kid, who turns out to be Willie Schmidt, who worked with Walter years later. Then they both split and they came back and there was a bunch of them; there were a couple of real cute girls. As a matter of fact, years later I met one of them; her name was Rose Marie Neuman. The girls were 15 and 16 at the time and most of the boys were younger. And there was a tall, thin fellow who came over and looked at me and said, "Sir, are you hurt?"

I didn't answer. I thought, "This is it. I'm dead."

He kept repeating, "Sir, are you hurt? May I help you?" In broken English. And I finally said "Yes. I'm hurt."

He said, "Let me help you up." He came down, stuck out his hand and I grabbed it and he helped me up.

Now all this time, all these kids are running around there, and they're oohing and aahing because they've probably never seen a guy with a four-day beard and hair standing straight up, beat up like I was. I hadn't shaved in a couple of days at that time. And all this time, I learned years later that up on the hill a little further on, I looked at and saw an SS man who was in charge of all these Hitler Youths, who were out picking up the pamphlets and the phony money. Apparently this SS man could have caused a lot of trouble, but he just let them go on and do what they did and kept his nose out of it. Fortunately for me.

This young gentleman that had helped me said, "I'll have to take you to the authorities."

I said, "I understand that."

We walked across this little bridge and onto the railroad track, and maybe after 15 minutes walking, two fellows came toward us, and they had uniforms on that looked like major domos. I thought, "Holy mackerel! Is that Heinrich Himmler or Hitler himself coming to see me?" So I asked this guy, "What is this, Gestapo?" And he laughed.

He said, "No, no. Police." And these two, as they got there I could see they were older gentlemen, not quite my age today, but they were in their late sixties or early seventies. And very nice. They didn't speak any English. But they took me to a two-story house, and the lady of the house had a little baby and she fled, because the propaganda had it that Americans beat little children, or something to that effect. I met that guy 40 years later, the little baby. He's not little any more, believe me. Bigger than I was. But they took me in and they interrogated me, and right across the street there was a house, and I heard them say a Dr. Blom is over there.

Pretty soon this fellow comes over, well-dressed, wearing a vest. He had been eating; he had a napkin tucked under his chin, and he was still chewing a sandwich he had finished. He introduced himself. He spoke English perfectly, and he explained the situation, that he'd have to question me.

I gave him my name, rank and serial number, and that was it. Then we talked for a while. It was very pleasant. Up to that point, it was more of a party, really, with these kids and everything. But they left, and these two policemen then said, "We have to take you into town." And I don't remember how I even got into the town of Bad Hersfeld. This was two or three miles down the road, near Friedlos. So they took me into this little town. I remember going into this jail, and there was a woman there, probably in her late twenties.

They shoved me in a solitary cell with just a board with some straw on it. My back was killing me. They stripped me and took all my stuff away, emptied all my pockets, my shoes, everything. Down to my underwear. Then they let me put my things back on and dress up. I had a prayer book. And as we had intended that night to go out, I still had my navigator wings on, and my first lieutenant bars. I had my nice green shirt on. I was hot to trot once we got back. So if they had any brains at all they knew I was a navigator.

After 10 or 15 minutes in this cell I hear, "Pssst. Hey, Yank."

Up above my bed is a little window, and I hear a voice coming through: "Hey, Yank. Come up to the window."

I thought, "They're not gonna get anything out of me; they're just trying to give me this phony stuff."

Earlier, two civilians came and interviewed me, and they were downright nasty. Those are the guys that made me strip – of course the girl was out of the room – and they kept telling me that I was a sergeant, not a lieutenant. I would say, "Nein. Nein, Oberleutnant, Oberleutnant." They were very solemn-faced, not at all like the two police officers, who were very nice. These guys were strictly business. I called one Mr. Moto. He looked like Peter Lorre. And the other one I called Sidney Greenstreet. One was big and fat and the other was short and thin. Finally they left after getting all the information they could from me, which was nothing. That's when I heard these voices, and it was these two Englishmen. One said, "Hey, Yank, wait till those two civilians go. We'll cook you up some hot cocoa and cookies."

I thought, "What the hell is this?"

By God, about a half-hour later the door flies open and here's one of these police officers and these two other guys. It turns out they were two British officers who had escaped from their prison camp. One of them had been captured at Dunkirk. That means he was in his fourth year as a POW already, and the other one, as I recall, was captured in Norway, which is about the same time. And they were jolly fellows even though they were a little as we say around the bend.

They said that they had been free for three or four days and got captured and were just waiting for their guards to come get them and bring them back to their camp. Everything was done on the up and up in those days. The Germans had a certain system and that was it.

Sure enough, they hold out cocoa and start to make hot cocoa, and we ate some cookies that they had. They had all kinds of food which they had saved up for their escape, which was confiscated but given back to them, and they in turn gave it to me. They said, "Our guards will be here tomorrow, they'll take this stuff away anyhow, so you take it." In the meantime, everybody laughed because when they had examined me, I had all those potatoes in my pockets, and they took my potatoes away from me.

The two British guys gave me their names and addresses, but when they wrote them down they said, "Don't let anybody see it. If anyone comes in, they'll confiscate it." And I ended up chewing on it and swallowing the paper when that young lady came into my cell. I woke up in the middle of the night, and the door flew open and she threw something on my chest, and here was my little baseball mitt. This young girl must have known it was a good luck charm and wanted to see that I got it back, probably with the approval of the police officers. But they had it turned inside out. All the stuffing was hanging loose and I had to shove it back together. I still have it, hanging on the wall.

A few hours later, in the wee hours of the morning, the door opened and a sergeant from the Luftwaffe came in. Tall, thin guy. He talked to the British officers because they could speak German. And they explained to me that I would be taken to another place, and from there I'd go to a camp.

I remember walking down this cobblestone street with this sergeant, across an old stone bridge over the Werra River. There was a full moon and I can still see it reflecting off the water. On the other side, we hopped into a car or a truck and drove off, and he took me to a Luftwaffe camp. Guys were Heil Hitlering all over the place; everybody's saluting everybody. He took me down to a barracks and I came into like a dungeon, and as I walked in and went down this hallway, lo and behold, coming toward me and being led by a guard was the navigator who was in Jim Schaen's ship, Corman Bean. We just looked at each other, never said a word. Didn't even blink an eye, like we had never seen each other before. And here we had breakfasted that morning together. He got shoved in a cell and I got shoved in a cell. I have no recollection of how long it was before they came and they got me out, but pretty soon they took me outside and Corman Bean's there along with ten or fifteen others from the group.

We all were taken from there to a railroad station, and when we were standing at the railroad station we heard these guys talking-marching, in German, eins, zvei, drei, vier, and here comes a whole bunch, maybe 35 guys, American, assorted sizes and shapes and guys beat up. I recognized some right away. George Collar was right in front. His face was swollen. His nose was broken. He had black eyes. They had beaten him up.

Now we sat down and we were taken from this railroad station and put in railroad cars. I remember one fellow, [Jerry Cathol] – he had been a football player; we thought he had a broken back, but I guess he just had some broken bones, and he was in such misery. We're in this railroad car and it was moving, and boy, were these guys surprised – they were all pretty hungry – when I opened up my pockets and pulled out this food. It didn't last very long, but the little bit that there was was most welcome. There was some cheese, butter, powdered cocoa, crackers, probably Spam too; I never could remember the names of those British boys.

The train took us to an interrogation center for all airmen in Oberrussel. It was called Dulag Luft. You would go in one at a time to these inquisitors and they would ask you, "What group are you with?" I just gave them my name, rank and serial number, and then they said to me – and probably to every other one – "Until you give us some more information you're just going to stay here in solitary." And you just shrug your shoulders and think, "They're not going to keep us in solitary too long; there's too many of us because a lot of planes went down." Twenty-five planes over the target. Also, at the same time the Kassel mission was taking place, the battle for the bridge at Arnhem was going on. A complete Polish parachute regiment had been captured by the Germans and they were in Dulag Luft with us, but they were on the other side of the fence, and the Germans were meaner than hell with them. They didn't bother us too much, but they were using bayonets on these guys' fannies if they didn't double time. I'd hate to have been a German when those Poles got loose because they were the toughest looking guys I've ever seen.

After about a day there, we were sent to Stalag Luft 1. We were shoved into a train that had compartments, six seats on each side and a luggage rack, so they put ten of us in each compartment and they gave us a Red Cross parcel each, which contained a week's rations.

It took six days to go 350 miles to our camp. We went through air raids. We'd pull off at sidings. They were strafing and bombing ahead and had the heck scared out of us in Frankfurt. When we went through Frankfurt an air raid was coming on and they abandoned us and let us sit there at the siding.

We had a German guard on each end on the railroad car. I don't know how many cars we had but we did have a commanding officer. He was Lieutenant Colonel McArdle, a British paratrooper, who was in charge of the operation at Arnhem. He had finally surrendered, because they were running out of ammunition and out of men. So consequently, there were a lot of paratroopers, and these were all officers – we were all officers headed for Stalag Luft 1 – so there's quite a few British officers from the paratroop regiments. And then us, plus others who had been shot down. One of the fellows in my compartment was from the 15th Air Force; he was shot down in Italy on a B-25. His name was Richardson. He had been burned; the top half of one ear was burned and his hair was burned off, but he was jolly. He had a big bandage wrapped around his head. He had a few cuts and scabs from when he bailed out. Talk about walking wounded, we looked like a fife and drum corps. Everybody in different clothes, some with shoes, some without shoes.

On the train, three guys would sleep sitting, two guys on the floor, and then the next night we would switch off. It was very uncomfortable. You didn't get much sleep. It's very demeaning. You're a prisoner of war. You've got two guys with guns at each end of the car glaring at you. You can't describe it unless you're there. And you never think about this when you're home until suddenly, Bingo! You think of what happened. And the hard part is worrying about what happened to the other fellows. We didn't know what happened to Virgil Chima, the co-pilot, or Omick, or the enlisted men at that point other than Joe Gilfoil. We knew he was hit; they announced that when they threw him out of the plane, hoping his parachute would open and he would be treated on the ground. And we were misinformed by someone that he was okay. One of the enlisted men came up to us right after we were captured and said they managed to get a doctor which they didn't. George Collar ended up picking up his body.

On our way from Oberrussel up to Stalag Luft 1, we were scared to death because of the bombings and things that were taking place, and then some guy came along and said, "Hey, we're safe, you don't have to worry, they're not gonna strafe us. It's all marked on top of each car, POW."

And some wise guy said, "Yeah, but suppose they come in from the other side?" And everybody just howled.

One night, we pulled over from the main railroad to a little siding, and it's probably 10 or 11 at night. Jackson and myself couldn't sleep. We were up shooting the breeze and all of a sudden we heard THUD! You could just feel the stuff hit the ground. I think we had been dozing, and that woke us up. And we wanted to know what was going on. We went and looked out the window, and we could see in the distance searchlights, explosions, you could feel them. The RAF was raiding this town. And the town was Berlin. We were on our way to Barth, which was 100 miles north of Berlin, and we're probably right now 25 or 50 miles south of Berlin. And we're sitting there watching them bomb Berlin. And we see explosions, we know an RAF plane's been hit, and these big blockbusters kept hitting, and all of a sudden the German guard comes up to Jackson and me and says something, and Jackson says, "He said something about an apple for some cigarettes."

I said, "An apple? Wow! Let's do it!"

We had cigarettes; they gave us five packs of cigarettes on that Red Cross parcel. We gave this German guard three or four American cigarettes, and the guard gave us each an apple. Holy mackerel! Next thing we know he comes back again and Jackson says, "He said he can get us some beer."

About 100 yards from the train were a couple of very dim lights, and I presume it was a gasthaus, because the German guard pointed to it. We gave him the cigarettes, and he came back with a German canteen full of beer. A German canteen was about twice the size of an American canteen. It must have been a liter. And we're sitting there chewing apples, drinking German beer, and watching them bomb Berlin.

I had to remind Jackson about that the last time I saw him. He completely forgot about it.

A day and a half later we ended up in our camp. When we got to Barth they dropped us off at the station and we started marching. It was in the evening. We had these guards with these monstrous German shepherds and Doberman pinschers. They were big and they were mean. Three or four hundred of us marched about three and a half miles, and some of us were in bad shape.

I had received a little medical attention at Oberrussel; I got to see a German doctor there in this hospital. There were a lot of German men there who were going into the service, and I felt sorry for those guys because they were in their fifties and they were being taken in the service. Some of them were in worse shape than I am now. When I got into this room, this German doctor took one look at my back, and he said, "Not much we can do," and then he just bandaged my feet. He said, "Your back is pretty bad. Do you want to see what it looks like?"

I said, "What do you mean?"

He said, "Take a look." And he had two mirrors there. That's the closest I came to fainting up to that point. My back was just the color of tar, all the way across the lower back, where I had been injured. The doctor had his aides give me a heat treatment which made me feel a lot better. I thanked him very much. At that same time, I remember them saying an American nurse was in the hospital there. She wasn't actually injured but she was taken there with some of the injured; she was flying in a plane that was shot down outside of Aachen. It was a hospital plane carrying troops out, and she was captured as a POW. About three years ago there was an article in the paper about this nurse up in Sacramento who had just passed away, and it was her. The only Army nurse that was ever captured over there. And I thought, "My God, here I am 40 miles away!" I never saw her over there but just the thought of all that was going on, what very brave young ladies they were.

Now I get to Stalag Luft 1. We were there for eight or nine months and it was hell. You're feeling just rotten, and when you're injured you feel worse. And your mental condition isn't the greatest. The winter was miserable. The food was poor. We lost a lot of weight. I lost 30 or 35 pounds. All of us were pretty skinny. And one thing about it: When you're hungry you don't think about anything else. It's always food, food, food. You dream day and night of food. And escape was not advisable. They said, "You know, it's not a game anymore, you're going to get shot if you get caught." And at one point, Hitler issued orders to take the American Jewish boys and separate them, and there actually was an order out to shoot them. Common sense at least prevailed and they realized that if anything like that took place there would be an interaction in the United States and we were holding a lot more of their prisoners than they were of ours. That's the general thought, anyway.

We had this one Jewish guy, his name was Gerber, and he was very swarthy, almost Arabic looking. He said, "They're not gonna get me, because I just changed my religion."

And we said, "What did you change to?"

He said, "I'm gonna say Hindu."

Everybody just howled. But they got him; they put him in the other barracks.

Our commanding officer in Barth was a Colonel Von Mueller. He had come from the States, from Long Beach, Long Island. He was what was called a Long Beach Nazi.

Colonel Von Mueller interviewed me when I first went into the camp. When I walked in there he said, "Ahh, Frank Bertram. You're married. Your wife's name is Mary. And you went to Commerce High School in San Francisco, graduated in 1938."

He's telling me this and I'm sitting there thinking, "What is this?" They knew all about me, as they did most everybody else. And he said, "You have no children."

I said, "We didn't have time."

He said, "Aahh, that's the trouble. In America, not enough children. In Russia, too many children. But in Germany just right."

Then he said, "You know, I could have you shot as a spy."

I said, "What?"

He said, "You write down your name as Bertram. But the dogtags you gave me said Burtram."

I said, "What?"

He said, "Take a look."

And sure enough, they had misspelled my name on my dogtags and I never knew it.

Then he said, "Of course, we wouldn't do that. We know who you are."


I knew nothing about the Second Air Division Association until about 20 years after the war, when a friend of mine who lived right around the corner from me in Stockton told me he belonged to it. I thought, "That sounds interesting." So I joined this organization and they're sending letters and newsletters; you'd come across names you knew, or people looking for information about someone you knew. But every once in a while I'd think, "Gee, what happened to me? I'd like to go back there and find the area where I was shot down." My wife, Mary, and I took several trips to Germany, but I could never find the location – and me, a good navigator, I didn't know where the hell I was. I knew the approximate area but I couldn't pin it down. We came within maybe 10 or 15 miles of the town; we probably passed through the edge of Bad Hersfeld, and we were in the town of Schlitz, where the original Schlitz Brewery was.

As I went through life, I kept in contact with a few of the fellows who were on my plane, but never anything personal. Until one time, in February of 1986, I come home from work and my wife doesn't say hello, she doesn't give me a kiss, and she says, "What was the number of your plane?"

I looked at her – now this is 40 years later – and I said, "What plane? I drove home."

She said, "No, the plane you flew in the war."

I said, "You want to know the number? All I remember is it was a B-24. I don't know what the number was."

She said, "Wait till you see this package."

Well, this packet was from Walter Hassenpflug. It had letters from the 8th Air Force Historical Society and from the 11th Armored Cavalry Regiment, which was in the town of Bad Hersfeld. And it said that Walter was researching what happened on this particular day over the town of Bad Hersfeld.

Walter's letter stated that as a boy of 12, he witnessed an airplane explosion in the air, and then he witnessed some parachutes coming down, and he said two days later they were walking through the forest and they came across this man lying by a creek. And I thought, "My God, that's me!"

His letter stated, "All I remember is that he was a first lieutenant from San Francisco."

Well, when you give your name, rank and serial number, how they ever found out about San Francisco, all I can think of is I had a little prayer book in my pocket that my mother gave me, and it had my address, 118 Delores Street, S.F., California.

I immediately wrote to Walter. Then we got to writing back and forth, and I told him I'd be there in April or May, but due to an injury – I fell through a trap door and pulled some ligaments or tendons in my leg, and had to put a cast on, so that postponed it till August. We met Walter, and much to my surprise he did not speak a word of English, other than "Hello." But he had a fellow named Carl Lepper who interpreted for him.

The Kassel mission has been sort of a mystery. When we came out of prison camp we got interviewed by Colonel Stewart – Jimmy Stewart – Brigadier General Terrill, who was the commanding officer when I was there, and Colonel Jones. And whatever you told them, they just let it go in one ear, wrote it down, and out the other, and they just passed on through the line. There were something like 22 of us in the line. The doctor would say, "How do you feel?" And you'd say "Fine." He'd say "Okay, pass." And that was it. They were just as anxious to get home as we were.

Something on this mission was screwy. If you talk to 20 guys you're going to get 20 different stories. The group in back of us, the 453rd, was supposed to follow us. They very wisely went to the target after their commanding officer called our commanding officer to tell him he was going the wrong way. And our man told their man to follow us, that we were on the right course, and I understand really cussed him out when he wouldn't do it. The 453rd did the right thing by going to the target. You couldn't see the target on the ground but you could see the group ahead of you going in, and you could see all the flak and the explosions.

I have maintained all through the years, mouthed off about it a few times – other people have said no, but I have people other than me that agree with me – that there was a deliberate turnoff to avoid going through that heavy flak. This is my personal opinion and that of several others that I know of. Too many things just don't add up on that mission. The one lead plane, of course, blew up, and the pilot was killed. The command pilot, Major McKoy, was killed. The lead navigator on that plane did get out before the explosion. He ended up in Stalag Luft 1 months after we did; whether he was injured or held prisoner somewhere I don't know. But I went up to talk to him about it and he insisted that they went in to the target. And I just don't understand it, because it was so obvious. But he insisted we hit the target. So I just gave up. The navigator was killed in an automobile crash shortly after he arrived home. So the one guy that really knew is dead.

The Luftwaffe were not aiming for us as a target. They were headed for the main body, the other three hundred and some planes that were going into Kassel, and they were a little late, as far as hitting them before the bombs dropped. These particular FW-190s were not made to do battle with the American fighters. They were heavily armored, and the pilots were heavily protected but did not have the maneuverability or speed of the regular FW-190. They were there for one purpose and that was to shoot down bombers. And they were ordered that when they came under attack by American fighters to get the hell out of there, no combat, just go. Which discouraged Ernst Schroeder, who I befriended and I still consider a good friend, if he's still alive. He said when he shot his second plane down, "In all honesty, Frank, I'll get the credit, but the damage had already been done" on the wave of planes that went in ahead of him and set these planes on fire. He said, "I put the finishing touches on them."

And he said, "I followed these planes down, and watched to see where they crashed, for confirmation." He said he was flying over some railroad tracks when he heard thump-thump-thump and he looked behind and there's a P-51 Mustang right on his tail. He said, "I turned around and came around at him, but I had no ammunition left and I just got the hell out of there."

Some of these German boys that were in those planes that day that were killed were on their first or second mission. Others were oldtimers. And I personally met them: Schroeder, Ossi Rahm, Werner Vorburg, who actually flew in World War I. Werner Vorburg is gone. Ossie Rahm is gone. And the last I heard of Ernst two years ago he was quite ill.

At its best, flying combat was nerve-racking. Even in training it was nerve-racking. We'd sweat out every takeoff and every landing and in between we'd pray. Without the fighter escort, we didn't have a chance. When I think of those poor boys on that Ploesti mission, because 160-some planes went in there and they lost 60 or 62. One of the boys in my room in the first place I stayed at Stalag Luft 1 was on the Ploesti mission. He was a bombardier in Killer Kane's crew. Which group was that? I think the 93$^{rd}$. He crash-landed in Turkey and they escaped from Turkey, and then he got shot down a second time and captured.

Now that must have been scary, flying 50 feet above the ground going into a monumental flak area. Ploesti probably was one of the most heavily defended targets in all of Europe, because of the value of the oil fields there and the refineries. If you got hit there, you're dead, there's nothing you could do. At least when we're up there at 25,000 feet you could jump out or get blown out, but I've seen pictures of these guys at Ploesti, they didn't have the chance of a snowball in hell once they got hit.

You know, that generation – of course I was involved – really did save the world, because Hitler, that German army was something else. They came so close, so very close. If we hadn't gone in there with all this bombing, we'd all be speaking German. They actually had rockets that could hit the United States, but they never used them because of lack of petrol. They almost took the British to their knees with those V-2s, after what those poor people in Britain went through in the blitz and then the V-1, which was going on when I was there. They were terrifying enough but these V-2s, there was no answer to them. You didn't know you were dead until 30 seconds after you died.

We wouldn't have that memorial if Walter Hassenpflug hadn't found me. I tried to tell him in English – and he didn't understand me – that he owes me a lot of money because since he found me, it's cost me all this money going back and forth to Germany. And Walter being real German doesn't have a great sense of humor; it takes him a little while to catch on. The second year we went there, I had brought my pilot, Reg Miner, and his wife, and with Walter we were going to go around to all the sites where these planes crashed and Walter couldn't show us because he had his hand all wrapped up in a cast.

I said, "What happened?"

He said he was out hunting and shot himself in the hand and severed some nerves.

I said, "You know, Walter" – he had an interpreter – "that's why you guys lost the war. You couldn't shoot straight." And for about 30 seconds he just looked at me and then he burst out laughing.

I talked myself into attending a Luftwaffe reunion with Ernst Schroeder. I got invited to this reunion of the Wild Boar Squadron, which was one of the ones that attacked us that day. I was the only one there that wasn't a fighter pilot. My wife and I went there. We had a great time. The only thing bad there was every one of them smoked up a storm up and almost choked us to death. But they were nice people. The wives were so nice and so pleasant, and very few of them could speak English, so the communication problem was there, too. There was no chance of getting too friendly because of the lack of communication.

When they started their meeting, they had as a gavel at the podium the joystick of an FW-190. They had it all fancied up there with the trigger guard like they used in combat. Of course I didn't know what they were talking about, and Ernst would tell me once in a while what they said. He was in charge. And I asked, "Could I see that FW-190 joystick?"

"Sure." He gave it to me, and all these guys were looking at me. And I turned it over, and I said, "Oh, made in Japan!"

You could have heard a pin drop. It took another thirty seconds before they realized it was a joke. "Nein! Nein! Deutschland! Deutschland!" We had a big laugh on that.

I've always been a joker. It's kept me alive, even through prison camp. I won't tell you what they called me in camp but it was like megaphone mouth or something. But you had to do that or you'd go crazy.

Throughout the years I've kept in close contact with my pilot, Reg Miner. He's probably one of the best pilots the Air Force ever had. Man, he could handle that bomber like it was a kite. And he was over there for one reason: that was to win the damn war and get home.

I don't want you to think that I'm pissed off at these dead guys who were in that lead ship. I had a fellow who thought we should court-martial those people. I said, "Hey, they died that day. How are you gonna court-martial them?"

"Well, posthumously."

I said, "Aw, come on. That will do no good." It's just the idea; you'd like to find out if someone really knew why this happened. It's too late to do anything about it; once it's done it's done. We could have gone in to the target and gotten killed there just as easily, although there wouldn't have been that heavy a loss.

On a previous mission to the Kassel mission – six missions before – we had flown one that was scarier than the Kassel mission, but with not quite the same results. We were shot up very badly over the city of Saarbrucken in Germany; that's just on the border with France. Our plane took a thumping that you wouldn't believe from flak; we must have taken five or six damn near direct hits. You could see the red interior of the shell. Our radio operator, J.G. Weddle, had a piece of his foot blown off.

We lost one engine over the target, and another one was windmilling. We couldn't feather it, and we dropped like a wounded bird. The group had us going down in France. They had us down in the English Channel. They had us down in England. They gave up on us. We were badly wounded and we were all by ourself, and we fired off some flares, and within thirty seconds we had an escort of P-51s. They would circle us and talk to us, and no German plane would go near us. We went all the way across the Channel. We ended up throwing stuff out of the plane into the Channel; we even threw our parachutes out to lighten the plane because we were down too low to jump. We threw everything out except the bombardier, he was next. And for one reason or another, we didn't make it, and we crashed. The pilot again did an inspirational job; how he did it I'll never know. But we crashed and it was quite an experience; we bounced around, very traumatic. The next day I was so stiff and sore I could hardly move.

On that particular mission, George Collar had been taken off our plane, and we had this guy Omick as our bombardier. And in the nose turret we had a first lieutenant, Richard Aylers, and he'd only flown on two missions. Now let me explain what happens; sometimes men get sick and they can't fly a mission, or the train was late coming from London or they slept in with some babe overnight and forgot to get up or some excuse, and most of them were tolerated, but they may miss a mission or two; whereas the rest of their comrades finished or got shot down or something, and there they sit. That's what happened to this guy. He had two missions to go, and actually he outranked all of us. He was a first lieutenant. We were still second lieutenants, although our promotion was in but we didn't know it.

He was in the nose turret. And the pilot said to me, "Give me a heading for the closest airport, quick!" I looked out right in front of us and there was a runway, and I said, "Straight ahead!"

He said, "Clear the nose and get out of there!"

I opened the nose turret door and tapped that guy on the shoulder and tried to pull him out. He got mad at me; he didn't hear the conversation. He was gonna take a swing at me because I jolted him. I got him out and got him in back, and I didn't quite make the bomb bay when we hit the ground. I was still in the bomb bay and got thrown out of the bomb bay into the waist. I kept bouncing around like a rubber ball; all the other guys were braced for a crash-landing. And Miner brought us to a safe, healthy conclusion.

Years later, the third navigator we picked up – the pilot's navigator, Jackson – claimed that he was on that mission with us. And I sure couldn't place him, because he was a pilot's navigator, and that's what this Lieutenant Aylers was. But Jackson insisted he was on the mission. He sure knew enough about it, because it was quite a thrill that day. So I found out where you could write to get some records. I wrote to the U.S. Air Force archives and asked if it was possible that on Lieutenant Miner's crew, flying a certain date which was Aug. 15th, I think, that you could get the crew members. Lo and behold, about three weeks later here it comes with the date, all the crew members – and this is the funny part: They did not have Jackson in there. So I knew I wasn't losing my mind. Aylers was flying that day, and Jackson wasn't there at all. But they did not have our tail gunner listed, and now they had me wondering if our tail gunner flew that day or maybe Jackson flew in the tail.

I thought, God, these guys are sharp after all these years, that they would have these records, so I wrote them back and asked for the disposition on the Kassel Mission of Sept. 27, 1944, and I never heard a word. Not a word. And someone else, I believe it was Lieutenant Ira Weinstein, had once before tried to find out, and I did too, and they stated that the files have been missing since 1950. Someone took them out. They don't know who, but there's not a thing regarding that mission back in their archives. So there's another reason that this thing should be down in some history book somewhere. Plus it was really a bad day, the worst day our group ever had. Every day was a bad day for some groups, but not like this one. It's funny how the mind works. I know in my case a lot of these things I don't even think about but once I get into it, it just keeps coming back and you're living it over and over.

I'm paying for it now. The knees in particular gave me a bad time for years, and the back, the last three years, it's just been getting worse every day, and all they can find is fused vertebrae at the base. But for many other guys it happened a lot worse. It was a good 40 years before I learned what happened to our co-pilot, Virgil Chima, and he was my best friend at the time. His body was not found until November 15th. Walter Hassenpflug dug this up, and what he found was that some women were looking for beech nuts up in the forest and ran across him, so he must have been laying there for six weeks, and yet, the mystery is, his parachute was missing. The shroud lines were cut. He was laying in the fetal position. But his body had decomposed so much by the time they got to him, I don't imagine that they ever figured out just what happened to him. But obviously, someone got the parachute, which was silk and was very valuable over there at the time. All you can do is surmise. I know what it was like coming through those trees. He could have made a worse landing than me and maybe broke his back and couldn't move and just died there. It's very doubtful that someone had beaten him because it was so far up in the hills where nobody would go for any reason, and no one had gone up there prior to these ladies going hunting for beech nuts for food. So I'm inclined to think he badly injured himself, although why would he be in the fetal position? Of course he could have just drawn into that, knowing he was dying, trying to keep warm. Poor little guy. Nineteen years old. And the most meticulous guy on the crew; man, he checked everything to make sure his parachute and harness and instruments were perfect. He had two brothers. One of them was a major in the 91st, which was the one with the Triangle A, the group that was in "12 O'Clock High." And then he had another brother who was a bombardier with the Third Group over there. There were four boys and three of them were in the Air Force and Virgil was the only one who didn't make it. And his mother never did get over it. He was the baby of the family. The same thing happened with our radio operator, Joe Gilfoil, who lost his leg and bled to death. He was the only child of an Irish family right outside of Boston. I guess his mother and father were at that time in their late forties or early fifties when he got shot down. Joe was 19. Joe and I had gone to communion that morning, as we did before each mission.

He was a good Catholic boy. I was a Catholic boy. And we had one other man in our crew, Alvis Kitchens – Cotton was his nickname – a very quiet kid, never said boo. Did his job. He'd go with the guys but he never smoked, he never drank, he was very religious. Very soft-spoken, just a good Christian lad, and do you know, 54 years later, he's still the same. All these other guys, including me, would go out and just raise all kinds of ruckus, drink and chase women, do all kinds of crazy things. Not him. Never.

When I went over and met Walter Hassenpflug in 1986, he introduced me to Ernst Schroeder. The guy shot down two of our planes that day, and I don't know how many he shot down during the war. He was the father of seven boys. He didn't speak a word of English, but he's very well-known in German circles as an expert on military fighters at that time. He was an expert on the FW-190 and the Messerschmitts. He had nothing but the greatest admiration for the Mustang. He said if it wasn't for the Mustang we'd still be fighting over there. He said that airplane changed the war; after they developed the drop tanks and they could protect the bombers going in. That changed the complete air battle situation. Actually the

German production of aircraft was greater in September 1944 than at any point up to that time. The big problem was the lack of manpower and the shortage of petrol. But as far as planes, they had them. And they were good. The Germans were very, very brave people. And what I noticed, they just could not believe how friendly I was, and others were towards them. They acted like we should hate them because of what happened 40 years ago, which I didn't even think about. I mean, you were just people; they just did their job and we did our job.

Walter Hassenpflug is one in a million; the hard work he's put in and what he's done. Not just this particular mission but primarily this one and other air battles that took place near his hometown, because he was orphaned by some bombs that dropped on his parents' home, and raised by his aunts.

The first time we were over there, I thought, Jeez, Walter has been investigating this for maybe five or six years now, which would take you back to about 1980, and I thought, why, after all these years, is he all of a sudden looking into this particular mission? This is a personal opinion – and I saw it over there when the newspaper came out on the anniversary of this particular air raid – this had nothing to do with our mission, but I think it's the one that took place in November 1944 in which his folks were killed, I think that is what set him off on this quest. And when you think of what it took to go back 35 or 40 years and to go to where all these planes had crashed, get all the information on those that survived, those that didn't. Walter did all this on every plane that went down. He could tell you exactly where it landed, who got out, who didn't get out, and generally what happened to them. Carl Lepper, his interpreter, told me he'd go back dozens of times, the least bit of a lead he had of anything, he would go there and photograph and talk to people, look it up, and go through records, and he did this for eight or ten years.

I can't think of anything else. I probably got a few things mixed up. You'll have to dig deep on this one. I don't know how long you were over there when you met Walter, but didn't you find that a nice little area? I thought it was great. I really enjoyed Bad Hersfeld, the little park they had there, and that old church, that old ruin there. I just found that area fascinating. The only thing bad about Germany was the driving. Probably if I was younger I wouldn't mind a bit, but boy, now it's scary.

*"In this building ... I met a forward observer from the artillery or the Air Corps – I don't know which – but he had a radio on and a whip antenna and he was directing artillery fire, or he was talking to aircraft because they were strafing with P-47s in the next block over. I was standing right next to him. He had to be from New York; he had a heavy accent, and he had big dark Coke-bottle glasses on. He hadn't shaved, the stubble was just black on his face, and whoever was calling to him on the radio was asking, 'Whose fire is that? Is that enemy or is that friendly?'*

*"And he said, 'Sir, I believe it's half and half.' "*

**Vern
Schmidt**
**Pfc.**
**Company E**
**358th Regiment**
**90th Infantry**
**Division**
**Interviewed**
**Sept. 2, 1995**
**San Antonio, Texas**

I was in a rifle squad. We had a B.A.R. man, we had a bazooka man, and then an assistant who carried three rounds for the bazooka. I did that for a time. But other than that, there were just the 12 of us. We had our own little war going on. You didn't know what was happening except you just followed orders, and we followed our sergeant.

I can't even remember my sergeant's name anymore. The first one I reported to became a second lieutenant; he received a battlefield commission. That was

Sergeant Mueller. I met him in the pillbox at Habscheid, and for several days I never met anyone of higher rank than he was. They were very under strength at the time. I came in as a replacement after the Battle of the Bulge.

We crossed the Moselle River in March. We had very little resistance crossing. We got to the other side in the area of Hatzenport. The hills rise almost immediately pretty high, and we went up into the woods. It was late afternoon, we were beginning to dig in, and we were fired upon sporadically. Then, as we got ready to dig in for the evening, it got pretty ferocious. We learned later that these Germans were part of the 6th SS Mountain Division, and they were a tough bunch.

I recall the night because it was miserable. The company jeep that carried our blanket roll never showed up. The bedroll consisted of a blanket for each of us, and we normally buddied up so that we would share two blankets between two guys.

We began digging holes. The digging was tough. There were rocks and roots from the trees. I got a hole probably 16 or 18 inches deep and I could see water already trying to find its place in the hole, to find the lowest spot. I'd dig that out and it would start filling up, so I built kind of a bench in there so I could sit on dry ground and then have my feet down in this hole, and as I kept digging a little deeper, the water seemed to come a little faster. I took my helmet off and every so often I just bailed this water out of there, to keep my feet halfway dry. It was miserable that night. It got cold, and my foxhole was getting soaked.

It got real quiet, and we had to form a night-time perimeter. We used a code for identifying one another. We'd use a movie star's name. We'd use the word "Gable," and the other one reported "Clark."

I finally crawled out of that hole and crawled under a big bush, probably five feet tall. I thought I'll crawl under there and at least I won't get soaked. I didn't have a blanket but I did have a raincoat and I pulled it up and made like a little tent in that bush. I lay under there most of the night, and what time it was I don't know – time went awful slow at night – the Germans came and began walking through our lines. I was barely 19 years old, pretty naive, really; I didn't know what to do. We knew they didn't answer to our code, but they walked in and amongst us during part of the night, and I think they probably were just as scared as we were. They didn't know how large a group we had. But we made it through the night. It was cold; we didn't have anything to eat. Nobody caught up with us with rations.

The next day we spread out into the forest, and I spotted a German soldier in the woods. I hollered at him and he started running. I challenged him to halt and he kept on running. I fired a number of times with my M-1. I don't know if I hit him or not.

A couple of days after that we were near Bingen, which is mentioned in many of the history books of the 90th Division. We were still in the woods. It seemed like we just fought in the woods all the time, which is real tough. There were deer there that would come crashing through, and you'd swing your M-1 around and get ready to fire; you didn't know what it was. One day we were in kind of a sitting, relaxed position. I had my M-1 pointed upwards, I had my hand holding the wooden stock, and this deer came leaping through and he knocked the M-1 right out of my hand; his hoof hit the stock and broke part of the wooden stock.

Just before we reached the Rhine, we were held up for an hour or two in the woods overlooking the Rhine. Then we moved out, and we went down into the town of Treftinghausen, which is near Bingen, right on the water. We had a guide there. He assured us that there were no Germans in town. But as we got downtown, there was a railroad track there and we could see across the Rhine. There was another railroad track on the east bank, and we could see Germans over there, and they could see us.

We flushed out the town; we didn't find any soldiers. They had all gone across as this guy had told us, and we occupied the town and stayed overnight. I remember sleeping between white sheets with dirty old muddy shoes, but it was kind of a neat thing to lay down in some white sheets. Still, we didn't dare take our shoes off. If you were attacked and were in a state of undress, you were in bad trouble. From January until March the 12th I never had my shoes off. I never had a shower. Never had a bath.

In 1964, I went back for the first time to visit. I took my wife along, and we went back into this little town of Treftinghausen. We were walking along, and I was trying to point out that somewhere along here is where we slept overnight. And here was a guy and his wife just leaning out the window. It was a sunny day in July, and they were standing at the window, with the veranda open, and I said in kind of halfway German, "Good day. How are you?"

And he spoke back in English.

I said, "Oh, you speak English?"

"A little bit." Then he said, "Who are you?"

I said, "We're Americans. We're touring here."

We started talking, and I said, "I was in this town as an American soldier back in 1945."

He said, "Is that right?"

And I said, "We came into this town about the 16th or 17th of March."

"No, you're wrong," he said. "The Americans didn't come here until April."

I said, "No. We were here about the 16th of March."

And he started arguing with me, kind of in a friendly way. Then he went and got his wife in the back room. He asked her in German, "Frau," he said, "when did the Americans come in this town?"

She said, "Between the 15th and 17th of March."

Well, he shut up. He knew he had made a mistake, and those people, they hate to be wrong. But we got acquainted that way, and he said, "Would you like to join me? We'll go down to the pub and have a drink together." So we went down there and sat around the table.

The first shower that I got was on March the 12th. And I didn't get a bath until the third week in April.

That one on March the 12th was just about a 10-minute shower in cold water. We were on a hillside and they said we're all going to get showers and clean clothes, and I said, "Man, that sounds fantastic!" They took our platoon, just us 12 men. We entered this tent; it was on the side of a hill. We walked in and they said, "Take your clothes off." Well, from March the 12th back to January I had never had my clothes off, and the food we ate – we had mostly K rations but once in a while you would butcher something along the way that probably loosened up the bowels – I had had a good case of GIs for quite some time. I thought, "Uh-oh, I'm going to be embarrassed here." I'd found a German knife, it had one blade in it; if you opened it up it looked almost like a butcher knife, it was big and long. I opened it up, and I started to take my underwear off, and it wouldn't come off, due to the GIs. So I had to use that knife and literally cut my underwear off my body.

Then we got clean underwear, and that was all. We still had our other stuff. And I got clean socks.

Then, about the middle or latter part of April, we were held up in a town overnight, and I had acquired lice by that time from sleeping in hay. We'd slept in so many places where the Germans had just left – in barns and in foxholes that had straw in them – that we acquired body lice. They don't bother you until you get real quiet and warm, and because we wore long woolen underwear, it had a lot of thick seams on it. You'd lay there real still and try to be warm and you'd feel one start over here, and it would go clear across that seam of your underwear, clear across the back and over to the other side, and pretty soon one would start around the bottom part of your underwear and he'd go around your belly or around your back.

A number of us were pretty lousy at that time. So we were held up in this town just long enough to get some fresh food, and one of the guys came and said, "Hey, we're gonna have a delousing deal here." We went down to a barn, and it was at nighttime. They closed the doors and put a candle there and lit it; no electricity. There were two tubs of water, and there was a sergeant, there was a corporal, and I was a Pfc. So you know who got in the water first. The sergeant got in that water. He washed his body with soap and then he stepped in the next tub and rinsed off, and meanwhile, his clothes went into a big garment bag and they stuck a bomb in there that was supposed to delouse your clothes.

Then the corporal took all his clothes off and stuck them in another sack and he put the bomb in there, and I was still waiting. The corporal crawled in that same tub of water and he washed off. Then he stepped into the next tub and rinsed off. And I thought – at home, when we were raised, on Saturday night you took a bath in a big tub in the kitchen. We didn't have running water at that time. I thought, "Holy smokes, they don't change the water here! My mom used to do that; she'd change the water for you."

I got up there and the guy says, "Take your clothes off, Schmidt." So I undressed. I hesitated … I was the third guy to crawl in that tub. The water wasn't even hot anymore. I washed off, and I kept thinking, there's two guys been here scrubbing themselves in there and I'm getting that same water.

I got in the other tub and rinsed off. That was kind of humiliating, but when you're 19 I guess you don't care too much, or you didn't have time to think.

Half an hour later they said, "Your clothes are okay now." We got nothing clean at that time. We put that same underwear right back on, the same socks, but supposedly our clothes were deloused.

I had been given a care package and it had a wool scarf; we'd wrap it around our neck at night time, or pull it over that little cap that we wore, and we'd wrap the scarf around our ears to kind of keep your ears warm. The guy there told me to throw the scarf away, and I said, "No. That's kept me warm."

He said, "There's a lot of lice in there, but I think we got 'em killed now."

So I kept the scarf.

It wasn't long before I had lice again.

Prior to crossing the Rhine, the first large town we attacked was Mainz. We approached it by the suburbs, and slowly came into town. We were in an apple orchard, and coming off of a farm. The ground was sandy, which made it nice that we didn't have to dig. But we were coming in this apple orchard and we could see that we were approaching a village because there were houses here and there. And we barely got in this orchard – of course artillery shells were going over back and forth, both ours and theirs – and all of a sudden we got opened up on with machine gun and small arms fire, and we all hit the dirt. I never was so happy to find a furrow that you could actually lay in. Then we stood again because we knew we had to take that perimeter of homes. And before we got up into a marching fire, an SS trooper came out of one of the houses and he came running toward us, and one of our guys fired on him. I don't know whether he was hit but he lost his balance and fell, and he lost his machine pistol. And one of the guys to my right – it could have been my sergeant – said, "Shoot the bastard!"

There were four or five guys who were closer to him than I was, and the sergeant kept yelling, "Shoot that guy! Shoot that guy!" And that SS guy stood up and cursed us, "Amerikanisch swine!" And to just prove how difficult it is to shoot someone in cold blood when you see their eyes – it takes a lot of guts. I told you about shooting at this guy in the woods, I didn't see him other than his body. But this guy we were close enough you could see his eyes. And finally one guy just went and took him prisoner, and he cursed us again. I couldn't believe a guy could be so close to death and still be defiant and curse you like that. But there were several SS, and they were keeping the fire coming to us from the regular German GIs on the edge of town. My sergeant was to the left of me in this furrow, and he took a sniper shot – he was laying prone in this furrow and the bullet entered his left shoulder and came out through the right cheek of his buttock.

We went into a series of little buildings; they looked like chicken coops, and the roar of the artillery barrage was getting so loud – ours you could hear whistling over, and theirs were arcing and landing behind us – and we kept moving forward hoping we'd get out of their fire. In this building which I called the chicken coop I met a forward observer from the artillery or the Air Corps – I don't know which – but he had a radio on and a whip antenna and he was directing artillery fire, or he was talking to aircraft because they were strafing with P-47s in the next block over. I was standing right next to him. He had to be from New York; he had a heavy accent, and he had big dark Coke-bottle glasses on. He hadn't shaved, the stubble was just black on his face, and whoever was calling to him on the radio was asking, "Whose fire is that? Is that enemy or is that friendly?"

And he said, "Sir, I believe it's half and half."

We got out of there and we went into marching fire, just leveling our M-1 about hip-height and firing to more or less harass them to keep them down. We got into the first row of houses, and my B.A.R. guy – a big, tall guy – was right alongside me and we started flushing out this house. We didn't see anything on the first floor, so we went upstairs. And as we came up to the second floor and went to the first window and looked out, right across – probably no more than 20 feet away – was another house, and in the second-story window right across from us were two big Germans looking right at us. The first thing we saw them do was duck, and I figured they probably thought, "These guys don't know we're here." So they went downstairs apparently and came around and came out through a cellar and were going to crawl into the cellar of our house. And this B.A.R. guy and I, we leaned out the window, and he said, "Watch me, Smitty." And he laid that B.A.R. right out the window there and he got both of them. They never made it to our building, but I swear, had he not gotten them they'd have come in there and gotten us. You hate to say you were out killing anybody but one thing we were taught at our Infantry Replacement Training Center was you either kill or you be killed.

The guys that trained us, at Camp Roberts, Illinois, were Rangers and guys that had come home from Normandy. They said, "Do you want to come home in a box? If you do, then don't pay any attention to what we're telling you." This B.A.R. man knew exactly what to do. These guys came out of there and he just pointed that B.A.R. down, and twenty rounds come out of there in about three seconds.

It took us all day to take that city of Mainz, and by dusk – there were three of us – we were going down one street and we flushed out 54 Germans. They became our POWs. They were all just plain GIs; there were no SS. We talked to them. They said, "The SS kept us up here until they knew they could get out, and then they left."

We had one guy, back in the Siegfried Line, he didn't believe in prisoners. He wore a tanker's cap. We called him Red because he had a very pronounced red mustache, and he was always chewing tobacco; you'd see it drip out the side of his mouth. He was an unkempt looking guy, especially when that beard would grow; he had a red beard and when that tobacco juice went down he had two long brown lines. They'd get a prisoner and he'd say, "Give him to me." And he'd march him off. You'd hear him yell at the prisoner. Then you'd hear a couple of rounds go off and he'd come back and say, "I got rid of him." That was contrary to the Geneva Convention, but a few of those guys had brothers or maybe an uncle or a close relative that had been killed either in the time of the Bulge or in Normandy, in a brutal way. The 773rd Tank Destroyer Battalion that was with us, one of the tank commanders had lost a brother in Italy, and he'd lost a sister in the nurse corps, and he didn't have any time for the Germans. He said, "You shoot first and ask your questions later." If we were ever attacked coming into a town, he'd just bring one of those tank destroyers up there, and he'd sit right up on the turret with that .50 and blast away and just take a house at a time and put a shell in it. And he said, "I'm getting revenge for my brother and my sister." That might not have been right, but he might have saved a lot of lives, too. You know, war is hell, and who's to say? My brother was a POW of the Germans. He came out 98 pounds, a big 6-foot-1 guy like myself; he didn't get skinny eating steak every day. And he helped bury a lot of guys in his POW camp.

He was captured in Hatten, which is a little town near Strasbourg. He was with the 42nd Rainbow Division. There's a French lady in the town of Hatten, she was just a young girl, she has written a book about this fight, and it is outstanding. My brother has met her. They brought her to the States and she spoke at one of their reunions. Of course the 45th has written several articles on that winter, there's an author named Bucher. He tells more of the capture of Dachau. The 42nd and the 45th and the 442nd Japanese, that regimental combat team, all three of those outfits apparently participated in the liberation of Dachau. However, the 45th claims that they were the first ones. In '93 we were there; there's a bronze plaque on the wall mentioning the 42nd.

Dachau was large enough, I'm sure, that it had several gates, and was probably approached from several angles. This guy that writes the story about the 45th Thunderbird Division tells it from his point of view and pretty well says that he was under orders from Eisenhower to specifically take Dachau. Now the 442nd, which was a Japanese regimental combat team – the ones in "Go for Broke," I went to one of their original meetings in Fresno where they're so predominant, that's where many of them live today – they say they shot the lock off the gate. So all three are actually claiming in various books that they liberated Dachau. And it's conceivable that all three of them could be right. This guy that writes the one about the 45th says the people were ordered to allow no one inside except their people. And my brother remembers the commanding general from the 42nd, his name was General Linden, he came up in his jeep, and this corporal of the 45th said, "Sir, you can't go in."

And he said, "What do you mean?"

He says, "I have orders to allow no one to go inside other than who's inside now."

General Linden reached to his holster and said, "By God, you're gonna let me in."

And this corporal lifted his M-1 and said, "You ain't going in or you're going in dead."

And General Linden I guess asked his name; he said, "I'll have you court-martialed."

Anyway, they were politicians, but I think they got together later and kind of squared the thing away. But it's pretty vivid reading in that 45th book telling about this incident. So I passed it on to my brother. I said, "I thought you guys went in there and he says you didn't." But yet there's a plaque there stating that they participated in the initial deal.

We liberated Flossenburg, the leading elements of my division. A reconnaissance unit actually liberated my brother on Easter Sunday of 1945; he was in Bad Orb. I had known he was a POW for about two weeks; I had been under the impression he was missing in action because that's all the information that was fed to me, so I didn't really know he was even in that particular POW cage until he got home and wrote back to me and we talked about dates and places that we were involved in.

He was captured in January of 1945. So in roughly four months he went down to 98 pounds.

He tells a story; there was a water trough outside and of course the winter being so cold it was frozen, and he said that they'd chip ice there and get a chunk of ice and then put it in their helmet and heat it inside for shaving or washing. He said, "We'd even melt it and drink it." And he said, "One day, we noticed that the water was thawing. When it thawed, there was a Russian soldier who had frozen to death laying in that trough."

He said, "I guess that's why that water tasted kind of bad." But you know, we had those halizone tablets, and we'd drink water out of the streams all the time and then put halizone tablets in. You'd walk upstream a ways and here were several horses that were used in pulling artillery pieces laying there with their legs stiff, probably shot for several days, or weeks, who knows, from aircraft probably. Bloated. It was just survival; if you didn't know it was there you didn't worry about it. Heck, we fished with hand grenades. You'd see a stream with fish in there, you'd just toss a hand grenade in and that sucker would go off underwater, and the fish would come right to the top.

The day after the war in Europe ended – we were in Czechoslovakia – a couple of us went and found a swimming hole, and we just peeled all our clothes off – we didn't have any inhibitions – we all jumped in this water, and a couple of gals came walking down there. Well, we thought, we'll just go out a little bit farther out where they can't see us. But you know, they crawled in too; it didn't matter to them.

The next day we found an irrigation ditch; let's just go to the kitchen and get us a bar of soap, and we'll really scrub down. We took our underwear, we stripped down naked, went in this  irrigation ditch, lathered up with soap – man, it felt so good just to watch soap ooze through your fingers, and to wash your hair again; your hair was just stiff and matted, and it just felt good to take a bar of soap and wash your head.

We're sitting there, three of us guys on the bank here stark naked, and we had meanwhile taken our underwear and we'd gone in the ditch. We'd scrub the soap on to hopefully kill the lice, so we had laid our underwear along the bank, and while we were halfway through washing, I thought, "I'll look and see if there are any more lice." I turned the seam of my flannel underwear inside out – man, there were six or seven of them. So we sat there and we cracked them with our fingernails. We sat there for hours just killing lice.

We didn't get rid of them all until we could actually get into a routine where we could bathe on a halfway normal basis, maybe once or twice a week. And then finally they brought us new clothes – we used to get clothes I'm sure that came off of dead guys or people who went back home who were wounded. A truck would stop by our headquarters just loaded with clothes. We'd crawl up on the pile and look through it until we found our size.

I grew up in and around Fresno. Worked on a farm during my off time from school. My father was a farmer by trade, and he was also a farm labor contractor.

My wife came to California and could relive the story of "The Grapes of Wrath." Her parents had been farmers in Texas and Oklahoma during the dust storms. They were cattle farmers, and the sand – I can't believe this but she tells me and I believe her – the sand that drifted back and forth got into the lungs of the cows to where they couldn't even breathe, and they'd just either die a slow death, or they killed them, and they just abandoned their farm. At that time they had five children, it was 1935, and they had a two-wheel trailer and a '29 Chevrolet car. They loaded everything up including two dogs, and the trailer was loaded with all their earthly possessions. They had two big trunks – they didn't have a mattress on top like you saw in the picture – and it took them nine days to get to California. She just laid her mother to rest last week, and we of course told this story at the funeral, how they came to California. They left on my wife's birthday, which was August the 1st, and got there on her mother's birthday, which was August the 9th. Her father had a dollar and 37 cents in his pocket when he got there. Kind of like some of the people we meet here from overseas; they say, "I came to America because I was sponsored here" – well, they weren't exactly sponsored to California but somebody knew them out there. And they drove to their place and said, "Here we are," and they said, "Well, you go inside, we have the table already set," and here this family of five kids, and mother and dad, seven of them, sat them all around the table, and they said grace, had their meal, and my father-in-law said, "We'll sleep someplace here on the floor and tomorrow we'll go out and find a job." And he did. And he knew it was going to take something to find a house, so he went to a distant relative and said, "I'd like to borrow fifteen dollars so I can get in a house. I'll pay you back." And he put most of the kids to work – my wife was nine years old at the time, and they went on up to 14, her oldest brother – they all went to work in the fields picking grapes and making a few bucks. He comes back to this guy and says, "Here's your fifteen bucks," paid him back in full. And he never lacked a day for aggressively looking for work. There was no welfare system. The people had a will to work and enough moxie to say, "I know how to work. I have to earn money for my family." And they did it. But theirs was just one of thousands and thousands of families that came. We lived on the edge of town. My dad, as I said, was a farm labor contractor. We had people pull in there that would work for my dad and they said, "Can we move our little house trailer in on your yard until we can find a permanent place?" And he'd say, "Yeah, park it over there, and connect the garden hose up there," so they'd have water. They'd run an electric cord over to the house, lay a bare wire across the back yard for their electricity. But these people, they wanted to work, and some today became wealthy by their hands and education. Our town was built around those kinds of people.

I graduated from high school in 1943 when I was barely 17 years old. We had an air base in Fresno called Hammer Field, and I was all set to enlist in the service. My brother enlisted in the Air Corps and I figured I could too, so I went to the enlistment board and said I want to become a pilot.

They said, "You've got to fill out these papers." So I filled out a questionnaire, and took an oral test, asking you about your skills and other kinds of questions. Then I took a physical. Passed all three, and they said, "We'll notify you."

At that time all the training was done in cycles; they were called classes, and they'd rotate. And I didn't hear for a while. Finally I got a letter that said that at the present time they were not scheduling any training because as casualties went up and down in the Air Force, that's how they chose their cycles. They said, "We suggest that you wait for the draft, or we'll call you."

They didn't call me, so I was drafted, and I didn't have much choice. I didn't want to go in the Navy. I hated water. And I didn't like being on a ship. I wanted to be able to put my feet on solid ground. So the Army was it.

We went to Presidio Monterrey, which was a permanent base. They wanted some volunteers who knew how to drive. I'd driven a truck for my dad that held fruit and stuff, so I said, "Yeah."

He said, "Step forward." And he took me down to the old man's stable; he had his horses down there, and they gave me a wheelbarrow and said, "Here, drive this." So I'm shoveling manure, the old man comes by there, here I'm in fatigues, he comes in the stable and I thought, "Let's see now, do I put this scoop shovel down and salute him?" If you're on a work detail there's supposed to be somebody saluting for you; you're supposed to keep working. And I didn't know what to do.

But I never finished basic. The Ardennes was beginning to take place, and casualties were mounting. I was in my 12th week of basic, and they just came to us in the nighttime and said, "Gather up your stuff; we're going into the base. You're all getting tickets tomorrow, bus tickets, train tickets, a delay en route, and you're on your way to an overseas assignment." So in 30 days I was on the front lines in Germany.

I went over on the Queen Mary. It took six days to get across. Then down to Southampton. Then we went across the English Channel on a ship to Le Havre. And then three days and two nights riding the 40 and 8s up to Metz. There they issued us rifles and ammunition, put us on a truck, took us up through Luxembourg and on into Belgium, and that's where I joined the 90th, right in the Siegfried Line.

We got off the truck and they led us over to a railroad siding and said, "You, you, and you, follow this man." He took us into the town of Habscheid, and we went into a church – the top of the church was all blown off – and he said, "You guys stay here until it gets dark."

After it got dark a runner came up, and three of us – one of them I had trained with at Camp Roberts, and the other fellow had come from Alaska; he had been in the antiaircraft up there, he wore real heavy glasses, like those Coke bottles, and he complained that he couldn't see. When it got dark it was just like he was blind. So this runner came down to get us and said, "You'd better stay close to me because it's dark and we're going up to a pillbox." And this guy from Alaska, his name was Wigten, he said, "Smitty, I can't see anything."

I said, "Just grab on the back of my belt and hang on." So he held onto my belt and this runner took us down into the pillbox, and we walked probably two blocks, and it was dark, I mean dark. We came into this pillbox – all the ventilation had been knocked out; you could just see the water coming down on the cement sides. And he took us over to meet this gentleman. He said, "This is Sergeant Mueller. He's in charge." And that was the highest ranking guy there; he was a staff sergeant.

And we were all fresh. We had lots of stuff on, and we were carrying a whole bunch of things. We had everything – blankets, overcoat, raincoat, overshoes. I had a whole carton of Dentine chewing gum, and a writing tablet and a pen and pictures. And he kind of oriented us a little bit. He said, "Fellas, you're part of the squad here, get acquainted. These are all your buddies."

Then he said, "Once you know where you are just find a place to sleep. We'll jump off in the morning."

Now, I didn't know what that meant, "jump off." At five or six o'clock, he woke us all up and said, "Get outside here," and we all got out and carried all our stuff. I'd left the gum, the pictures, and my toothbrush inside. I said, "Sergeant, are we coming back here tonight so I can pick up this stuff?"

He said, "Not unless they're carrying you back."

I said, "You mean, we're not living here?"

He said, "No, that was last night."

And I can't believe how naive I was. I said, "Would you give me just a minute?"

He said, "Hurry up."

So I went back in, and I thought, "Let's see. I want my fountain pen." And I'd just become engaged to my wife and I have her picture, a five by seven, I've got to have that. And I grabbed the toothbrush. And that was about it. Stuffed them inside my field jacket, and came back out. And I said, "You're sure we're not coming back here tonight?"

And he said, "Not unless them Krauts push us back." So I left a carton of Dentine gum for somebody.

The first day we went off and attacked, but it was more or less a mopping-up exercise. During the day there was tank movement and I thought, "Boy, if you get behind one of these things, you've got good protection!"

I could feel that warm exhaust coming off, that felt good. I could smell that diesel, it reminded me of home. I said, "Man, that feels good."

And the sergeant hollered, "Hey, Schmidt! Get away from that tank! That thing draws fire. The Krauts will zero in on it and blow you to pieces."

It took a couple of days to learn that you didn't hang around them. But you always liked to have those tankers; they were so good to us, gave us food. They got 10-in-1 rations, they ate pretty good, because they could carry everything with them.

My first day I was so scared. I had a carbine. I had trained as a cannoneer. At Metz I said, "I'm a cannoneer, so I get a carbine." Everybody else had an M-1. Here we are going down the road and my sergeant said, "Where'd you get that popgun?"

I said, "I got it in Metz."

He said, "You'd better trade that off for an M-1, or something that you can depend on."

And I said, "What's wrong with this?"

He said, "That's a popgun. Get rid of that thing." So I traded with the guy that was carrying the bazooka or one carrying the machine gun. He gave me his M-1 and I gave him my carbine, and from then on I carried the M-1. It was more reliable, and you could get it pretty full of dirt and it would still fire.

I never got wounded. In Mainz I got shot in the shoe; it merely grazed the heel and lifted me off the ground Another time, I was a second scout in the woods and next to me was my sergeant, he was the third man in line, and there was a sniper up there. We found this out later – he let us two scouts go – he was smart, he knew that we were probably scouts and the next one would probably be a sergeant or someone in charge – and he nailed him there.

I visited his grave in France. And the two fellows that I walked up to that pillbox with that first night – on the 19th of February, right near the same area; we had only covered a few kilometers a day – we were up on a ballfield and took direct 88 treebursts, and both these two guys, the one with the heavy glasses, who couldn't see, he and Roper, the fellow I trained with at Camp Roberts, both were cut to pieces, almost like a sieve. One was almost decapitated from this treeburst. The sergeant just about a day before had given me the little radio to carry and he said, "You stay with me, wherever I go." He dove in a hole and he said, "Schmidt, get in this hole with me!" I went in this hole and these three other guys, just like that, were killed instantly.

I made it clear into Czechoslovakia without being wounded. I credit a lot of that to my father; he was a very devout Christian. Being a farmer, he didn't punch a clock but he worked. He'd spend hours of the day in his work, saying my brother's name and my name in prayer. He believed in God, and I did, too. I still do. But he had a fervor. He would read the Scripture, the 91st Psalm, a thousand fall at your side, ten thousand on the right hand, but it shall not come nigh thee. He stood on that prophecy.

On my trip to Germany in 1993, we visited a little home in the Siegfried Line where my squad had stayed for three days while holding a bridge over the Prum River.

We knocked on the door, and this couple came to the door. I said, "I was in this house in 1945," and the woman said, "You were an American soldier?"

I said, "Yes." We came on in. They were overwhelmed that someone would come back and visit. And she said, "Can I tell you a brief story that took place, that you may not have put together?"

She said, "When you came in" – our squad had a big, tall Texan as a sergeant; I can't remember his name, but it might have been Webster. When we'd go into a building we'd generally throw a grenade in to clear the place out until we knew it was safe.

Somehow, this big tall Texan walked in, and he saw a cellar. He walked down to the cellar with his M-1, and it was dark. It was a square cellar. He shined his light, and there were 24 civilians sitting on the dirt floor and their eyes were wide, wondering, "What's this guy going to do?" And then he saw that on the wall opposite him was a crucifix. He said, "Are you Catholic?"

And the lady who we met when we returned, her father said, "Ja, Ich bin Catolisch." And it was like it was a magic word. The GI dropped his rifle, he reached into his pocket, and he pulled out a rosary, and he said, "I'm Catholic, too." And for three days, the people in this cellar were taken care of. We gave them food, we took care of their wounds, and reminiscing back almost fifty years, this lady put her arms around us and hugged both my wife and myself, and said, "You know, doesn't this do wonderful things in our life? It brings us together. Once we were enemies, and now we are friends."

*"No matter where you were you had to be careful because [the ship] was so crowded with soldiers. You could hear guys saying, 'When I get back home I'm gonna do this, I'm gonna do that.' And the soldiers, who had his shoes off, nobody had their helmets on because you're inside the ship, and they all knew it was just a dry run. That was what they knew. But they never knew it was the real thing."*

**Patsy J. Giacchi**
**94ᵗʰ Quartermaster**
**Railhead Company**
**Survivor, sinking of**
**LST 507 during**
**Exercise Tiger**
**Interviewed in**
**Clifton, N.J.**
**April 25, 1998**

I was born and raised in Hackensack, New Jersey. I went to Hackensack High School for a couple of years. And then I quit to make a living, because things were rough in those days. I helped the family out. I met my future wife, Emily, and then Pearl Harbor was bombed, the war broke out, I turned 18 and I got drafted.

I went for my physical in Newark. There were ten busloads that went from the Bergen County Courthouse in Hackensack. I passed my physical. Then they gave me ten days to clarify things, like I was working in a supermarket, to tell them that I'm going into the Army.

Then I went to Fort Dix. I stayed there about a week. From there I went to Camp Lee, Virginia, where I took my basic training. After that, they gave me a furlough for 17 days. I came home, went out with Emily, had a good time. Then I went back to Camp Lee, and within a week I moved on to Camp Chenango, Pennsylvania, that's where they issued me my steel helmet, the carbine gun, a gas mask and everything else.

We stayed at Camp Chenango another week. From there I went to Orangeburg, New York, and we took a ferry across the Hudson River to a big ship called the Mauritania. That was a Cunard liner.

It took a couple of hours to get on this troop ship. My number was 13. And as they get to Number 13, you've got to call your name. I said, "Patrick J. Giacchi!"

And as I'm getting on board, there's military police on each side so you can't escape. You'd see some of the guys break down; they don't want to go, but you have to go.

The Mauritania took us to Liverpool, England. I stayed there for a while, and we started to train, train, train. Then, after six or seven months, they take us out and then bring us to a marshaling area.

There they started to examine my teeth, they examined my eyes, and if I needed a pair of eyeglasses it would be made special to fit the gas mask.

Before you know it, from this marshaling area they took us to Brixham.

I said, "What is this for?"

"We're gonna be in a program called Tiger Exercise."

"What's Tiger Exercise?"

"We're going to make a fake run to go on land in Slapton Sands."

"Where's Slapton Sands?"

"By the time we get down there you'll see what it is. What we're gonna do is we're gonna have a fake problem."

But on the ship, they load us up with tanks, we got the Ducks [amphibious vehicles] and everything else, as though it was a real invasion. And there were three or four companies of the boys. I was in the 557th Quartermaster Railhead Company. So we got on this LST, and the first thing I did, I went down to the tank deck. They said, "Go find a place to sleep." We slept on top of the trucks. We slept anywhere we could find a place. I found a stretcher on the side where the two big doors open up. I stayed there in a corner.

Up above there was another stretcher, and my friend Patty Moreno took that. He was in the motor pool, and was from Brooklyn. We start talking. In the meantime you look at the ship and the ship is about 300 feet long, about 50 feet wide. You see all the tanks and the trucks and everything down there, and the guys are all sitting down, who's writing to their loved ones, who's playing the harmonica, a ukelele, little things, just to pass the time.

The lights were on. And no matter where you were you had to be careful because it was so crowded with soldiers. You could hear guys saying, "When I get back home I'm gonna do this, I'm gonna do that." And the soldiers, who had his shoes off, nobody had their helmets on because you're inside the ship, and they all knew it was just a dry run. That was what they knew. But they never knew it was the real thing. And you look around, you see guys talking, some guys are sleeping. I was scared. I didn't sleep that night. I lay down on the stretcher. Patty Moreno was writing a letter to his grandfather, and I was looking at the two big doors, and I could see little puddles of water where the big doors open up. Then I looked around and I said, "Let me see now, the steps are over there, just in case," and then, boom-boom-boom, I heard a couple of noises, boom-boom, whatever it was, outside. I don't know what it was, the guns were shooting, other LSTs were shooting. I waited a while, and then the second time I heard something, and it jarred the ship. I said, "Patty, I'm going."

"Aw, Pat, don't go! It's only a dry run."

I put my helmet on. I put my life belt on, and I checked it. And I started to go up the stairs. As I got to the top, I couldn't believe it. I saw the ocean was on fire. It was the real thing! I said, "This can't be a joke!" Behind me comes another guy, his name was Bradshaw, and we look around. He said, "Oh my God! What's this?"

Then we got a direct hit. BOM! And I knew that who was down there, forget it. I knew right away because I flew up, ten, fifteen feet, I came down. Bradshaw landed on the side of me. My forehead hit the corner of a piece of sharp, square metal, I don't know what it was. I hit that and I started to bleed. But I said, "I'm all right! I'm all right! I'm gonna make it!" I was dizzy. I got up. Bradshaw looked at me. We turn and look and we can see the ship, the 507, was in half.

Bradshaw says, "Pat, we've got to get off of here!"

Only one torpedo hit the 507. I thought the second explosion was a torpedo but they tell me it was something else. But whatever it was, had it been a moment earlier, as I was coming up the steps, I wouldn't be here. Had I been down there I'd have been with those guys.

I had a gash in my forehead and I was bleeding. I lost my helmet. I had it with the strap loose, and when I went up and came down, it fell off.

I remember another thing vividly. We had a bugler; his name was Eintracht, and he was near us at the edge. On the edge of the LST you've got a bar that goes around, and to jump off you've got to go over that bar. All of a sudden this bugler is coming near me and anything you do, if you don't do it fast, you're gone. You're in a daze, you can't move, you're like doped up. All of a sudden he's coming by me and he's trying to grab my life belt, because he had no belt. And I'm trying to push him away. I didn't have much strength left, but Bradshaw gave him a push, and he fell down. Then we went over the side. I don't know what happened to Eintracht. It was just in a split second. Some guys were brave but some guys, they'd kill you to get that life belt.

When I came up, I saw a Navy man; they had gray helmets, we had green ones. He was wrapped around a gun, dead. He must have been firing the gun when the torpedo hit. He was wrapped around the gun and there was blood all over him.

As I was looking at him, I saw a vision of my mother. She said to me, "Save yourself!" in Sicilian. "Patsy, save yourself!"

This is the truth. That's the feeling I had.

Bradshaw was on the side of me, and as I turned around I saw the Navy man killed on the 40-millimeter gun, I saw the ocean on fire, then a split second, wow! It was like an angel. And my mother said to me, "Patsy, save yourself!"

I said, "Mom, I will!" I never said anything to Bradshaw. I was too excited. And I feel this – I never gave up. I hit that water and never gave up. And I was not a good swimmer. I feared water. That belt saved me. When we hit the water I swallowed so much salt water, because I wasn't prepared for that part.

We start to drift away. And as we're pulling away, we held hands, and we could see other guys in the water. The water was on fire, there was a gasoline smell, but the worst thing was the death cry of the sailors and the soldiers, "Helllp! Helllp! Helllp!" And there's nobody to help. These are guys that were wounded. I was all right. I mean, compared to those guys. The blood was coming down my forehead, but I didn't care, I knew what I was doing. We held on together, Bradshaw and I, and we started to drift, and by that time, you could see the difference between us. He looked at me and said, "Patty, hold on, we're doing fine."

[Mumbling] "Yeah, I know. ..."

As we drifted, every now and then you'd see something like a shadow off in the distance; it could have been an E-boat going back, whatever it was. But the four or five hours we were in the water seemed like four or five days.

Bradshaw was a year or two older than me, about 22 or 23, and you know how the Southern boys speak very softly. "Patsy," he says, "we're gonna beat this thing."

I said, "Oh, yes, Bradshaw, oh, yes, we're gonna beat this!" But I had that doubt in my mind: "What happens if nobody picks us up, what if we drift into the middle of the ocean?" I didn't know what part of the Channel we were in. Then we saw a light off in the distance, and it came close, oh, we were saved! I told Bradshaw, "I don't care if it's the Germans. We've got to get out of this water or we're gonna die."

He said, "All right, Patsy. If it's the Germans, we'll go. We'll do what they tell us to do."

The light got bigger and bigger, and before we knew it it was right on top of us. It was a British corvette. They let down a big special wire with a big bucket. Bradshaw was in better shape than I was, so he put me in the bucket first. It pulls you all the way to the top. They pull it inside, and it's a big corvette, with beautiful red rugs and British pictures of Her Majesty the Queen.

"Hiya Mate," they said. "We'll take care of you, Mate, right away." They took off my clothes that were soaking wet for hours and hours, they gave me a needle, they gave me a shot of scotch, they gave me dry British clothes. Then they picked up my friend. By that time it was almost morning, and as we're going in, the British corvette can't help it because they've got quite a few soldiers that they picked up. As they're going in, you could hear the boat hitting the bodies in the water. "We can't help it, Mate, we've got to go, we can't help it, Mate."

Before you know it, it's the next morning. Me and Bradshaw are in this room, and they've got a tremendous table set up. And on the table there's all wallets that they've picked up, because they had two colored companies going out, graves registration, with grappling hooks to pick up bodies. On the table they had all kinds of wallets with money and pictures of loved ones, pictures with their wives and their kids. All kinds of money was piled, singles, soaking wet with the salt water. Fives, tens, twenty dollars bills. They asked me, "If there's anything that belongs to you, take it." A big pile of false teeth, eyeglasses, you name it, yes, they were there. Nothing was mine.

Now we're on land. They had sent an LST out to pick up some bodies, and they came back and opened up the two big doors. You looked in and you could see piles of soldiers and sailors, dead. They closed the doors right away because the port was loaded with English police and civilians, and they didn't want everybody to see what was going on because it was supposed to be hush-hush. This was a tragedy. It never should have happened, especially with D-Day five or six weeks away.

They chased everybody away, and they took us and put us in another company. They didn't say anything to us, so we thought we were coming home, because at the slightest noise I went crazy. Bradshaw said, "You'll be all right."

I said, "Yeah, Bradshaw, I think we're gonna go home."

"We're finished," he said. "We saw our action."

Then, a few days later, a buck sergeant came and said, "Survivors of the 507, follow me."

We follow him. We're waiting for him to tell us we're going home.

We get into a truck. We ride and we ride; before you know it, we're back in the area of Brixham.

I said, "I can smell the gas! I can smell the oil. I can smell the water! What is this?"

The sergeant said, "Sorry, boys. My orders were to deliver you here. You're going on an LST. You're going back."

"Going back WHERE?"

This was May 28th. Two or three days later, we're on an LST again, and then before you know it, you look out there, and by the hundreds the LSTs are all lined up. Then they waited till it got dark that night, the night before June 6th. So we're taking off. I go on the tank deck of the LST. I stand there. The officer comes out; he says, "Soldier, what are you doing here?"

I said, "I-I was told that I could stay here, I'm one of the survivors."

"Oh, okay." He says, "Do you feel better?"

"Yes," I said. "Please."

By that time everybody started to gather around me, all bunched up. Then the chaplain comes up. And the boats are all going. You could look out, it's starting to get light. By the thousands! LSTs and other ships! Which one I was on to make the invasion of D-Day I don't know, but I know I was with the 94th Quartermaster Railhead Company.

So we're going, and there's a priest there. He says, "To all faiths, to all you service boys on this ship, to Catholics, Jews, whatever your faith is, may God speed, may God bless you, and let's hurry up home!"

Now we're starting to go. It's getting lighter and lighter. Then we start to hear, "Boom! Boom-boom-boom-boomboom! Rat-tat-tat-tat." And as you get a little closer, it gets louder and louder.

Okay. We're starting to come in. The LST goes as far as it could go. They have the ropes on the side. Big, thick ropes. I start to come around with a full field pack and am coming down the cargo net on the side. Someone gets his foot caught and is hanging in midair. "Forget him! They'll get him down! You keep going!"

As we're going in, guys are being hit and we say, "Oh my God, I hope the next one's not for me." You keep going in. As you get onto land you can see the engineers with the minesweepers. And then you see the medic guys trying to put up a big Red Cross hospital. As they're putting it up, a Luftwaffe plane comes down and strafes the hell out of them, right near us. We're running on the side. But luckily, no bullets hit us. So we kept on going. And they got those guys who were setting up the hospital.

Then as you're coming in, you've got to follow the rest of the guys; they tell you where to go. Then we hit on the side like where the big hedgerows were. We stayed there, and we were soaking wet, and in the meantime they're firing away. We were there for one or two days. Then they told us to move, and as you're getting up you looked out, and you can smell all the dead bodies. The Germans and the Americans. They tried to pick up the Americans as fast as they could because it knocks the morale down when you see an American soldier there.

I was going to look up the Morenos; it took me fifty years. There are a million Morenos in Brooklyn. I never did. I wanted to tell his family exactly what happened.

After Tiger Exercise, I was assigned to the 94th Quartermaster Railhead Company. Our job was to go down to the LSTs. They had big cranes that would take a big pile of K rations or whatever it was, and put it on a Duck. The Duck would drive from the water, then when it gets on land, it drives away. They would bring it back to our area, and we would stack the stuff and cover it with camouflage. Our job was to bring the supplies to the boys. We weren't rear echelon; we were right up there with the guys. We weren't actually in combat hand to hand, but we were right there. They were doing the fighting, the infantry and the engineers and so forth, and we had to supply them.

And a few times – this was later on, after me being torpedoed – they hit an ammunition dump. You ought to have seen that thing go up. All kinds of ammunition, the big blockbusters, they used to store them, and we used to dig holes around it, in case there was a fire, so it wouldn't go beyond that big, deep hole.

We went through Ste. Mere Eglise. Now, we were quartermasters; we went through with the guys we were attached to 18 or 20 days after D-Day. But the paratroopers landed there H-Hour on D-Day; we used to hear stories about those guys, that they're coming down, the Germans were strafing them, they had them like sitting ducks. A lot of them got killed as they were coming down. And we heard that a lot of them drowned. The Germans opened up the reservoirs or something like that, and when they were dropping, they drowned, because they had a full field pack, and they drowned in water four or five feet deep. They found a lot of paratroopers the next day bloated up from drowning. I heard those stories.

And then we used to hear stories about the Germans with their artillery gun called the 88. The 88 was so damn accurate they used to pick up an American soldier walking maybe two or three miles away; they could pick him up by himself, that's how accurate their guns were. We used to hear this every day. And we knew that their burp guns were sensational, their machine guns. Everything they had was more superior than ours.

I remember I thought, "Wow, the war's just started, we've got a long way to go." And then, every now and then we'd see maybe three, four, five hundred German prisoners, they were taking them away and bringing them to England. They'd be saying, "No! No! We want to go to America! Because in America they'll spare us. The English will kill us." They were very afraid of the English. And then I'll never forget, on D-Day I saw some Japanese in German uniforms.

But then along the beach on D-Day you'd see all kinds of LSTs there, and then you'd see the barrage balloons all over, so that the Germans can't get in with their Luftwaffe to strafe them, to keep them high above and away like that. And then every night at the beach there, while we were having our K rations, or you'd be trying to walk down the beach, the Germans would drop flares that used to make our area look like Broadway, and if it lit up they told you, no matter what you're doing, freeze, because if you moved they could spot you with the planes.

I pulled guard duty on D-Day. I was scared. They go by alphabetical order, my name is G, Giacchi, and mine was the last one to be picked.

In the meantime everybody's scared on D-Day. You could hear the guns going bom-bom, tat-tat-tat-tat-da-da-da. All of a sudden I pulled guard duty. And my job was to go up there and watch the K rations. There I am with a steel helmet on, I've got the gun, and then they said that if you hear anything, there'll be another soldier near you, just give your call. We had the signal, we had the little information like the cue card to tell us what to say. All of a sudden, they started to bomb up above us, and the flak was coming down; you could see the hot flak, and we're standing there. A piece of shrapnel came down and started to light a fire on the grass. I put it out. I was so scared. The Germans are here! So finally, that's it, one hour, it seems like about 50 hours. The corporal comes. "Pat? It's me. Corporal Gray. Yeah. You're gonna be relieved."

"Oh thank God!"

Another guy asked me, "Pat, how is it?"

I was scared, scared, because there were Germans all around us. But I was lucky because if I ran into a German I don't know what my reaction would have been. If they told me to stay awake, I would stay awake; some guys were sleeping on guard duty, that I would never do. But I wasn't firing my gun. I was just holding and protecting it.

I think the first time I took my shoes off was after about 21 days. So when some of the guys took their shoes off, uggh! Things like that. Some guys had swollen feet. But with me, we used to wear the paratrooper boots, because I was assigned to the combat engineers. These guys always were right near the front.

I was a loader. I would lift up stuff and put the rations onto the trucks. All of us had to do it. We had to bring the supplies up to the guys. And every now and then, somebody would come in – some soldier maybe got drunk, he wound up getting some cognac – somebody would come in, they'd have two chickens, somebody would say, "I'll kill those chickens, give them to me," and we'd eat them. Because we never had chicken like that. We always had the K rations, the special chocolate that's got vitamin this and vitamin that.

I was in the service for almost three years, but from the time I left the States, I couldn't believe, everything happened so fast. I went in one day, a week later I'm in Pennsylvania. I'm there, the next day I'm in Camp Lee, Virginia. Thirteen weeks of basic. Come home. Take a furlough for 17 days. Go back. Before you know it, I can't believe it, I'm on the high seas. They said over the loudspeaker, "Okay, we can tell you where you are, now that we are outside the jurisdiction of the United States. You boys are now going to the ETO." What the hell's the ETO? ETO means European Theater of Operation. "Oh thank God, we aren't going to fight the Japs!" Because the Japs are dirty, they don't care. The Germans are more civilized. The Germans used to value their lives, too. But they were good fighters.

I got seasick, very bad. I pulled KP on the Mauritania. I pulled KP, my second day on this tremendous ship, and here I am with all the other guys, downstairs in the kitchen, all of a sudden, "Boom! Boomboomboom-boom!" I dropped that pot. "Man your stations! Man your stations!" You've got to go by a certain station where the lifeboats are. It was a fake drill, to show us what to do.

Then they told us while we were there to turn around and look at the back of the boat, and you could see the path in the water. It was never a straight line. It was zigzag, zigzag, zigzag. You can't torpedo a boat zigzagging like that.

I said to a couple of British guys, "Tell me the truth, are we being chased?"

"Are we being chased? They're on our tail!" The German submarines, I don't want to exaggerate but they came close many times near New York. They picked up strange noises. And I believe the Germans could do that. Probably they followed a lot of the boats going out.

My parents both came from Sicily, but they got married in Paterson, New Jersey. In those days, the boat would come in to Ellis Island and the Statue of Liberty, and they separated them there. They went to Paterson. I heard the story from my older sister and brothers; they're all dead now, but I would hear the story that they had come to Paterson. Then they moved to Hackensack.

My father was a farmer. When it was tomato season and celery and so forth, he used to make so much a week. Of course their pay was very little then for farming, but long hours.

I had two brothers. My brother Johnny died of a heart attack. And Joey is my other brother, he's about now 68, because I'm 75 and Johnny would have been about 80 if he was living. I had five sisters. Half of them died of bad hearts and whatnot. Because in those days they didn't do much about rheumatic fever and murmur of the heart, you'd die. Today they can conquer it. And my mother died when she was about 80.

My father died while I was in Germany, in a town called Schweigenhausen. My father passed away, and the thing that I want to say is that my mother was always a sickly person. She had a stroke when I was 12 years old; she had rheumatic fever. So when my sergeant came to me and said, "Captain Ashley wants to see you," I said,

"Ohhh, don't tell me I made corporal again!" So when I went there – they slept in the pyramidal tents; we slept in a foxhole, they slept in a big tent. All of a sudden he chased everybody out of the tent. It was just me and the captain. He's got a letter, and it's all burnt on the edges. So I'm nervous.

He says, "Patsy, how long have you been in my company?"

"Well, Sir, from the time after I got torpedoed."

And he says, "Now I've got to tell you something. You've been a very good soldier. ..."

"Well, gee, thank you, Sir."

He says, "I've got a little sad news for you."

I go crazy right away. Some guys could take it. I just can't. I looked at him. "Sir, is it my father or my mother? I know. My mother."

But it wasn't my mother. He told me it was my father. But I thought it was my mother. Because my mother was always sick. He says, "This letter is addressed from your parish, St. Francis Church," which is in Hackensack, on Lodi Street, it's a Catholic church. He says, "I've got a letter here from the priest. He says your father has passed away."

I said, "Gee, I know, she was very sickly."

He says, "No, not she. It's your father."

"Oh, I'm sorry, Sir."

"Your mother's living, it's your father."

He opened up the letter. He showed it to me; it was all burnt. But the letter was already seven months old. My father was dead seven months! They couldn't get to me because we used to move up so goddamn fast. When he showed me the letter, it said that the priest said, "Patsy, we're very sorry to inform you that your father has passed away," but this was seven months later they brought it to my attention! My father had been dead and buried for seven months. And I said to myself, "No wonder I'm not getting any mail from my sisters and my girlfriend" – she was my girlfriend then, Emily, that I married. Because they were writing to me. But then when I got the mail, whoa! They had a whole special truck for me alone. "Patsy! We've got a big box for you!" From Emily, loads and loads of letters, from my sister Jane and everybody else. They said they tried everything to save my father but they couldn't. At that time they didn't know too much about cancer of the throat. He smoked. Here I thought it was my mother. And they were good about it, they sent me back to the rear echelon and gave me two weeks off. Then I came back and kept on moving. By that time, I didn't realize it but we were getting closer to the end of the war.

When the war ended, I was in Germany, in a town called Ulm, U-L-M; we say Ulm, but they say "Oohlm," the Germans. Out of the clear blue sky over the loudspeaker they say, "The war has ended! The war has ended!" Here I am in a foxhole talking to one of my buddies. "What did they say?"

"Pat! The war has ended!" You'd see there were some of them out there going crazy. Guys were shooting each other by mistake! GIs, yes, they were shooting themselves, from the excitement. They tried to tell everybody, "Calm down! Be careful!"

And I was in a foxhole down there. "The war is over! The war is over!" I was crying in the foxhole from joy, I couldn't believe it. The following morning they called formation outside, they said, "The following names, please step forward." Finally, "Pfc. Patsy Giacchi!" I step forward.

"Okay," the captain says, "you guys are all going home. "

Boom. One guy passes out from the excitement. I couldn't believe it. I think I was 21 years old then.

The following day, it was a clear blue sky. "Cover up your foxholes." Before you know it, they put us on trucks, the big Army trucks, they load you up in there, hold the back door, the driver takes off, and he's going for miles and miles and miles, before you know it, you're riding almost a whole day. You ride from one part of Germany to another part. You bivouac. Five in the morning you get up, take your tents down, they give you coffee. Boom! We start to travel. Before you know it we're deep into France. Another couple of days we're in Le Havre. And there's the big liberty ships waiting. But before all that they had to give you the inspection, because a lot of guys caught venereal disease. If you had a venereal disease, they took you out of line. They put you in the hospital, and they cured you there, then they would send you home. A lot of guys were pulled out, who had syphilis, the clap. A lot of soldiers caught VD over there. They taught them how to use prophylactics, but a lot of guys were stupid, they got drunk.

Now I'm on a liberty ship coming home; I can't believe it. All of a sudden, after about a week, they said, "Here it is, boys." We come around a big bend, and they say, "You guys want to see it? Go up on the top deck, you can see it."

What is it? We're hitting Newport News, Virginia. And you look, as you come in, you can't believe it, the United States! And there's a big sign that says, "Welcome home, boys! Well done!" I'm on the deck there, I'm crying, I can't believe it.

All of a sudden you start to line up. I said, "Pat, be careful now, Pat be careful, you made it through the whole war. Don't get killed, don't fall off the ship or get hurt."

Then they call your name; you step down. When I got off, I kissed the ground. I cried.

Then, "All the guys from New Jersey, line up on one side. You're going to Fort

Monmouth." All the guys from another state, they line up somewhere else.

So I went to Fort Monmouth. The following morning we had to go to a big church. You had the organist up there playing songs.

They said, "When your name is called, step up, salute the officer who's giving you your discharge papers, make a turn, go back, you're discharged from the Army."

"Pfc. Patsy J. Giacchi."

"Pfc Patsy J. Giacchi!"

A guy goes, "Hey, that's you!"

"Oh, yeah! Yeah!" I go up there, nervous. They give me that paper. I walk back.

"You don't go back and sit down! Get the hell out of here, you're discharged!" I see an officer go by, I salute him. He says, "You're not a soldier anymore."

"I'm sorry, Sir."

"That's okay."

I'm the only guy that's coming toward Hackensack. They told me where to get the next bus to go from Fort Monmouth to Newark.

I'm on the bus a couple of hours, and then the driver says, "Newark, Penn Station!"

Penn Station! I remember that from when I was a kid! Penn Station in Newark.

I got off the bus. I went to a telephone booth. There were many guys there. My time came. I took out my wallet. Now I didn't know my phone number, because when I left it was three years ago. So I opened up my wallet to look for my phone number. I had my mustering out pay. They gave me three hundred dollars when I got discharged, plus I had another two hundred dollars. That's 1945. That's a lot of money. I'm nervous. All of a sudden, "Hello. Who am I speaking to?"

"You're speaking to Nellie." Nellie's one of my sisters.

"Nellie, please, now don't get excited. This is your brother Patsy."

"Who?"

"Patsy."

"Who?"

"Patsy!"

Boom. She dropped the phone. She passed out.

Jane picks up the phone, my older sister, and she says, "Who's this?"

"Jane, please, it's your brother Patsy. Please, don't get excited. I'm in Newark, New Jersey."

"Oh my GOD!" We'll send somebody."

"No, no, no. I'm coming home. I'll take care of it. I'm coming home."

"Patsy, please be careful. Oh my GOD!"

I left my wallet there. I had some change in my pocket, and a couple of bills.

I got on the bus. I took the bus from Newark to Hackensack. Then from Hackensack on Main Street I took a taxicab to West Street, where I lived.

As I'm coming around the corner, they've got a big sign for me in front of my house, "Welcome home, Patsy!" All my Italian neighbors are waiting for me. I get out of the cab, and they're grabbing me, my mother's trying to grab me, my father – no, my father's dead – my mother was trying to grab me, my sisters were there. The neighbors were there. Across the street the DeLorenzos. "Ohhh, Patsy, it's good to see you" and everything else. Who's pulling me here, who's pulling me there.

After about two hours, some of the neighbors disperse, we go inside, we start talking.

Then Jane says, "Gee, Patty, have you got any pictures?"

"I've got one or two pictures. … JANE! My wallet! I left it in Newark."

"Oh my God! How much was in it?"

"Five hundred!"

"Five HUNDRED?!!!" Then it was like five thousand.

We call up Newark. They say, "Would you please come down?"

We get down to Newark. I go where I made the telephone call from. Behind the counter, there's a couple of cops there, security or something else. They said, "Soldier, we get this every day. You're going to have to give us some real good detail. Everybody tells us "black wallet, brown wallet," something like that. Tell us if you can what's in your wallet.

"Well," I said, "I've got a couple of this, a couple of that."

"Keep going." The other guy's writing it down.

I said, "Okay. I've got it! Okay, now look." I was always excited.

"Take your time now," he says.

"Okay. You'll see a picture of my girlfriend, an Italian girl with long black hair. She's got a dress on" – I bought her this dress – "and the dress has got an emblem of a little parrot."

That did the trick. They gave me the wallet, with the money in it and everything else.

"Sir," I said, "who returned this for me?"

He said, "A little old lady. She said, 'Some poor bugger left his wallet here with all his money. Please see that he gets it.' "

I said, "Can I give her a reward?"

He said, "She doesn't want a reward. Just take care of yourself, she said."

**the end**

# Acknowledgments

Normally, I would use this space to express my gratitude to people like Susan English, whose editorial guidance helped shape the "voice" of this book; and Elizabeth Lynn of the Bookaccino for encouraging me to hustle it into print; people like my goddaughter Avery Harken for her suggestions on the cover design, and the author George Forty for his recognition of my work. Instead, I'm going to turn the remainder of this page over to Jim Koerner, whose story provided both the inspiration and the title for "Nine Lives."

Jim would like to see his story dedicated:

"To my beautiful wife, Helen, who has put up with me all these years through bouts of depression, stubbornness and moodiness. I love you so very much – I just wish I did a better job of showing it.

"To our children, Elaine, Jimmy, Dave and Keith, and grandchildren, Eric, Dana, J.J., Joy, Zachary and Joey, Melissa and Elise, Sean and Nicollette. I hope you will read these pages and understand the price of freedom.

"To my brother, Ted – I couldn't have asked for a finer brother. You have been my best friend.

"And to all the dedicated men and women of the Lyons VA Medical Center in New Jersey. It took me 50 years to find this great hospital whose doctors and nurses and fellow vets minister with such kindness to those who pass through their doors – doors which are in danger of being shut down forever. I know that I speak for all when I say that we shall ever be grateful for your help in dealing with the horrible memories of the war atrocities that haunt us, and the accompanying physical ailments we bear from serving this great country in her time of need.

"God Bless America!"

**9 Lives**
*An Oral History*
**By Aaron Elson**
author of
*"A Mile in Their Shoes"*

# About
# the cover

Clockwise from the bottom: The Kassel Mission memorial in Friedlos, Germany, on which are engraved the names of 118 Americans and 23 Germans who died as a result of a battle in the skies overhead; Kay Brainard Hutchins in 1999 (with a photo of Douglas Fairbanks, Jr., for whom she worked as a social secretary); Hutchins when she was a Red Cross girl during World War II; Patsy J. Giacchi being honored at the 1999 annual dinner of the Exercise Tiger Foundation; a photo of the Schilling family of Oberwampach, Luxembourg – the little boy in the foreground was mortally wounded during an artillery barrage; Sergeant Hassel C. Whitfield of the 90th Infantry Division, who was mortally wounded trying to save the child, and who posthumously was awarded the Distinguished Service Cross. The photo in the middle was taken by the gun sight camera in a German fighter plane, and shows an unidentified B-24 beginning to break apart on the Kassel mission of Sept. 27, 1944, when the 445th Bomb Group lost 25 planes in less than six minutes. Kay Hutchins' brother, Lieutenant Newell Brainard, survived the battle itself, but was murdered on the ground by slave labor camp guards.